KT-212-917

September 1993
Newark, NJ.

Jesus Acted Up

Jesus Acted Up

A GAY AND LESBIAN MANIFESTO

ROBERT GOSS

HarperSanFrancisco
A Division of HarperCollinsPublishers

JESUS ACTED UP: *A Gay and Lesbian Manifesto.* Copyright © 1993 by Robert Goss. All rights reserved. Printed in the United States of America. No part of this book may be used or reproduced in any manner whatsoever without written permission except in the case of brief quotations embodied in critical articles and reviews. For information address HarperCollins Publishers, 10 East 53rd Street, New York, NY 10022.

FIRST EDITION

Library of Congress Cataloging-in-Publication Data
Goss, Robert.
Jesus acted up : a gay and lesbian manifesto / Robert Goss.—1st ed.
    p.   cm.
Includes index.
ISBN 0–06–063318–2 (alk. paper)
1. Homosexuality—Religious aspects—Christianity. I. Title.
BR115.H6G66 1993   92–56415
230'.08'664—dc20   CIP

93 94 95 96 97 ❖ RRD–H 10 9 8 7 6 5 4 3 2 1

This edition is printed on acid-free paper that meets the American National Standards Institute Z39.48 Standard.

To Frank H. Ring, Jr.
A life dedicated
ad majorem dei gloriam

Contents

Acknowledgments

Inspiration for this book comes from numerous sources. I want to thank my longtime companion, Frank H. Ring, for his love, support, and criticisms of this book. It was out of our shared vision of love making and justice doing that this book was generated. His life and legacy of compassion, what Jesuits call the spirit of "more" (*magis*), live in the words of this book. Our Sunday eucharists were peppered with prayer and the challenge of the more, the vision of generosity that Ignatius of Loyola inspired, and the vision of justice-love that Jesus lived. He lived the fact that God is HIV-positive and to be found in our midst and he now lives the justice-love of Easter.

I am indebted to numerous readers and their critical suggestions: Dr. Anthony Saldarini, Dr. Sharon Welch, Rev. Susan Nanny, Rev. Paul Diederich, Rev. Michael Broadley, and the late Rev. Robert Williams. I also want to acknowledge the faith and commitment of ACT UP and Queer Nation in St. Louis. Their courage and commitment to justice informs the pages of this book. I share their hopes of a liberated and just society grounded in compassion. I share as well their commitment to eliminate AIDS-phobia and homophobia.

I want to thank friends and members of an AIDS base community of care providers and HIV-positive people in St. Louis: David Salter, Barbara Krazl, Nino Giovanni and Jim Peters, Larry and Lois Horack, and David Bolinger. I also want to thank the clergy and leaders who encouraged the project. They remain unnamed because of the climate of ecclesial terrorism, silencings, and sanctions.

Finally, I am grateful to Harper San Francisco's commitment to theological truth. I am indebted to my editor John Loudon and senior editorial assistant Joann Moschella for their critical comments, suggestions, excitement, and challenges. They have both been integral to this book.

Originally, the title of this book was *The Battle for Truth: A Gay and Lesbian Political Theology.* "The battle for truth" alluded to Michel Foucault's notion of "the insurrection of subjugated knowledges" against the powerful deployments of socially created truth. It encapsulated for me the struggle of gay/lesbian truth from the margins of society against homophobic Christian discourse. After several incarnations, the staff at Harper and I agreed upon *Jesus Acted Up: A Gay and Lesbian Manifesto.* I want to thank Yvette Bozzini for suggesting *Jesus Acted Up;* it summarizes the central metaphor and practice of the original title. For the wonderful cover, I want to thank Gerald Bustamente of Studio Bustamente. He successfully captured the "in-your-face" attitude of lesbian and gay theology. I am also indebted to Mimi Kusch, the production editor for the book. Finally, I want to thank the marketing staff and Steve Hanselman for their vital contributions.

Introduction

I have especially wanted to question politics, to bring to light in the political field, as in the historical and philosophical interrogation, some problems that had not been recognized there before. . . .

MICHEL FOUCAULT[1]

What does it mean to speak and practice Christianity from a gay and/or lesbian perspective?[2] I attended a "Stop the Church" action meeting in St. Louis in February, 1991. It was a coalition of women's, gay/lesbian reformist, and activist groups. People were split into two divisions. Some men and women felt the pain of trying to maintain a fragile relationship with their church(es) while being a woman, a lesbian woman, a gay man, or an HIV-positive individual. These women and men acknowledged the pain caused by the church but did not want to demonstrate publicly against the church. They desperately wanted to be loved, be accepted, and be part of their church. They perceived the church as the presence of God's reign, albeit an imperfect presence. They hoped that institutional change would take place by a conciliatory attitude and by internalizing the pain of nonacceptance. These individuals would not participate in any staged protest against the church.

The second division of men and women felt a variety of emotions, from alienation to anger to rage. They articulated their pain of being rejected or excluded by the church for being a female, a lesbian female, a gay male, an HIV-positive individual, or a person living with AIDS. They perceived the church as the "reign of God," as the absence of

God, and as a political oppressor. The church sanctioned social violence against them and refused to allow their sexual difference. They favored a staged action in front of the Catholic cathedral on Easter Sunday to proclaim that they were crucified by the church and that Easter was their day of liberation. They would take back Easter as their own.

Both groups were angry. The first internalized its anger with a spiritualized language; the second externalized its anger with a political language. The first group internalized the church's homophobia, whereas the second externalized and rejected that homophobia. Both groups of men and women experienced the damaging effects of oppression and the violence wrought by ecclesial homophobia and heterosexism. However, all participants in the meeting shared a degree of consensus on the damaging effects and the oppression of the church. Though the target was ostensibly the Roman Catholic church, it could well have been any number of the mainline Protestant, Orthodox, or fundamentalist churches.

For many lesbians and gay men, Christianity is perceived as the enemy. It is seen as socially oppressive, overtly antagonistic, and deliberately hostile. It legitimizes cultural oppression and social violence:

> For churches to baptize and confirm the homophobic insights of society, and indeed for theology to be exposed as the root of many such notions, is the scandal that has driven many people far from the pews. More significantly, to justify the virulent attacks on lesbian/gay people by an appeal to Scripture and tradition further undercuts any reason why lesbian/gay people would relate to Christianity as anything but an adversary.[3]

Christian discourse and institutional practices are rejected by a great number of gay men and lesbians, for they remain at the root of much of their familial pain and social and political oppression.

Yet the gay and lesbian community is deeply spiritual. Many lesbians have sought out the spiritual experience of sisterhood and the Goddess. Many gay men and lesbians have become Buddhists, Hindus, or members of one of the new religious movements. Other gay men and lesbians have tried to remain within the various traditions of Christianity. Some lesbian and gay Christians became nuns and priests; ministers and presbyters; deacons, bishops, and elders.[4] Some felt that they could quietly reform their churches from within their structures. Some believed that they could be gay and lesbian privately while continuing a public Christian "persona." Others who dared to break their silence were marginalized, silenced, or excluded. Others have formed marginal communities of resistance to reform their churches; some created alternative churches where gay men and lesbians could practice their faith openly and be themselves. Some lesbians joined nonlesbian women in forming the Women-Church. Other gay men and lesbians have joined political action groups, forming coalitions with women's groups and AIDS action groups to fight for justice.

What all these gay men and lesbians have in common is the deep conflicts that they have experienced and continue to experience with institutional Christianity. The Christian churches are immersed in a cultural discourse of hatred and the institutional practices of oppressing those who are sexually different. Lesbians and gay men have suffered discrimination, exclusion, condemnation, terrorism, and violence. They have been denied ordination (unless they play ecclesial games about their sexual identity), the blessing of their unions, and even participation in the institutional practices of their churches.

For those insiders and for those outsiders who remain in conflict with Christianity, I write this book as one who has struggled with this conflict for nearly two decades. I struggled with homophobic and misogynistic forms of Christianity as a gay male and AIDS activist, as a feminist-dialogue partner (meaning my active commitment to listen to the experiences of feminist women and theologians and to allow these experiences to inform my theology), and as a theologian and historian of religion. I am an apologist neither for Christianity nor for the gay and lesbian community. I value my experience as a gay Christian, and I write as an openly gay Christian theologian who participates in a base community that works for compassion and justice. I write to encourage the continued struggle for justice and the hope for liberation from oppressive exclusion and violence.

Christianity itself is not the enemy. Rather, institutional forms of Christianity continue to oppress gay and lesbian people. Institutional Christianity remains conceptually impoverished in its theological discourse about gay men and lesbians (also regarding men and women in general). Its social practices are often unjust, exclusionary, and violent. Institutional Christianity has to be criticized and prophetically challenged to be faithful to Jesus' message and practice of God's reign. This challenge has recently taken the multiple forms of resistance, struggle, reform, challenge, rejection, and provocative alternatives from the pluralistic gay/lesbian movement and the feminist movement. Gay men and lesbians must articulate a theological discourse sensitive to the experiences of gay/lesbian Christians, to empower their practice for liberation.

Liberation Theologies

The thesis of this book is that contemporary Christian theological practice concerning gay men and lesbian women has not been contextual or even pertinent to their own experiences. Christianity has institutionalized a particular discourse and practice of heterosexist power relations. By claiming that they are universal, Christianity has excluded many particular social groups. More specifically, such particular discourse and practice have actively contributed to homophobic oppression and violence. The question for Christian theology in a postmodern era is not whether it has vested interests or not, but rather where do its interests lie. Feminist critics have leveled charges that the grand Christian discursive claims are patriarchal, exclusive, particularist, oppressive, and necrophilic.[5] African American critics have charged that Christian claims are white, racist, and enslaving.[6] Latin American critics point out that these claims emerge from Eurocentric and North American Christianity, reflecting the established political and economic patterns of colonialism.[7] Feminists, African Americans, Latin Americans, and other groups deny the dominant claims of Christian theology as universally applicable to their particular experiences. Christian global claims exclude the experiences of the majority of peoples on this planet.

All liberation theologies dismantle dominant Christian claims of universal systems, grand or "meta" narratives, and global theories. They emphasize their own particular social experiences in order to question the universal claims and to unmask the oppressive particularity of universal claims. Their theological discourse is postmodern. It is critical and deconstructionist. Liberation theologies emerge within their world of oppression, focusing on the need for political change and practicing actions for political change. Theologian Sharon Welch points out that "universal discourse is the discourse of the privileged."[8] Liberation theologies challenge dominant Christian political regimes of universal truth with the concrete, lived situation of oppressed peoples and their liberative practices.

Likewise, a gay and lesbian liberation theological discourse can only be understood contextually: "Contextual theology is a method of theologizing which is aware of the specific historical and cultural contexts in which it is involved, and senses that it is directed to experiences and reflections of others."[9] A contextual gay and lesbian theology can proceed only from critical analysis of the social context that forms our experience, our struggles, and our emergent, innovative, and transgressive practice. A gay/lesbian theology is an organic or community-based project. It includes gay/lesbian sexual contextuality, our particular social experiences of homophobic oppression, and our self-affirmation: "Nothing that is of us can be alien to our theology."[10] Gay/lesbian Christian discursive practice emerges from the painful and often lethal struggle against homophobic power relations. This means that no one "not involved" in and committed to the struggle for gay/lesbian liberation can write a gay/lesbian liberation theology. Nor can anyone who is not out as gay/lesbian write a liberation theology. There is no apologizing in an authentic gay/lesbian liberation theology.

Gay and lesbian critics have rejected the universal claims of heterosexist Christian discursive practice as homophobic and heterosexist. Christian homophobia is legitimized in a few insignificant biblical passages—in the holiness code in the Pentateuch, the Genesis legend of Sodom and Gomorrah, and a few citations in Paul's letters and the catholic letters, all of which are subject to varying interpretations. In some churches, Christian homophobia is based on outdated theological constructions of natural law. Gay and lesbian people have rejected the Christian claims that they are sinful, deviant, sick, objectively disordered, or intrinsically evil. Such homophobic Christian claims legitimize and contribute to the social organization of hatred within our society. The failure of institutional Christianity has resulted from an impoverished theological discourse toward sexuality and a failure to commit itself to practicing justice. Institutional Christianity has failed to listen to the truth of gay and lesbian lives, the truth of their sexuality, and the truth of their Christian witness.

A gay/lesbian liberation theology begins with resistance and moves to political insurrection. It resurrects what theologian Hans Küng calls the "dangerous memories and liberating memories" of Jesus in the Gospels.[11] Retrieval of the "dangerous memories" of Jesus is appropriated into gay/lesbian narratives of resistance. The memories of Jesus' suffering and memories of their own homophobic oppression fuel insurrection. Political insurrection surfaces from being aware of the power of the homophobic truth and the social mechanisms used to deploy that truth in society. Gay men and lesbians need to understand how homophobic power is produced and how it operates within society. Then they can comprehend how their practice of truth can potentially effect change:

> Liberation is also defined as a process of naming and analyzing. It is a process in which dominated groups discover their history of oppression and resistance and articulate their conception of themselves and their vision of a just society. Liberation is a process in which oppressive groups acknowledge their responsibility for structures of domination and the forces that lead to repentance and conversion.[12]

Gay/lesbian liberation theology is a critical and political practice of truth, bringing about change in the social fields of exclusionary language, homophobic discourse, and oppressive practices.

A Queer Theology

I tread a perilous course by naming this theology both gay and lesbian. Mary Hunt is weary of any false inclusionary categories that collapse the experiences of women into the experiences of men. She claims that gay men and lesbians do not have the categories to understand each other's experiences:

> The backlash against AIDS increases the need for lesbian and gay people to work together. I must also say that as they work together it is increasingly clear that fewer and fewer claims can be made that apply to both women and men. Experiences of loving persons of the same sex may be similar insofar as both sexes are oppressed by the larger society. But there the differences end because of a patriarchally constructed society. . . . My sense is that trying to talk lesbian/gay anything is like trying to speak of a Judeo-Christian culture. It simply obscures the differences and results in muddled and disrespectful discussions. It ought not to be done.[13]

Hunt and other lesbian critics are correct that the categories of understanding differ between lesbians and gay men. However, as a dialogue partner with lesbians, my experience differs. Lesbians and gay men are now creating a common language of understanding in their political struggles against homophobia/heterosexism. They are learning from one another; they are talking to each other about their own pain, about what it means to be a woman and a lesbian and about what it means to be a gay man. The lesbian/gay alliance is sensitizing gay men to feminist critiques of heterosexism/sexism. Many gay men are now confronting their own sexist socializations. Likewise, many lesbians have actively worked in AIDS service organizations responding to the ravages of HIV infection among the gay male population. The new coalitions between lesbians, feminist women, and gay men form an ongoing learning process, a dialogue that achieves relative understandings and effects social change. In this dialogue, lesbians and gay men have adopted the common term *queer* to describe themselves and their sexuality diversity. *Queer* is a term of political dissidence and sexual difference. It is part of the movement to reclaim derogatory words from oppressive culture. Julia Penelope, a lesbian-feminist theorist, says, "The attempt to claim words is the attempt to change the dominant shape of reality."[14]

I try to construct in this book an inclusionary theology that is both queer and feminist. I will refrain from making particular claims about how lesbians experience or what they feel. Feminist/lesbian social analysis and theological criticism inform all my theological constructions. I have learned much from my dialogue with feminist women on some of the issues addressed in the following chapters. Moreover, I do not speak for women or for lesbians, but I try to let them speak for themselves in their own writings as much as possible. I value their pioneering analyses in gender and sexual identity politics, their commitment to challenging "heteropatriarchy" and their oppression.[15] The contours for a queer liberation theology emerge from my own experience as a queer Christian and in coalition with feminist/lesbian critique and practice.

The term *homosexuality* was coined by medical discourse to describe clinical pathology. I use *homosexual* and *homosexuality* only in homophobic discourse or when used in a specific quotation.[16] My political preference is for the colloquial usage in the gay/lesbian community, *lesbians* and *gay men*. I frequently use *gay/lesbian*, such as "gay/lesbian discourse" or "the gay/lesbian community." I recognize the unique and individual experiences of gay men and lesbians within a heterosexist and homophobic society. I do not abridge their sexual differences.[17] *Gay/lesbian* refers to the sexual differences between gay men and lesbian women and their common experience of homophobic oppression. *Gay/lesbian* refers also to the evolving, mutual understandings between lesbians and gay men. Gay men and lesbians have consciously united in their resistance to homophobic and heterosexist deployments of power relations. They live in a society with sharpened definitions of gender and sexual identity. Although lesbians and gay men have their own distinct experiences of social resistance, they bring their separate experiences to enrich one another and find a common social identity forged in resistance and the struggle for freedom. Lesbians and gay men are forging new possibilities of understanding between men and women. They are creating a new erotic "truth" for social analysis as they form coalitions to struggle to change heterosexist/homophobic society.

Another important element that I employ in constructing a queer theology is the critical method of the gay historian and philosopher Michel Foucault. Foucault's genealogical method provides a framework for social analysis of homophobic discourse and practice. It is a method that calls attention to, or as Foucault puts it, "surfaces" alternative forms of knowledge to dominant constructions of discourse. His method activates the "insurrection of subjugated knowledges" by examining the local memories and resistances that are present in the text. He attempts "to maintain events in their proper dispersion; ... to identify the accidents, the minute deviations—or conversely, the complete reversals—the errors, the false appraisals, faulty calculations that gave birth to those things that continue to exist and have value for us."[18] In other words, Foucault's method surfaces what is marginalized, disregarded, or ignored by dominant forms of cultural discourse, such as gay/lesbian writings. For Foucault, power and knowledge are not external to one another; rather, they operate in history to generate one another. They form a network of opposing relations, continuously in tension within all human activity. Power and knowledge together create particular discourses and institutional practices, and they have particular social effects.

Foucault's genealogical analysis highlights the forgotten or alternative voices within discourse and those excluded from particular social practices. It dismantles the illusions of universal claims and categories of truth. Foucault's genealogical criticism is suitable to the critical work of constructing a queer Christian theology. For a critical feminist theology, Sharon Welch argues, "Genealogy is a mode of investigation appropriate for a theology that understands Christian faith as a commitment to eradicate oppression and to establish justice, and understands theology as the analysis of the conditions and motives of such work for justice."[19] Genealogy is a mode of investigating history for queer social critics. I refer the reader to a more detailed explanation of it in the appendix. Foucault's method of social and cultural analysis has been invaluable to recent feminist and queer social analysis of homophobia/heterosexism, power, truth, gender, and sexual identity. His method has deeply affected gender and sexual identity studies.

Finally, this book will center around eight major topics: (1) the social organization of homophobia; (2) the social formation of queer discourse and practice. These two chapters are pivotal to understanding the remaining chapters. They make primary what is ignored or condemned by Christian theology. The remaining chapters try to retrieve Christian truth from homophobic/heterosexist theological constructions: (3) A queer retrieval of Jesus from oppressive Christologies; (4) a queer biblical hermeneutics; (5) the construction of queer Christian basic community; (6) The practice of conflict; (7) God as love-making and justice-doing; (8) prophetic queers act up. What motivates me to construct a queer liberation theology is the homophobic truth and violence produced by Christian theology and practice. I engage in a queer battle for the politics of Christian truth and a battle for sexual justice. This book is written for those queers who have internalized Christian homophobia and for those who have externalized their anger to fight back and stop the homophobic/heterosexist churches. It is a battle for queer truth, the truth of our love-making and the truth of our justice.

The Social Organization of Homophobia

Blatant homophobia mutilates you without pretense: it forbids you to talk, it forbids you to act, it forbids you to exist. Invisible homophobia, however, convinces you that closetedness is your destiny and impotence is your nature: it convinces you that it's not possible to speak, not possible to act, not possible to exist.

PARAPHRASE OF A QUOTE FROM EDUARDO GALEANO[1]

I find I am constantly being encouraged to pluck some one aspect of myself and present this as the meaningful whole, eclipsing other parts of self.

AUDRE LORDE[2]

In this chapter, I analyze the ways that homophobic power and oppression impinge upon the lives of lesbians and gay men. I begin with the fact of homophobic oppression in our society. I then critique the particulars of institutional oppression: How are prejudice and hatred and violence practiced at the institutional level against lesbians and gay men? I practice a genealogical analysis, paying attention to the exclusions, the irrational fears, prejudice and hatred, and the violence toward gay/lesbian people within institutional discourses and practices.

Homophobia is the socialized state of fear, threat, aversion, prejudice, and irrational hatred of the feelings of same-sex attraction. Homophobia can be specific to individuals, groups, social institutions, and cultural practices.[3] Beneath the organization of homophobia into social practice lies a perceived fear or threat. One of the most often stated accusations against gay men and lesbians is that they subvert or threaten "traditional" family values or the family itself.

In fact, homosexuality threatens only what traditional family values are based upon—the dualistic politics of gender and sexual identity. People are born male and female, and they are socialized into masculinity and femininity, which are politically instituted cultural roles. Same-sex genital practice threatens notions of masculinity and femininity upon which gender roles are constructed and differentiated. It challenges also the conventional patterns of male dominance and female subordination, which in our society are germane to the politics of gender. Cultural definitions of maleness and masculinity reinforce the social identification of maleness with power relations. Men sexually attracted to men and women sexually attracted to women pose a direct political threat to this heterosocial network of power relations.

Heterosexism socially organizes and maintains the institution of "compulsory heterosexuality," the mandatory privilege given to social practices built upon patriarchal definitions of male and female, their sex role differentiations, their sexual practices, and the creation of opposing networks of power relationships.[4] It compels people to play their sex-stereotyped gender roles. Heterosexism produces a network of power relations that privileges the male over the female in familial, economic, social, and political institutions. It defines women only as they relate to men. Its network of power relations is tightly interwoven with these institutional and cultural practices.

People are not born homophobic. They are socialized to homophobia as they learn heterosexist roles and values. Homophobia is embedded in heterosexism: "Heterosexism is to homophobia what sexism is to misogyny and what racism is to racial bigotry and hatred."[5] Homophobic discursive practice is based on the same binary oppositions as heterosexism but conflates them with an additional set of oppositions, heterosexuality/homosexuality. With this addition, homophobia and heterosexism merge into a social whole. Homophobic oppression becomes the product of the same heterosexist network of power relations whose deployments, rules, and strategies oppress women. Our society is both brutally heterosexist and brutally homophobic. Its social effects are recorded in the increased incidences of violence against women and gay and lesbian people.

Same-sex sexual practices challenge not only the politics of gender but also the politics of sexual identity. Gay and lesbian sexual practices generate gay and lesbian identities. These sexual identities are constructed in relation to heterosocial definitions of gender, sexuality, and social roles. Gay and lesbian sexual identities form a counterpractice that deconstructs the rigid definitions of masculinity and femininity and social constructions based upon these definitions. They transgress many dualistic strategies that support heterosexist sexual identities. For example, the United States Olympic Committee sued the Gay Olympics for proprietary usage of the word *Olympic,* whereas they did not pursue similar actions against the Special Olympics for the disabled or the Senior Olympics for senior citizens. The rigid definitions of masculinity within the U.S. Olympic Committee were threatened by the conjunction of *Gay* with *Olympics.* Lesbians, likewise, threaten heterosexual women by their independence from male control. Their independence intimidates women who have internalized heterosexist dualities.[6]

Gay/lesbian power arrangements challenge the unequal production and distribution of heterosocial power in our society. Lesbians and gay men through their sexual identities challenge homophobia deployed in heterosocial arrangements of power. Our society could not change its homophobic discourse and practice without affecting heterosexist social, economic, and political institutions. Particular homophobic discursive practices will affect other forms of discourse and practice; they interlock in a mutually generative matrix to produce homophobic power and truth claims. Homophobic power is the social and cultural matrix through which our social selves are formed. We will now shift to examining the social effects of homophobic power upon gay men and lesbians.

The Language of Hatred

Society teaches hatred of gay men and lesbians. Society labels as deviant those who are different. In our own society, gay men are called "sissies," "fairies," "queers," "perverts," "inverts," "fags" (faggots), "sodomites," "pansies," and so forth. Heterosexist discourse stereotypes gay men as limp-wristed, underdeveloped men, effeminate, not interested in typical masculine interests, and as child molesters. Lesbians are called "dykes," "witches," "butch," and "men haters." There is less labeling of lesbians by homophobic discourse because they are initially perceived as less threatening, or even invisible. It is only when lesbians assume roles outside of traditional femininity and assert their

independence from men that they pose a threat to androcentric social structure. Their utter lack of investment in the male power structure challenges the very foundation of male domination over women.
For example, any feminist who challenges the male power structure
is often labeled a lesbian by that structure. Lesbians are also subject
to the same labeling definitions and stereotyping degradations that all
women experience in our culture.

The distribution of power within any given society is rarely balanced, and more often than not it is unevenly distributed. This is particularly evident in our own contemporary society. Deviance is a label
used for social and political control by the prevailing heterosexist discourse and institutional practices.[7] In his study of deviance, sociolo-
gist Howard Becker observes, "Social groups create deviance by
making rules whose infraction create deviance. . . ."[8] Gay/lesbian sexual behavior is considered deviant. Yet deviance is applied not only to
their behaviors but also to lesbians and gay men themselves. Labeling thus becomes a means of creating deviance. It assigns gay men and
lesbians negative moral meanings and political statuses. It is an act of
political retaliation for transgressing heterosexist rules and social
boundaries.

Gay and lesbian behaviors are labeled sick, criminal, perverted, and
sinful. Such derogatory labels as "fags" and "dykes" are extended to
us as a group. Labels have been effective in controlling and maintaining heterosexual behaviors since childhood.[9] Children's literature reinforces heterosexual behavior through the traditional family values of
the Dick and Jane reading primers. Cultural diversity has begun to influence the educational materials of grade school children; however,
sexual diversity has not. These educational materials continue to reflect intense homophobia as well as intense heterosexism.

Heterosexist social rules attempt to socialize people's perceptions
and behaviors to interests consistent with their own position. Gay
and lesbian people who break heterosexist rules find themselves not
only labeled but also stereotyped. Stereotyping is punishment designed to degrade those who violate heterosocial codes. Gay/lesbian
violators are stripped of their social status by removing the symbols
of that status. For instance, they may be fired from their jobs, excom-
municated from their churches, imprisoned, hospitalized, given a
dishonorable discharge from the military, denied housing, or treated
as second-class citizens by the legal system. Violators are stigmatized;
they are identified as morally spoiled, socially undesirable, or politi-

cally threatening. They have been marked off from society, marginalized, and excluded from full participation in its network of power relations.

Heterosexist networks of power are jealously protected from those who do not fit or who are different. Lesbians and gay men in their differences are controlled, punished, made silent or invisible through exclusionary mechanisms of homophobic discursive practices in our society.

The Medicalization of Homosexuality

In *The History of Sexuality*, volume 1, Foucault observes how Catholic confessional practice gave rise to a proliferation of discourses on sexuality in the nineteenth century.[10] One form of discursive practice—"the psychiatrization of perverse pleasures"—examined sexual instinct with a clinical eye. Sexual instinct could function naturally; it could also be perverted, inverted, or distorted. A whole new field of discourse on sexual experience emerged in the practice of German psychiatry.[11] The word *homosexual* entered the vocabulary of contemporary Western society through German psychiatric usage in the nineteenth century. Foucault notes,

> The psychological, psychiatric, medical category of homosexuality was constituted from the moment it was characterized—Westphal's famous article of 1870 on "contrary sexual relations" can stand as its date of birth—less by a type of sexual relations than by a certain quality of sexual sensibility, a certain way of inverting the masculine and the feminine in oneself. Homosexuality appeared as one form of sexuality when it was transposed from the practice of sodomy onto a kind of interior androgyny, a hermaphrodism of the soul. The sodomite was a temporary aberration; the homosexual was now a species.[12]

Whereas sodomy had been understood as a "sin against nature," psychiatry now understood homosexuality medically as a set of symptoms or as a pathological illness. Religious discourse about the "sin against nature" was replaced by scientific discourse about the unnatural, the abnormal. The perverted was transformed into the pathological:

> The nineteenth-century homosexual became a personage, a past, a case history, and a childhood, in addition to being a type of life, a life form, and a morphology, with an indiscreet anatomy and possibly a mysterious physiology. Nothing that went into his total composition

was unaffected by his sexuality. It was everywhere present in him: at the root of all his actions because it was their insidious and indefinitely active principle, written immodestly on his face and body because it was a secret that always gave itself away. It was consubstantial with him, less as a habitual sin than as a singular nature.[13]

Thus the modern category of "homosexuality," along with its binary opposite, "heterosexuality," emerged in the West through medical discourse. The homosexual was created with a case history. New categories of sexuality appeared in the fields of medicine, psychiatry, and law centered on homosexual/heterosexual definitions in order to correct or remedy a social illness.

Now sexual behaviors could be chronicled, detailed, and classified along a scale of normality and abnormality. People could be circumscribed within sexual discursive categories. Heterosexuality was biologically, psychologically, and culturally normative. The medical discourse on homosexuality/heterosexuality implied the notion of a cure. Once a diagnosis of pathological sexual behavior was made by a clinician through observation and surveillance, established practices could be applied to correct the pathological behaviors and restore normal behavior.

Heterosexual doctors and psychiatrists exercised their clinical power and expertise to define homosexuality in professional journals. They saw it as pathological or sometimes pathogenic, always against the standard of normative heterosexuality. Their scientific discourse for the most part ignored any gay or lesbian definitions of themselves.[14] Pathological aspects of the most extreme behaviors of gay men and lesbians became the narrow diagnostic norm for defining all gay and lesbian experience.

The medicalization of homosexuality made possible medical and legal forms of social control. Homosexuality had to be observed clinically, corrected through treatment, and eradicated with the cure. A host of corrective medical and psychiatric treatments were applied from the late nineteenth century until recent times. They included involuntary hospitalizations, surgical castration and vasectomy of male homosexuals, hysterectomy and the surgical removal of clitoris and ovaries of suspected female homosexuals. These practices continued well into the twentieth century in the United States, when new corrective technologies of hormonal injections, pharmacologic experimentation, electric shock, lobotomies, and aversion therapies were applied to homosexuals.[15]

Homosexuality was treated both as a crime and a disease. Until the early 1960s homosexuals who were arrested were given the choice of prison or medical treatment. Many gay and lesbian people chose medical/psychiatric treatment to contain their sexual impulses. They were subjected to all forms of brutal aversive therapies, including drug-induced nausea, electric shock, and chemical therapies. Other behavior modification techniques of desensitization, heterosexual arousal techniques, hypnosis, and individual and group therapy attempted to regulate homosexual behavior and/or change homosexuals to heterosexuals. Homosexual groups based on the Alcoholics Anonymous model were formed to control homosexual impulses.

Conservative Freudian psychoanalytic societies replaced the more gross forms of social control with subtle forms of psychoanalytic control. For the crude tortures of aversion therapies, they substituted intense self-examination of parent-child relationships in order to understand the etiology of homosexual dsyfunction and behaviors. Irving Bieber and Charles Socarides were the leading psychiatrists in homosexual research at the time of the Stonewall Rebellion, the beginning of gay/lesbian liberation. They forcefully characterized homosexuality as profound psychopathology. For Bieber, exclusive heterosexuality was the biologic norm. Homosexuality emerged from the pattern of a domineering mother and detached father.[16] Socarides, likewise, pushed the origin of homosexuality back to the pre-Oedipal stage. Homosexuals were more profoundly disturbed individuals; they compulsively searched for an ever-elusive masculinity in their sexual partners and desperately avoided merger with their pre-Oedipal mothers.[17] For both Bieber and Socarides, the homosexual couple was nothing more than a pathological union of pain and disappointment.

Culturally produced definitions of normative heterosexuality within psychiatric practice, however, prevented clinicians from appreciating that people have a wide range of sexual diversity.[18] These culturally produced definitions of the normative were elevated to clinical discursive practice. Even today, much of the research into the causes of homosexuality is intrinsically hostile to gay and lesbian people. It is motivated by the premise that homosexuality is pathological.[19]

Psychiatric homosexual discourse influenced the American penal and legal system, affected the military screening and discharge of recruits, buttressed Christian pastoral and doctrinal positions, and shaped American culture.[20] The neo-Freudian and the behaviorist psychiatrists failed for the most part in their reparative therapies of homosexual orientation. Homosexual men and women can change their sexual behaviors through coercion or pressures—albeit psychiatric, familial, or religious. All human behaviors can change or be modified. Sexual orientation, on the other hand, is a different matter. It is difficult for homosexuals or heterosexuals to change who they really are. Psychiatrists studied a very specific segment of the homosexual population confined to prisons, hospitals, and those maladusted to their own sexuality. They failed to study a more representative segment of the homosexual population.

Another failure of psychiatry was its inability to listen to the discourse and practice of gay and lesbian people. Foucault observes that the medical and psychiatric discourse called forth a "reverse discourse: homosexuality began to speak in its own behalf, to demand that its legitimacy or 'naturality' be acknowledged, often in the same vocabulary, using the same categories by which it was medically disqualified."[21] In the next chapter, we will examine the counterdiscourse of the gay and lesbian community and its struggles with the American Psychiatric Association.

Medical/psychiatric discourse on homosexuality came to signify something of the truth of a person. Homosexual bodies became the focal point of sociological, anthropological, economic, religious, and political discourses. The medicalization of homosexuality lingers on in the fields of medicine and psychiatry. A significant number of doctors and psychiatrists still would like to find the causes of homosexuality and eradicate them. This medicalized dream may be possible as technological advances in genetic engineering become more real. Homophobic society may someday realize a "medicalized dream of the prevention of gay bodies" with a genetic cure.[22]

The Holy Crusade

Christian inquisitions, witch hunts, tortures, imprisonments, and executions of men and women who practiced same-sex sexual behaviors have now been replaced by more sophisticated forms of violence. Within Christianity negative definitions of people with homoerotic interests have been sustained since the twelfth century.[23] Contemporary Christian discourse has, in fact, facilitated and legitimized other homophobic practices of discrimination and violence. Roman Catholics and Protestants are less tolerant of homosexuality than members of non-Christian religions and nonaffiliates.[24] The social organization of homophobia produces homophobic people. Social scientists have discovered that homophobic people were "more authoritarian, more dogmatic, more cognitively rigid, more intolerant of ambiguity, more status-conscious, more sexually rigid, more guilty and negative about their own sex impulses, and less accepting of others in general."[25] These attributes can be correlated to homophobic institutions as well.

Christian discourse has organized and fostered an atmosphere of intolerance and hatred. Under the constitutional separation of church and state, offensive and inflammatory Christian discourse is legally protected speech. Literalist or fundamentalist Christian discourse has carried on a relentless assault on gay and lesbian people. This form of discourse is found in the mainstream Protestant, Catholic, and Orthodox churches. These ecclesial systems contain strong literalist or traditional positions on homosexuality. A few denominations—Quakers, Moravians, and Unitarians—are exceptions to the literalists' discourse on homosexuality.[26] Not all voices within the mainstream churches agree with their institutional positions on homosexuality.[27] Nonetheless, the major Protestant and Catholic churches consider homosexual relations to be sinful. They refuse to ordain openly gay/lesbian ministers and priests; they refuse to recognize and bless their unions. They fought the application of the Metropolitan Community Church (MCC), a gay/lesbian church, to the National Council of Churches.[28] Their institutional discourse on homosexuality either punishes gay and lesbian members or condones institutional homophobic social practices. They have not institutionally spoken against the increased incidences of violence against gay and lesbian people.[29] Nor do they support the gay and lesbian victims assistance organizations.

The Christian Right includes the rapidly growing fundamentalist Christian churches. The Christian Right is hateful in its discourse and violent in its practices. In initiating her "Save Our Children" campaign, Anita Bryant declared, "God puts homosexuals in the same category as murderers."[30] Her campaign organized the social hatred of the Christian Right, fostering a campaign based on social stereotypes: "Homosexuals cannot reproduce so they must recruit. And to freshen their ranks, they must recruit the youth of America."[31] Bumper stickers in Dade County, Florida, sported the slogan: "Kill a queer for Christ."[32] On television, Dean Wycoff of the Santa Clara, California, branch of the Moral Majority coupled homosexuality with murder and called upon the government to execute homosexuals. Larry Lea, a charismatic minister, announced that fundamentalist Christians would wage spiritual warfare against the gay and lesbian community in San Francisco: "We're talking about doing some serious damage to the evil strongholds of this area."[33] The Christian organization of social hatred and violence is no more apparent than in an appeal from the Reverend Jerry Falwell, the leader of the Moral Majority: "Stop the Gays dead in their perverted tracks."[34] At the 1992 Republican Convention, Pat Buchanan and the Reverend Pat Robertson leveled vitriolic attacks on lesbians and gay men in defense of traditional family values.

Jonathan Dollimore, cultural historian and critic, offers a social theory of displacement to explain the intense hostility of Christian churches to gay/lesbian people. Displacement often leads to demonizing the socially or the sexually different. The dominant social group places social blame for crisis on the social deviant, who becomes the focus of anxiety:

> In periods of intensified conflict, crisis is displaced on the deviant; the process only succeeds because of the paranoid instabilities at the heart of dominant cultural identities. Further, such displacements of non-sexual fears onto the sexual deviant, be he or she actual, imagined, or constituted in and by the displacement, are made possible because other kinds of transgression—political, religious—are not only loosely associated with the sexual deviant, but "condensed" in the very definition of deviance.[35]

Throughout Christian history, there has been been a tendency to equate the heretic, the Jew, the infidel, the witch, the papist, and the insurrectionist with the "sodomite." Sodomy was conflated with all that was considered as terrifyingly other or with different manifestations of social evil.[36] Christian groups felt a strong need to contain social deviance and prevent its spread and contagion. Same-sex practices have been portrayed as a grave danger to Christianity; they are still conceived as antithetical to Christianity:

> The homosexual subculture and AIDS threaten perhaps more profoundly than any other problem, the very survival, both physical and social, of the West and of America in particular. . . . Homosexuality is the cultural culmination of rebellion against God. It represents the "burning out" of man and his culture. This is true because the homosexual strikes at the very cornerstone of human society. . . . A homosexual culture is opposed at every point to Christianity. It must therefore be fought with every available weapon.[37]

Dollimore's notion of social displacement provides a framework for comprehending past and present intense ecclesial hostility to sexual difference and its conflation with heresy. Sexual difference threatens the church's social and political use of power. Sexual difference is conceived as a wholly illegitimate form of human expression. Gay and lesbian people are perceived as the "demonized other" by Christian fundamentalists who already feel threatened by the tremendous social shifts in the United States during the latter part of the twentieth century.

Institutionalized Christian homophobia has shaped many organizations whose mission is to eliminate homosexuality. Exodus International is a worldwide association of Christian organizations dedicated to leading homosexuals out of bondage into liberating union with God. Within its ranks are homophobic organizations such as Regeneration, Homosexuals Anonymous, and Metanoia Ministries.[38] Christian discourse about homosexuality in each of the organizations follows a similar pattern of reasoning. Exodus International defines homosexuality as "the adult condition of having preferential, emotional and erotic attractions to members of one's own sex."[39] It upholds heterosexuality as the intent of God's creation and disputes the idea that homosexuality is an unchangeable orientation, dismissing all scientific theories on the genetic etiology of homosexuality. The argument follows a homophobic biblical creationism: homosexual tendencies are one of the many disorders that has beset fallen humanity. How could God condemn a behavior and not provide a means of escape? Therefore, homosexuals are made, not born. If homosexuals are not born but socially made, then they can be unmade. God defines homosexuality as sinful abomination. Therefore, if homosexuality is an act of sin, it can be repented of. For fundamentalists, Christ offers the healing, heterosexual alternative that God wishes for all humanity. Exodus and its affiliates maintain that redemption is heterosexuality: "Redemption for the homosexual person is the process whereby sin's power is broken, and the individual is freed to know and experience true identity as discovered in Christ and His Church. That process entails the freedom to grow into heterosexuality."[40] To be a new person in Christ means that a person is no longer gay or lesbian; to live in Christ is to become heterosexual. The Christ becomes a symbol of compulsory heterosexuality or heterosexual redemption.

The practices of these heterosexual missionary organizations are based on the psychiatric discourse that attempted to change homosexual behaviors. These ideas have now been transferred to Christian pastoral counseling. Christian psychologists such as Elizabeth Moberly draw on them to legitimate their pastoral practices of healing homosexuality and restoring heterosexuality.[41] The choice of homosexuality produces loneliness, alienation, symbolic confusions, emotional hurts, fears, and confusions, she says. Long-term, loving, or integrated same-sex couples really do not exist. Homosexuals are completely driven by their sin choices, and they need to be healed within a highly structured environment.

The practices implemented to heal the homosexual or restore the homosexual to a heterosexual orientation are numerous. Homosexuals Anonymous, for instance, has adapted the Twelve-Step program of Alcoholics Anonymous to a fourteen-step program for restoring a heterosexual orientation. The language of the fourteen-step program is enmeshed in confessional and self-control practices: "We admit, we come to believe, we come to see, we repent, we learn to claim. . . ." The practical application of biblical principles creates a homophobic spirituality that informs the participant's activities. The homosexual avoids the so-called addiction of homosexual behaviors.[42]

Homosexual orientation is broken down into its components of sexual behavior, identity, and lifestyle. Group support, pressure techniques, and aggressive, homophobic biblical interpretation become the means for change. These aversive practices are oriented toward the social and Christian construction of heterosexual behavior, identity, and lifestyle. They target and solicit unhappy gay men and lesbians. Other techniques include confessional practices, pastoral counseling, group support, workshops and retreats, family and peer pressure, daily phone messages, reading, prayer, and faith healing. These techniques for social control aim at suppressing homosexual behaviors and motivating a homosexual to renounce a homosexual identity and separate from gay/lesbian culture. Like aversive psychiatric practices, these practices may change behaviors but are unable to change sexual orientation. Exodus International and its affiliated organizations produce and distribute a vast amount of Christian homophobic discourse appearing on tapes and in books, newsletters, and pamphlets.

The official Catholic position is that homosexuality is a "disordered inclination." In 1975, the *Declaration on Some Questions Concerning Sexual Ethics* from the Vatican Congregation for the Doctrine of the Faith, previously the Office of the Inquisition before Vatican II, made the distinction between "homosexual tendency" and "homosexual acts." In the following year, the United States bishops produced a pastoral letter, *To Live in Christ Jesus*. In that publication, the bishops spoke of a "homosexual orientation." In 1986, Cardinal Ratzinger's *Letter on the Pastoral Care of Homosexual Persons* employs the term *homosexual orientation* three times. The 1986 document frequently uses *condition, inclination,* and *tendency* in place of *orientation*. *Orientation* in the 1986 document is used within a narrow philosophical framework based on natural law. (I will address the natural law issue in a later chapter.) Gay men and lesbians are described as "intrinsically evil" and "objectively disordered."[43] This is apparent in section 16 of the document, where it describes "sexual orientation" as reductionistic because humans are made in the image of God.[44] There is only fundamental human identity of God's children. The official Catholic position maintains natural law as the norm of human sexuality and opposes all social constructions of human sexuality through the social sciences. In the process, it upholds a patriarchal image of human sexuality wrapped in a patriarchal image of God. This enables the Catholic hierarchy to dismiss all social and cultural constructions of human sexuality as a reduction of the mystery of God.

The institutional position distinguishes between the "homosexual inclination" and "homosexual acts." Homosexual inclination is not sinful but "objectively disordered," whereas homogenital actions are an "intrinsic moral evil." In their 1990 document, *Human Sexuality: A Catholic Perspective for Education and Lifelong Learning,* the American Catholic bishops repeated the Ratzinger letter and described homosexuality as an "objective disorder."

According to the bishops, only in heterosexual marital relations can the use of the sexual faculty be morally good. Only a heterosexual orientation and only heterosexual marital acts are natural, that is, "intrinsically ordered." The fundamental identity of God's children becomes heterosexual, based on an erroneous reading of Scriptures and a faulty view of sexuality based on natural law. The Catholic position demands a life of celibacy for those with a homosexual condition. Courage and Diocesan Gay/Lesbian Outreach were formed by Catholic bishops to provide an emotional and religious support system for homosexual Catholics to live a celibate life. They were created to counter the Conference of Catholic Lesbians and Dignity, two Catholic organizations resistant to official church teachings on homosexuality.[45]

The 1976 pastoral letter, *To Live in Christ Jesus,* condemned violence and acts of malice against homosexuals. Yet the Catholic bishops lack credibility when they repeatedly oppose legislation for gay/lesbian civil rights. The cardinal primate of the Netherlands, Adrianus Simonis, stated that a Catholic could refuse to rent an apartment to gay men and lesbians.[46] The hierarchical position with a few exceptions has been that in the absence of laws prohibiting homosexuality, people will view it as morally acceptable. This hermeneutical principle has been applied to any civil law that prohibits anti-gay/lesbian discrimination and the hate crimes bills that include sexual orientation. Catholic bishops claim that such laws constitute moral approval. In 1984, Cardinal John O'Connor opposed the New York initiative, "Executive Order 50" of Mayor Koch, that prohibited any institution receiving funds from the city to discriminate because of sexual orientation. In 1986, Cardinal O'Connor vehemently opposed the New York City legislative initiative, "Intro 2," that banned discrimination on the basis of sexual orientation in housing, employment, and public accommodations. Without reading the proposed bill, he publicly accused it of supporting "sex between men and boys," child molestation, and giving homosexuals preferential treatment. He charged that the bill approved of homosexual acts and that this was contrary to church teaching.[47] After fifteen years of opposition from the Catholic church, "Intro 2" passed on March 21, 1986.

The Catholic hierarchy has claimed that any normalization of homosexuality fosters it and makes it more public. The 1986 Vatican document banned support of any Catholic group that did not teach that homosexual actions are immoral and sinful. Many American bishops have evicted over fifty chapters of Dignity, a national gay and lesbian Catholic interest group, from church properties. The Vatican forced the removal of Dr. Charles Curran from the faculty of Catholic University for his moderate ethical position on homosexuality.[48] John McNeill, who had been silenced for writing *The Church and the Homosexual,* broke his silence to speak out against Cardinal Ratzinger's letter; the Vatican forced his expulsion from the Society of Jesus.[49] Moreover, the Catholic institutional discourse vigorously maintains that any normalization of homosexual behavior erodes family life and remains contrary to natural law.[50] The Catholic bishops have contextualized their own position as "profamily" and identified homosexual rights with an "antifamily" position. Similar antifamily discourse is found in the rhetoric of the Christian Right. In 1991, the Catholic archbishop of Denver, Francis Staffer, opposed the city ordinance that would prohibit discrimination based on sexual orientation. In a letter to his diocese, the archbishop cited that passage of such a nondiscrimination bill would promote homosexual marriages. Cardinal Bernard Law has strongly condemned a proposed Boston ordinance, the Family Protection Act, that would recognize domestic partnerships and extend work benefits to spouses of city workers. He has condemned the proposed bill because it would lead to the civil recognition of same-sex marriages.[51] Because of stiff Catholic opposition, the Boston City Council rejected the ordinance by a vote of 11 to 2.

The 1992 Vatican document *Some Considerations Concerning the Catholic Response to Legislate Proposals on the Nondiscrimination of Homosexual Persons* urges the American bishops to take a public position of just discrimination against gay men and lesbians. This discrimination is compared to the state's authority to restrict the exercise of the civil rights of mentally ill persons to protect the common good. The notion of homosexual orientation as an intrinsic evil or objective disorder becomes comparable to mental illness. Gay men and lesbians are dehumanized:

> Among other rights all persons have the right to work, to housing, etc. Nevertheless, these rights are not absolute. They can be legitimately limited for objectively disordered external conduct. This is not only licit but obligatory.[52]

Furthermore, the Congregation for the Doctrine of the Faith points out that homosexuals who have not come out do not suffer public discrimination.[53] Only those who are public about their disorder are rightly discriminated against. The Vatican document ends with a call to protect family values by active public opposition to extending family status to gay/lesbian unions and extending health benefits to domestic partners.[54] Gay/lesbian bashers find in Rome's pronouncement a religious justification for their homophobic violence. Homophobic Catholic youth in Boston carried signs saying GOD HATES FAGS, aimed against Irish gay/lesbian marchers in the St. Patrick's Day parade. Homosexuals represent the devil to the religious right.

Institutional Homophobia

Homophobia permeates our social practices. Discursive fields of knowledge and practice link up with other fields to produce an interlocking system of power. For instance, there are close social and financial linkages between the churches and the Boy Scouts of America. This has led to the exclusion of "known or avowed homosexuals" as Scouts and Scoutmasters. The Boy Scouts of America promotes traditional family values, which are deemed inconsistent with a gay sexual identity.[55] The meaning of "morally straight" contained in the Scouts' oath has been reconfigured as "heterosexual," while the phrases "clean" and "reverend" from Scouts' law have been used to support traditional religious values. The Boy Scouts of America organizes and promotes social homophobia despite the fact that its founder, Lord Baden-Powell, had a male lover, Kenneth McLean.[56]

Our educational system presumes heterosexual children and does not allow for differences of sexual identities. Gay and lesbian children grow up in an educational system designed on rigid gender differences and oriented toward heterosexual social identities. Compulsive heterosexuality is embedded in the social and educational system within which they are socialized. Within a nonpluralistic and frequently intolerant system of socialization, they struggle to develop healthy self-images.[57] This compulsive heterosocial environment has led to severe isolation, alienation, and depression of gay and lesbian youth. They are compelled to hide their same-sex feelings from peer ridicule and sanctions. They learn to keep silent about their perceived differences. Gay and lesbian youth face a hostile environment of intolerance, misinformation, and hatred from their peers, teachers, coaches, counselors, and administrators. With a few exceptions, the educational system is neither gay affirming nor lesbian affirming in the formation and development of gay/lesbian sexual identities. Many teenage suicides result from an inability to deal with this compulsive heterosexual system. The educational system is the product of a heterosexist society that safeguards its mechanism for socialization and social integration. Yet this educational system works against the development of healthy gay and lesbian self-identities. Attempts at introducing more positive lesbian/gay sex education curricula have been actively opposed by the Roman Catholic hierarchy and the fundamentalist Right.

At colleges and universities, openly gay/lesbian students encounter a wide variety of responses from acceptance to intolerance and harassment. However, increased incidences of campus violence have been documented over the last eight years by the National Gay and Lesbian Task Force. Their 1990 report cites numerous incidents of queer bashings, harassments, and threats on campus.[58] At Marshall University, for example, several students placed signs on campus that read, "Queer Bashing '90. Bored? Join us in the yearlong crusade to maliciously harass Marshall homosexuals."[59] Until recently, college students involved in ROTC programs were required to fill out a "Worksheet for Administration and Retention in ROTC" that included the following question: "Have you ever engaged in, desired, or intended to engage in bodily contact with a person of the same sex for the purpose of sexual gratification?"[60] The ROTC worksheet equated sexual orientation with sexual activity and was designed to weed out gay and lesbian candidates for the military.

Each year thousands of good men and women receive dishonorable discharges from the United States military because they are gay or lesbian.[61] The rationale is clearly stated in the policy of the Department of Defense:

> Homosexuality is incompatible with military service. The presence of such members adversely affects the ability of the Armed Forces to maintain discipline, good order, and morale; to foster mutual trust and confidence among the members; to insure the integrity of the system of rank and command; to facilitate assignment and worldwide deployment of members who must frequently live and work under close conditions affording minimal privacy; to recruit and retain members of the military services; to maintain the public acceptability of military service; and, in certain circumstances, to prevent breaches of security.

The Department of Defense claims that the presence of gay men and lesbians would be disruptive to the military services and they would be less effective in performing their duties. Continuing an argument from the McCarthy era, the Defense Department groups homosexuality with communism as a threat to national security that must be rooted out of the federal government.[62]

A study conducted by the Navy in 1957, *The Crittenden Report*, found that gay servicemen actually displayed superior performance in contrast to their heterosexual counterparts.[63] The Department of Defense has not been able to cite a single instance of gay or lesbian military personnel being blackmailed to reveal military secrets. In fact, a 1989 study by the department's Personnel Security Research and Education Center (PERSEREC) concluded that homosexuals were no more a security risk than heterosexual personnel.[64] Despite the fact that over two million gay men and women served heroically during World War II and the Korean and Vietnam conflicts and that currently two hundred thousand enlisted personnel are lesbian and gay, the

Department of Defense continues to abridge the civil rights of gay men and lesbians to serve their country.[65] The Department of Defense bases its policy on inaccurate stereotypes of lesbians and gay men and a failure to understand the demographics of the spread of HIV infection in the United States. Recent political attempts by President Clinton and legal gains against the military policy of discrimination have drawn fire from the Department of Defense and the conservative/religious Right.

Employment discrimination continues within the federal government in sensitive areas of the Defense Department, Justice Department, CIA, State Department, and other agencies. From the time of the McCarthy era, the courts have upheld denials of employment and security clearances based on the arguments that homosexuals are likely to be blackmailed or are untrustworthy or violate criminal law.[66]

In other areas of public employment, the constitutional protections of due process, equal protection, and the first amendment of free speech prevent the federal government from arbitrarily hiring and firing individuals.[67] Such constitutional employment protections are not extended to the private sector for gay and lesbian people. Unlike other minorities who are protected under Title VII of the 1964 Civil Rights Act, there are no legal mechanisms to prevent the denial of employment or dismissal because of sexual orientation within the private sector: "Employment decisions based on sexual orientation result in second-class status for gay and lesbian people in society, solely because their personal lives or affectional preferences do not conform to those of the majority."[68] Employment discrimination against gay/lesbian employees is legal in all but a handful of states and a slowly growing number of city jurisdictions. Homophobia is widespread in educational employment in the public school system because of stereotypic prejudice.[69]

Gay and lesbian people are penalized in all aspects of their legal lives because of their sexual orientation. Until recently, aliens have been denied and refused naturalization because of their sexual orientation.[70] The Reagan Justice Department ordered the Centers for Disease Control to prevent homosexuals from entering the country by imposing a medical quarantine on self-professed homosexuals on psychological grounds.[71] In nearly half of the states, sodomy laws are retained and used against gay men and lesbians. These laws deny gay men and lesbians the right to have sex with consenting adults and render what gays and lesbians do in the privacy of their bedrooms illegal. They reinforce widespread anti-gay/lesbian sentiments. Gay and lesbian parents are denied custody of their children because of their orientation, or their lovers may not be allowed to live with them if they are to maintain custody.[72]

San Francisco's openly gay supervisor, Harvey Milk, was assassinated in 1979 along with Mayor George Moscone by the homophobic city supervisor Dan White. Mayor Moscone had signed into law Milk's comprehensive gay rights bill in 1978, barring housing and employment discrimination. Supervisor Dan White opposed the bill. Harvey Milk was assassinated three weeks after a statewide referendum defeated Proposition 6, the Briggs initiative that prohibited gay and lesbian teachers from teaching in the public school system. In the Dan White murder trial before an all-white and all-heterosexual jury, the charge of premeditated murder was reduced to manslaughter with the famous "Twinkie food" defense of diminished capacity because White had gorged on junk food before committing the murders.[73] No evidence of Dan White's history of homophobic antagonism or his 1977 election campaign based on hate rhetoric was ever presented by the prosecution.[74] White received a sentence of six years in prison for murdering two men who espoused gay-affirming values.[75]

Prior to 1961, homosexual sex between consenting adults was illegal in every state of the union. Now more than half the states have repealed their sodomy laws. In 1986, the Supreme Court upheld the constitutionality of Georgia's sodomy laws in *Bowers v. Hardwick.*

The right to privacy and equal protection under the Constitution were abridged for gay men and lesbians. According to the majority opinion of the Supreme Court, there is no fundamental constitutional right to commit consensual homosexual sodomy. The majority opinion refused to cast aside millennia of Judeo-Christian moral teaching. *Bowers v. Hardwick* thus legitimized social stigmatizing of gay and lesbian people on the basis of private acts between consenting adults. Former congressional Representative William Dannemeyer of the conservative Right calls for the restoration and enforcement of the states' antisodomy laws against what he calls the "homosexualization" of America.[76] The issue is power—whether the state or gay men and lesbians have social control over their sexuality.

The effects of *Bowers v. Hardwick* are felt in employment and housing discrimination, parenting issues and custody rights of children, legal abridgement of privacy in HIV testing, and discrimination against people living with AIDS. There is no legal recognition of same-sex couples; therefore, there are no legal protections for same-sex couples.[77] The lack of social and legal recognition makes it far more difficult for same-sex relationships to exist. With the advent of AIDS, many insurance companies use demographics to profile potential gay applicants and deny them coverage. Insurance companies screen out unmarried males who live in particular zip codes, who work in stereotypically gay occupations, or who name an unrelated male as a beneficiary. Legal protection for gay men and lesbians as such is almost nonexistent in America. Only a few states and a hundred or so cities and counties have laws forbidding discrimination on the basis of sexual orientation. San Francisco has legally recognized domestic partnerships and extended benefits to partners of city employees.[78]

The editors of the *Harvard Law Review* concluded in their study of sexual orientation and the law: "Despite some improvement, discrimination on the basis of sexual orientation persists throughout American society and the American legal system. The situation is unlikely to change until anti-gay discrimination is recognized as a legitimate issue and lesbian and gay concerns enter mainstream legal discourse."[79] The right to privacy and equal protection under the law need to be extended to gay and lesbian people to correct the second-class status that they experience as American citizens. They are not recognized as a legal minority and thus forego legal protection under federal legislation.

Passage of the Colorado Amendment 2 legalizes discrimination against lesbians and gay men. In effect, it implements the content of the 1992 letter from the Vatican Congregation for the Doctrine of Faith that calls for public measures of discrimination against gay men and lesbians. Amendment 2 removes any legal recourse to gay/lesbian persons who are denied employment, housing, accommodations, or services. It in effect creates a class of citizens who are singled out for public discrimination. Amendment 2 attempts to silence gay men and lesbians through fear and intimidation. With passage of Amendment 2, there has been a substantial increase in hate crimes and violence in Colorado directed against gay men and lesbians. The parallel of Amendment 2 with Nazi legislation restricting Jewish rights and increased violence against Jews is striking.

In the public media, lesbians and gay men are rendered invisible or portrayed negatively. Many forms of media repeat cultural stereotypes. General Motors produced a Chevrolet truck commercial where a customer referred to a foreign model pickup truck as "some little faggot truck." A rap song released by the group Audio Two featured this lyric: "I can't understand why you lookin' this way / What's the matter witcha boy, are ya gay? / Yo, I hope that ain't the case, 'cause gay mothers get punched in the face / I hate faggots / They're living in the Village like meat on some maggots."[80] Syndicated radio talk shows and local disc jockeys incite homophobia and AIDS-phobia. Comedians like Eddie Murphy continue to repeat queer jokes and make tasteless comments about people living with AIDS. President Bush's White House Counsel, C. Boyden Gray, remarked to a local Republican group that a Federal Home Loan Board examiner was a "fag."[81] Corporate business, the public media, government officials and religious leaders, and the entertainment industry all contribute to an atmosphere of social hate and intolerance. They organize, promote, and distribute social hatred and prejudice; these contribute to the increasing anti-gay/lesbian violence in our society.

AIDS and Homophobia

AIDS has been constructed through language to designate the medical effects of HIV entering and severely affecting the human immune system. Discourses of medicine, scientific research, and popular culture have contributed to its definition. From the initial cases of AIDS of 1981, the social construction of AIDS influenced scientific discourse and response to the disease. In the medical world the disease was initially called GRID, "Gay-Related Immune Deficiency" by early clinicians. It was called the "gay cancer" and then the "gay plague" in the general media in the early 1980s. The venerealization of AIDS—its categorization as an STD (sexually transmitted disease)—linked homosexuality and AIDS in the public mind. Homosexuality was viewed as the cause of AIDS, and this widely held belief delayed scientific, public health, and political responses. As long as biomedical scientists in the public and private sectors perceived AIDS as a gay male disease, little attention was paid to its spread.[82] AIDS discourse was far more moralized as a discursive practice than medicalized.

In *And the Band Played On*, gay author Randy Shilts points out that scientific discovery of the virus came quickly once the research bureaucracy began moving. He documents the bureaucratic infighting of research agencies that delayed the discovery of HIV.[83] The National Institutes of Health waited two years before funding AIDS research projects. It was already twenty-two months into the spread of HIV infection before the National Cancer Institute formed a task force on AIDS. And not until October 1985 did the Centers for Disease Control issue a definitive statement on the transmission of the HIV virus.

From the first appearances of AIDS among gay men in 1981, local and national organizations failed to respond adequately or appropriately to the health crisis. Homophobia had an effect on public health policy; New York City public health officials and government officials did not begin funding services until late 1984, even though they perceived how deeply the spread of HIV infection would tax city resources. The Reagan administration, committed to reducing domestic expenditures and increasing military funding, refused to spend monies appropriated by Congress for AIDS research programs. The administration was influenced by a vigorous Moral Majority lobby that violently opposed expenditures for homosexuals. But homophobia was not limited to the Republican Right. Mario Cuomo and Michael Dukakis, both liberal Democratic governors, were also reluctant to spend monies on a "gay plague." A cultural homophobia impeded effective public policy formation to counter the spread of HIV infection through the mid- to the late eighties. In 1985, influenced by the Republican Right and the Moral Majority, the Reagan administration blocked the use of CDC money for education to prevent the spread of HIV infection among gay men or IV drug users. Public officials were reluctant to deal with the explicit issues of "safer" sexual practices or the use of condoms because of the opposition from church groups, the Moral Majority, and conservative interest groups. The only bright light of the Reagan administration was the courageous efforts of Surgeon General Dr. C. Everett Koop, who, because of his sense of medical responsibility and Christian compassion, and despite his very conservative religiousness, spoke out for education in the midst of administrative silence. The failure of key organizations at the national, state, and local levels to intervene has contributed to the widespread belief in the gay and lesbian community that the identification of AIDS as a "gay plague" delayed effective response and the development of public AIDS policy.[84] It was only when AIDS threatened the nation's blood supply and started to spread to the heterosexual population that national organizations finally responded.

Misinformation and homophobia are more often than not intertwined with AIDS discourse. The media has sensationalized the myth of "risk groups": gay men, hemophiliacs, drug addicts, and Haitians. It has misinformed the public by focusing on risk group stereotypes

rather than risk behaviors. Stereotypes are conduits for social prejudice, not for medical information. The media construction of AIDS has
given large segments of the American population who are involved in
risky sexual behaviors a false sense of security. Since the 1980s the demographics of the spread of HIV infection have radically changed
from its earlier profiles to heterosexual urban minorities and heterosexual youth.

The powerful social discourse surrounding AIDS is inscribed with
homophobia. AIDS discourse reflects the practices of social stigmatizing, fear of contagion, and exclusion of the infected. AIDS hysteria
has fueled social violence and hate campaigns. Senator Jesse Helms
called for a quarantine of those with HIV infection. The columnist
William F. Buckley called for a physical branding of the infected:
"Everyone detected with AIDS should be tattooed in the upper fore-
arm, to protect common needle users, and on the buttocks to protect
the victimization of other homosexuals."[85] Cory Servaas, a Reagan
appointee to the Presidential AIDS Commission, announced that it
was patriotic to test negative.[86] The reverse implication is that to test
positive is unpatriotic, un-American. A number of American Catholic
bishops and cardinals have called for compassion for the "innocent
victims of AIDS." They have divided people living with AIDS into the
innocent and the guilty. There are those who get AIDS through no fault
of their own; included here are hemophiliacs, infants, and spouses.
The guilty, by contrast, have brought the punishment of AIDS upon
themselves. In his letter on *The Pastoral Care of Homosexual Persons,*
Cardinal Joseph Ratzinger states that the practice of homosexuality is
the cause and the vehicle for spreading AIDS to large numbers of people. The entire community is put at risk because of the moral depra-
vation of gay men.[87]

Homophobia and AIDS-phobia are closely intertwined. One surgeon stated, "We used to hate faggots on an emotional basis. Now we
have a good reason."[88] AIDS-phobia has inflamed and exacerbated
cultural homophobia. Since 1986, AIDS-phobia has led to a yearly increase of homophobic violence. On September 15, 1990, a security
guard at Disneyland in Anaheim repeatedly harassed a gay and lesbian
group with the words "I wish they would all die of AIDS."[89] Student
leaders of gay and lesbian organizations at the University of Utah received threatening letters with the messages "Death to Gays" and
"Thank God for AIDS."[90] In 1989, the house of one of the actors in Larry
Kramer's AIDS play, *The Normal Heart,* was burned in Springfield,

Missouri. Gay and lesbian hate crimes have increased geometrically with the emergence of AIDS.

AIDS discourse in our culture often masks genocidal homophobic fantasies. Religious language that places God on the side of the righteous, not with the HIV-infected sinner, may reveal such genocidal fantasies. This discourse envisions a postgay world, where homosexuality is eradicated by God. AIDS becomes God's way to rid the world of homosexuality and restore the world to Christian compulsory heterosexuality. In the words of Jerry Falwell,

> AIDS is a lethal judgment of God on America for endorsing this vulgar, perverted, and reprobate lifestyle. . . . God also says those engaged in such homosexual acts will receive "in their own persons, due penalty of their error." God destroyed Sodom and Gomorrah primarily because of the sin of homosexuality. Today, He is again bringing the judgment against this wicked practice through AIDS."[91]

In 1983, Ronald Godwin, an executive of the Moral Majority, opposed government funds for research and treatment of AIDS: "What I see is a commitment to spend our tax dollars on research to allow these diseased homosexuals to go back to their perverted practices without any standards of accountability."[92] Roman Catholic cardinal John Krol echoes Falwell's sentiments: "The spread of AIDS is an act of vengeance against the sin of homosexuality."[93]

Fundamentalist biblical discourse about homosexuality interlocks with AIDS discourse, producing and intensifying hatred. Institutionalized Christian homophobic discourse has, since the spread of AIDS, become fused with biblical discourse on plague and God's punishment. Homophobia and AIDS-phobia blend into a single discourse.[94]

A genocidal fantasy of killing off the gay population is deeply embedded in fundamentalist AIDS discourse. For Christian fundamentalists, the HIV virus becomes the new angel of death passing over and eradicating the gay population. Falwell comments,

> They [homosexuals] are scared to walk near one of their kind right now. And what we [preachers] have been unable to do with our preaching, a God who hates sin has stopped dead in its tracks, by saying do it, and die. Do it and die.[95]

According to fundamentalist discourse, God has inflicted a plague on American society to stop the sexual revolution and punish homosexual men. HIV as the wrath of God becomes an instrument for creating a new purified Christian society that supports heterosexist power. Moreover, a certain glee underlies fundamentalist Christian discourse about AIDS and the eradication of gay men. Christo-fascism has contributed to and blessed homophobic violence.

Anti-Gay/Lesbian Violence

In the United States, most institutional discourse—from state, educational, legal and penal, medical and mental health, military, ecclesial, familial, economic, and media establishments—tries to prevent the development of gay and lesbian people. These various forms of discourse produce interlocking networks of power relations aligned against gay men and lesbians. There is a direct link between the production of these powerful networks and the production of violence. The same structures that maintain compulsory heterosexuality also enforce invisibility of gay men and lesbians. Gary Comstock has observed, "The greater visibility of lesbian/gay people and their neighborhoods, the social activism of the lesbian/gay movement in most social institutions, and the attention of the media to both has been paralleled by a documented increase in anti-gay/lesbian violence."[96] The social organization of homophobia not only makes it difficult for lesbians and gay men to live openly; it makes it dangerous to be openly gay or lesbian.

The National Gay and Lesbian Task Force Policy Institute (NGLTFPI) has compiled incidences of anti-gay/lesbian violence since 1983 from police reports and local gay/lesbian victimization assistance programs. In its compilation of antigay crimes from six cities, the NGLTFPI reported an increase of intimidation and harassment, physical assault, vandalism, police abuse, extortion, homicide, bomb threats, and arson.[97] Each year shows an alarming increase in the number of incidents from the preceding year in all six cities studied. No group in the United States has experienced such a rapid increase of violence and hate crimes as the gay/lesbian community. The NGLTFPI lists a litany of other recorded national crimes, and it speculates that the rising numbers of violent incidents may be the result of a homophobic backlash against the visible gay and lesbian population.[98]

At the University of Delaware, the Homophobic Liberation Front has harassed gay and lesbian students with abuse and threats. White supremacists—the Aryan Nation, the White Aryan Resistance, the American Front—and skinheads continue to commit violent hate crimes against gay and lesbian people. The NGLTFPI concludes from its study,

As with other bigoted attacks, each anti-gay episode sends a message of hatred and terror intended to silence and render invisible not only the victim but all lesbians and gay men. In effect, such violence denies to gay people, and all who are perceived to be inferior, their full measure of equality, including the rights to speak out, associate and assemble. Unchecked, these crimes of hate create an atmosphere of fear and intolerance that undermines not only the lesbian and gay community but the democratic and pluralistic foundation of our society.[99]

Though many leaders in government, law enforcement, and churches support legislative efforts to end violence, many also resist legislative efforts against hate crimes. Twelve states have enacted laws that penalize crimes based on sexual orientation; ten American cities have statutes that address anti-gay/lesbian violence. However, homophobic legislators in a number of other states and cities have blocked or defeated hate crime bills because they protect lesbian and gay people.

On April 23, 1990, President Bush signed into law the Hate Crime Statistics Act, which requires the Justice Department through the FBI to compile the statistics on all crimes based on race, religion, ethnicity, and sexual orientation. Anti-gay/lesbian violence may be contextualized in the upswing of hate-related crimes against African Americans, women, Jews, and other ethnic minorities. In the future, we may have more accurate compilations of hate crimes against gay and lesbian people.

Most American social and political institutions actively work against gay and lesbian people. They foster prejudice and discrimination, the tools used by heterosexist society to maintain its control, production, and distribution of power. American society has a low tolerance for difference. The editors of the *Harvard Law Review* draw a parallel between racial prejudice and anti-gay/lesbian violence: "Anti-gay [and lesbian] violence resembles racial violence in that both serve to intimidate and disempower their victims and others like them."[100] Hate crimes seek to deny and reverse the social gains for equal rights, returning gay men and lesbians to social invisibility. Homophobic violence is a means of political control, a way of keeping gay and lesbian people in their place, in their "closets." Homophobia does not tolerate sexual difference or dissidence from heterosexist conventionality. It uses social control and violence to keep in check those who are different and has mainstreamed violence against a visible gay/lesbian community. Homophobia pervades every aspect of American life. It stands in violent opposition to the civil rights and sexual freedom of lesbians and gay men.

2

Gay and Lesbian Silence Is Broken

The struggle for sexual self-definition is a struggle in the end for control over our bodies. To establish this control we must escape from those ideologies and categorizations which imprison us within the existing social order.

JEFFREY WEEKS[1]

Gay men and lesbians were a silenced and hidden minority through the earlier part of the twentieth century. They were silenced by the power of homophobic discourse and sought the shelter of social invisibility against homophobic social pressures. Tens of millions of men and women in the United States felt forced to hide from or to hide their sexual orientation. However, resistance occurred to the network of heterosexist power. In my discussion of the medicalization of homosexuality, I noted Foucault's observation that medical/psychiatric discursive practice made it possible for a "reverse discourse: homosexuality began to speak in its own behalf, to demand that its legitimacy or 'naturality' be acknowledged, often in the same vocabulary, using the same categories by which it was medically disqualified."[2] The effects of the medicalization of homosexuality were not only to create a species but to incite it. These effects created an emerging population. The effects of the deployment of homophobia led to ever greater resistance; it led to the production and circulation of gay/lesbian bodies and voices. Far from silencing gay/lesbian sexual discourse, homophobic power produced its articulation. It generated a rebellious public discourse with specific forms, particular behaviors, and definite cultural sensibilities.

In this chapter, I will discuss to the "reverse discourse" of gay men and lesbians. The sources are drawn, whenever possible, from gay and lesbian writings. Their disqualified voices speak to the effects of institutional homophobia. Gay/lesbian reverse discourse includes gay and lesbian resistance after World War II, the movement from invisibility to visibility, and the movement of silent resistance to political activism. It is about the production of gay/lesbian bodies and voices. It is a story of courageous resistance to homophobic oppression and violence, to its definitions and categories. Gay and lesbian discourse challenges the negative heterosexist definitions of ourselves; it transgresses those social definitions to produce our own discursive practice.

"Closeted Sexuality"

Homophobic cultural practices have punished men and women for centuries for daring to be themselves or daring to express their same-sex attractions. Conscious of same sex-attraction, gay men and lesbians remained invisible but ever aware of their difference. They were socialized into the political network of compulsory heterosexuality[3] and educated to the same heterosexist values in their families, schools, and churches. Their role models were parents, teachers, and ostensibly heterosexual adults. They experienced their social world as the organization of values, policies, structures, and organizations that benefited only heterosexual people. Lesbians and gay men internalized homophobic values. They felt shame about their bodies and conflicted feelings about their attraction to the same sex. Being homosexual was their dirty little secret kept to themselves. Gay/lesbian teenagers have the highest suicide rates because of the shame of being different and the generalized cultural intolerance to difference.

The term *closeted* refers to the hiddenness of being gay/lesbian because of the dreadful repercussions inflicted by homophobic oppression. The metaphor denotes something hidden from public view or display, something kept secret and privatized. Living in the closet carries the constellation of feelings of fear, dread, shame, guilt, and self-hatred. It is internalized homophobia[4]. Internalized homophobia is a difficult and pervasive problem for many gay men and lesbians. Homophobia is a powerful force within their society; it exerts tremendous power in the social construction of their institutional and cultural practices.[5] Many gay men and lesbians have internalized the negative judgments of heterosexist society, turning those judgments against themselves. They feel deep self-loathing, self-hatred, and self-rejection. They are afraid of their same-sex attractions and feelings, and they do everything in their power to hide, suppress, or deny those feelings. Gay men and lesbians generally feel isolated and different from those around them. They are intimidated by men and women who are open in their sexual orientation. Sometimes they transfer their internalized self-hatred and fears upon those who are more open about their sexual orientation. Closeted lesbians and gay men desperately do not want to be labeled one of "them." Their hostility masks their own insecurities and self-loathing.[6] In their desperation, closeted gay men and lesbians seek out reparative pyschotherapies; they accept the repressive controls of religion. In fear, they hide from their own sexual truth.

The experience of closetedness is a social effect of oppression. Closeted sexual identity is the self-experience of internalized homophobia. It may include complete denial of one's gay or lesbian sexual orientation to oneself or to one's social network. Or it may be a partial, private admission of sexual identity to a limited social circle. Living in the closet often includes living a double life and is destructive to the person. Many gay men and lesbians are forced to fully or partially conceal their sexual orientation for fear of dreadful repercussions. Many enter marriages to try to change their orientation toward the same sex. Some studies have found that one-fifth of gay men were once married and that over one-third of white lesbians and over one-half of black lesbians were married.[7] More often than not, the reasons for marriage were a "desire to conceal one's true sexual orientation, to test one's heterosexual responsiveness, and to deny one's homosexuality to oneself, or more actively, to vanquish the homosexual impulse."[8] Many Catholic men and women entered the priesthood and religious life. They sensed that they were not "called" to heterosexual marriage and saw ministry as a viable nonheterosexual option.[9]

Moreover, some of the worst oppressors of the gay and lesbian community are closeted gay and lesbian people. Internalized homophobia is a complex social disease. It is expressed in the fear of discovery of the hidden secret of same sex attraction and the negative social sanction directed toward same-sex attraction. Some closeted people will go to any extreme to prevent self-discovery, even the oppression of gay and lesbian people. Other closeted people feel such self-hatred for their same-sex feelings that they violently strike out at openly gay and lesbian individuals. The psychosocial dynamics of this last group are very similar to the externalized homophobia of gay/lesbian bashers.[10]

An essential mechanism of closeted experience is "passing" within the "straight" or heterosexist world. It is the privatizing of gay or lesbian identity to homophobic social structures. For instance, gay male personal ads in gay printed media often contain the words *straight appearing*. *Straight appearing* is the opposite of *gay appearing* or *lesbian appearing*. In using the term, gay men and lesbians buy into the social stereotypes that the homophobic culture has placed upon them. They hide their sexual identity and pretend to be something or someone they are not. They may marry or enter the military, religious life, or professional sports to mask their true identity. Closeted gay men and lesbians assume heterosexual dress and behavioral codes to be "heterosexually acceptable" to a homophobic society. Some gay and lesbian people have to pass because of familial fears, economic necessity, professional identity, or corporate culture. Others buy into passing because deep down they believe that the labels and stereotypes affixed to them by the heterosexist world are true. They believe those stereotypes and desperately want to be normal. Closeted people desperately want to be accepted. They internalize homophobia and remain invisible to society. They pass at the cost of their own self-esteem and hiding gay/lesbian truth.

World War II: The Emergence of Gay/Lesbian Bodies

World War II brought together one and a half million gay men and lesbians into the military service. The psychiatric screening of recruits by the Selective Service Boards and the military, the same-sex segregation of service personnel, the discovery of large numbers of people with same-sex preference, constant antihomosexual campaigns, and pride in their service in defending their country created gay and lesbian bodies.[11]

Many veterans who had received dishonorable or "blue" discharges for homosexuality found themselves forced to come out to families and communities. Other institutions could use their discharge to discriminate against them or deny them GI benefits. Faced with such social discrimination, many of these veterans formulated the idea of homosexual rights.[12] Others migrated to large urban centers where they could live anonymous gay and lesbian lives within invisible circles of intimate friends. Prominent coverage of the antihomosexual terror campaign of the federal government during the McCarthy era led to homosexual crackdowns in all states and cities. The campaign contributed to a repressive climate designed to keep the mass of gay/lesbian veterans and people invisible.

However, the postwar years brought new opportunities. Antihomosexual crusades brought new possibilities for visibility: "For a generation of young Americans, the war created a setting in which to experience same-sex love, affection, and sexuality, to participate in the group life of gay men and women."[13] The postwar generation stretched its closetedness to include small intimate circles of friends and saw the emergence of gay and lesbian bars and the expansion of the small gay and lesbian publishing market. Alfred Kinsey's study of the sexual behavior of American males confirmed the experience of gay veterans from World War II that the number of males who engaged in homosexual activities was vastly underestimated.[14] Many of the gay and lesbian veterans in urban centers began to form "homophile" organizations, many of which were secretive and closeted. The visibility of the gay and lesbian subculture emerged from the closet with the formation of the Mattachine Society in 1950 by Henry Wallace and the Daughters of Bilitis in 1955 by San Francisco women. Gays and lesbians were becoming visible to a society that campaigned to keep them invisible and closeted. Gay and lesbian voices were beginning to be heard with the publication of One, The Mattachine Review, and The Ladder.[15] These early groups and publications laid the foundation for the emergence of the gay and lesbian liberation movement.

Various chapters of the Mattachine Society and the Daughters of Bilitis espoused a reformist strategy of changing society's perception of homosexuality. They worked with social scientists and psychiatrists to challenge public opinion and decriminalize homosexuality. They popularized the psychiatric discourse that homosexuality was an illness in order to subvert legal social practice that homosexual acts were criminal. If ill, homosexuals were not morally responsible for their sexual orientations. The Mattachine Society adopted a policy of neither condemning nor condoning sexual variation.[16]

In 1956 Edmund Bergler published his book Homosexuality: Disease or Way of Life? Bergler, a psychiatrist, attacked Kinsey as a "medical layman" whose findings had led to the outspoken demands for minority status by homosexuals.[17] Bergler's book was greeted with outrage by the Mattachine Society. By now large numbers of the members of the Mattachine Society were rejecting psychiatric discourse that homosexuality was a disease needing treatment and cure. They were shifting to a discourse of self-acceptance and self-adjustment and became more critical of the efforts of psychiatric treatment.[18]

The political climate of the early 1960s—the emergence of the civil rights and the women's movements—affected the Mattachine Society. Many gay and lesbian people participated in the black civil rights marches in the 1960s. Many lesbians pioneered and participated in the women's movement. The passage of the Civil Rights Act of 1964 proved that civil rights activism was an effective strategy.[19] Gay and lesbian identities were produced in their critical and resistant posture toward psychiatric discourse and their search for identity in the 1950s and the early 1960s. Gay and lesbian people who participated in the civil rights and the women's movements brought their activist strategies to the gay and lesbian movement. In 1965, the Mattachine chapter in Washington, D.C., under Frank Kameny issued a statement that homosexuality was not a sickness but a sexual preference or orientation on a par with heterosexuality.[20] As resistance to the specific effects of heterosexist power within psychiatric discourse emerged, so gay and lesbian resistance shifted toward gay/lesbian civil rights. In 1968, the North American Conference of Homophile Organization unanimously adopted the resolution introduced by Frank Kameny: "Gay is good."[21] Gay and lesbian political discourse was born. Gay and lesbian identities were produced from the social effects of homophobic discursive practice.

The Stonewall Rebellion

Social change had emerged from the many gay men and lesbians who served in World War II. Gay and lesbian organizations had grown in the decades of the fifties and sixties. These changes, coupled with an active civil rights movement initiated by the African American community, the sexual revolution, the antiwar movement, and the emergence of a vigorous feminist movement, led to the Stonewall Rebellion in 1969.

On June 27, 1969, the Stonewall Inn in New York's Greenwich Village was raided by the New York City police in a typical campaign of financial extortion, harassment, and entrapment.[22] For years prior to that night, the gay bars and residents of Christopher Street had been constantly harassed by the police without any legal recourse. That night at the Stonewall, many of the patrons were ejected after showing proper identification. The remaining patrons and employees were arrested. On the streets outside, a group of drag queens and other patrons of the Stonewall Inn gathered in anger. Their numbers swelled with hundreds of other gay men and lesbians. As the police van arrived to take away the employees and other detained patrons, gay and lesbian anger erupted. The assembled crowd started throwing pennies and street debris at the police officers. They uprooted parking meters, gathered rocks, trash cans, and whatever materials were available and attacked the police, driving them back into the Stonewall Inn. The police barricaded themselves in the bar until reinforcements arrived to disperse the crowds. A full-scale riot of outraged drag queens, gay men, and lesbians broke out; for the next four nights, thousands of gay men and lesbians fought riot police on the streets of Greenwich Village. Christopher Street now belonged to the gay and lesbian community. The campaigns of police extortion and shakedown, the harassment and entrapment would be resisted.

The Stonewall riots marked the beginning of gay and lesbian pride. A drag queen, Sylvia Lee Rivera, recounts the incident:

> The cops, they just panicked. They had no backup. They didn't expect this retaliation. But they should have. People were very angry for so long. . . . I saw other people hurt by the police. There was one drag queen, I don't know what she said, but they beat her into a bloody pulp. . . . They called us animals. We were the lowest scum of the Earth at that time.[23]

Gay men and lesbians have been treated badly by the New York City police for decades. That June night, they took back Christopher Street from the police and the oppression they represented. Stonewall ended our desire to be accepted as normal. Another gay man stated:

> On the fourth of July, gay men used to get dressed up in suits and lesbians in conservative dresses. In silence, we paraded around the Liberty Bell in Philadelphia. We hoped for acceptance. After Stonewall, we realized that we were different. We demanded acceptance of our difference.[24]

Stonewall was a catalytic event that ignited the gay and lesbian movement with a new contagious militancy that swept across the cities of the United States. Homosexual silence was transformed into gay and lesbian power. Tens of thousands broke the silence created by the discourse of hatred and the institutional practices of homophobia. They rejected the term *homosexual* used in heterosexist discourse and *homophile* adopted by the earlier pre-Stonewall organizations. They named themselves; they were gay and lesbian. Empowered by rebellion, outraged by police harassment and social oppression, they demanded gay and lesbian civil rights. The gay and lesbian movement became publicly visible with a transgressive self-identity. Visibility has been a key component of gay/lesbian politics ever since.

Social changes in the gay and lesbian movement followed the Stonewall Rebellion. The liberal assimilation movement for civil rights ended. The Gay Liberation Front formed. It became a prototype for a proliferation of militant gay and lesbian groups across the United States. Gay and lesbian radicals as part of the political culture of the New Left and the antiwar movement called for a complete restructuring of the social, economic, and political system. They tried to align themselves with revolutionary groups of the New Left, but the Black Panthers and other leftist groups did not want to be aligned with "faggots." The New Left viewed gay/lesbian sexual identities in Marxist terms as evidence of capitalist decadence or counterrevolutionary behavior. For the most part, the New Left of the 1970s trivialized homophobic oppression. To conservatives, the gay/lesbian movement threatened capitalist society; to the New Left, it looked like bourgeois behavior.

Despite this, the gay and lesbian liberation movement became a political force. Gay and lesbian consciousness centered on sexuality in radical terms. The movement for rights and protections for a sexual minority accelerated. It led to the emergence of a visible movement with a great deal of diversity, strength, and militant activism. The Gay Activists Alliance broke away from the revolutionary Gay Liberation Front to reform cultural and political institutions. The Gay Activist Alliance carefully staged public confrontations with key political figures or social institutions. Members of the alliance infiltrated political gatherings and made themselves heard. They "zapped" politicians with questions about what they were doing about the oppression of gay and lesbian people.[25]

The Radicalesbians and Lesbian Feminist Liberation Inc. formed their groups to pursue same-sex and feminist politics.[26] Sexism was rampant in Gay Activist Alliance. Jean O'Leary commented on the sexism in the GAA:

> The men actually treated women like surrogate mothers, lovers, and sisters. There were few women in leadership positions, and women were consciously kept out of them. The men were listening, but they weren't hearing what we had to say.[27]

Many gay men in GAA continued their stereotyped views of women, and some opposed feminist issues. Critical feminist issues had to be pursued for a time in separate lesbian organizations before gay men and lesbians would be able to forge coalitions to fight for justice.

Nonetheless, the gay and lesbian movement in its diversity developed a focused ability to respond to overt oppression. It adopted the tactics of sit-ins, marches, angry protests, and disruptive demonstrations. Lesbians and gay men continued to find common ground in their struggles with homophobic/heterosexist discrimination and the drive for gay and lesbian civil rights.

The legacy of the Stonewall Rebellion took shape in a Gay and Lesbian Pride parade in Central Park that celebrated the first anniversary of Stonewall and the end of the closet. That first parade in 1970 was celebrated by over ten thousand men and women. By the end of the decade, every major American city held a similar parade. Millions of men and women broke silence and celebrated their sexuality, refusing to be controlled by the social structure of the closet. These parades with their carnival-like celebrations flaunted and flouted gay/lesbian stereotypes, parodied them, and demonstrated their falsity when applied universally. Cultural icons that formed the social control of the closet were parodied and transgressed. "We are everywhere," chanted pride demonstrators.

Stonewall's legacy was the coming out of the gay and lesbian movement. Pre-Stonewall years were characterized by closeted existence for gay men and lesbians. Currents of resistance, growing anger, and pride awaited a catalytic event. Stonewall was that event: an event of self-definition. Gay men and women were no longer homosexuals or homophiles; they were gay and lesbian. Activists ruptured their closet boundaries. They overturned its control and deformation, its silence and secrecy, its isolation and pain. They embarked upon their own self-definition in the area of public discourse. They constructed a visible community that supported a positive affirmation of lesbian/gay identity.

Coming Out

The imperatives of Stonewall led to the rupture of closeted existence for many gay and lesbian people. The closet would no longer be a predominant feature of their lives. They challenged distorting stereotypes, forcible controls over their lives, and institutional heterosexist violence. Coming out was incorporated into what it meant to be lesbian and gay, a political action of declaring affectional preferences openly. They intended to be seen and heard, and they were aggressively seen and heard.

In the post-Stonewall decades, coming out means making gay and lesbian experience public. Coming out is both a personal and a political statement. The personal process is easy for some and difficult for others. They come out first to a sexual awareness of themselves, facing the necessity of redefining their social reality and themselves. They name themselves as gay or lesbian. They begin to end the denials and begin to affirm their sexual orientation. For some people, coming out is a long and painful process. It is full of imagined and real dangers created by an internalized homophobia. They are confronted with the real possibility of rejection as they inform friends or family members.[28] However, with the ending of "passing" and the restrictions of closeted existence, they begin to construct the truth of their sexual identity. They live with open sexual and political differences within a heterosexist society.

Gay men and lesbians seek out other queers to claim their sexual identity. The gay and lesbian community provides a place where they can discover themselves and find self-affirmation.[29] It is a place where they can produce their identity, test it, and affirm it against the damaging effects of homophobia. It is also a place where they can reconstruct their new self-definitions vis-à-vis our society. Frequently, they may need the supportive context of therapy to undo some of the damaging effects of internalized homophobia.[30]

The formation of gay/lesbian identity is a political act. It is the transformation of silence into power and the production of truth. It breaks heterosexist truth claims that being gay or lesbian is a dirty secret. It breaks the cycle of hiddenness, isolation, anxiety, and pain that gay men and lesbians have experienced from internalized homophobia. In public, gay men and lesbians can challenge a culture's fears of difference, its production and distribution of power relations. They affirm their own gay/lesbian identity. They represent a potential change and a threat to privileged heterosexist domination. They become visible and shed the cloak of invisibility. They speak the truth that gay/lesbian is good and that it is healthy.

Silence and secrecy were the price lesbians and gay men paid for remaining safe in the period before Stonewall. However, safety was the illusion of closeted existence. Violence occurred in every aspect of their public lives. Homophobic oppression controlled their lives. It regulated their sexual identity with stereotypic distortions, powerful discursive practices, and violence. It kept their identity secret. Coming out is a political action. In coming out, gay/lesbian discourse and practice become public. Every act of gay/lesbian visibility is an act of political resistance against homophobic oppression. Every public gay/lesbian discourse defies the heterosexist regime of truth. Coming out begins a political struggle for gay/lesbian truth.

Reformist vs. Transgressive Politics

Gay men and lesbians exist on the social margins. Our community has formed to struggle with compulsory heterosexuality. Our survival as a community depends upon our ability to continue and expand that struggle. Since Stonewall, two major strategies have been used within gay/lesbian political discourse: reformist and transgressive. Both arise out of the experience of homophobic oppression and social marginalization. Both discursive strategies aim to defend our civil rights and achieve freedom. Some activist groups are predominately reformist; some are transgressive; some try to blend both strategies.

The reformist strategy aims at transforming existing cultural and political institutions. Since the 1986 Supreme Court decision *Bowers v. Hardwick*, privacy rights and equal protection groups have emerged in most states, working for repeal of state sexual misconduct laws and passage of hate crime bills and gay/lesbian rights bills. In Washington, D.C., reformist political associations such as the National Gay and Lesbian Task Force, the Human Rights Campaign Fund, and various national AIDS associations are trying to educate the public and elected officials about lesbian and gay issues. They use the standard tactics of a political action group—lobbying, petitions, voter registration drives, and write-ins. They educate the public on gay/lesbian issues through speakers, workshops, pamphlets, and the public media.[31] They try to build electoral power to actively change discriminatory practices based upon sexual orientation. Gay/lesbian groups have emerged within a number of Fortune 500 companies promoting diversity training programs for employee tolerance. They try to demystify stereotypes and the threat of sexual difference. Growing visibility has made corporate America aware of potential gay/lesbian market power. Levi Strauss withdrew its corporate sponsorship of the Boy Scouts of America because of the latter's blatant discrimination against gay Scoutmasters and gay Boy Scouts.

Reformist organizations extend their political agenda to other institutions. In the religious sector, a number of organizations have arisen within their denominations: Integrity within the Episcopalian church, Dignity and Conference of Catholic Lesbians within the Catholic church, Affirmation within the Methodist, and several others. Gay and lesbian synagogues have emerged within Reform Judaism. These religious organizations assist their churches in understanding gay/lesbian issues and try to reform them from their institutionalized homophobic practices. Gay/lesbian student groups and faculty have assisted in the development of gay and lesbian studies in several universities such as Harvard, Yale, MIT, Tufts, Brown, City University of New York, and City College of San Francisco. AIDS service organizations have started to change the social construction of AIDS through education and pioneering efforts to develop a compassionate response to all people with HIV infection.

The other current of gay/lesbian political discourse is transgressive. This current has created a new language around which to construct gay/lesbian lives, to articulate their identities, to express their freedom, and to resist oppression. Transgressive activists assert that the reformists endanger the gay and lesbian movement with their assimilationist tendencies, that is, becoming acceptable or "passing" to liberal heterosexist society. These activists view themselves as revolutionary inheritors of the Stonewall Rebellion and the blatant gay/lesbian activism of the Gay Liberation Front, Radicalesbians, and Gay Activist Alliance. Transgressive activists identify themselves as nonassimilationists; they refuse to make concessions to heterosexist society in the interests of acceptability. They refuse to accept compulsory heterosexuality as social practice. They flaunt their cultural separateness, maintaining a distinct gay/lesbian identity and challenging gender politics and sexual politics.[32] They delight in playing up stereotypical images, shocking rather than persuading society. Transgressive activists look to the creation of a distinct gay/lesbian culture with its own discourse and practices.

The transgressive current is the path of direct action, provocation, nonviolent civil disobedience, and offensive parodies. Transgressive discourse is contemptuous of controlling heterosexist values and homophobic practices. It expresses itself in the refusal to remain silent or to follow proper protocol. It interrupts institutional discourse with angry expletives, shrill noises, a chorus of boos and hisses, chants, whistles, and shouts. It shows disrespect to the secretary of Health and Human Services, the Catholic cardinal of New York, or the homophobic senator from North Carolina. Transgressive activists are fully conscious that they are engaged in a historic struggle against the increasing violence of homophobic American social structures. It has become a struggle against genocidal policies and practices.

Queer Nation has taken transgressive stances against homophobic practices, first of all by reclaiming in its name a homophobic label. *Queer* has long been used as a heterosexist/homophobic epithet against gay men and lesbians, and it has evoked shame and fear in many queers. Queer Nation has reclaimed the word, taking homophobic power away from it. A friend of mine in Queer Nation tells a story about several Queer Nationals who were arrested and thrown into a holding cell with other detainees. Some Queer Nationals were wearing T-shirts with the words *queer* and *faggot*. The T-shirts flustered some homophobic detainees and took the power of naming from them. The only epithet remaining was *sissy*. *Queer* is transformed from a word coined against gay men and lesbians into an empowering, postmodern word of social rebellion and political dissidence.[33]

Queer is also a coalition word that gay men and lesbians can use together to designate their political action. *Queer* has become an empowering symbol for living sexual differences within a homophobic society. It has become a socially constructed and inclusionary term for gay men and lesbians and people of color who believe that the words *gay* and *lesbian* are "white" political labels. It has been adopted by bisexual, transsexual, and transgenderal members of Queer Nation.

Queer Nation was formed by several gay men and lesbians in New York City who were "gay-bashed." It was formed to fight back against homophobic violence and compulsory heterosexuality, to increase queer visibility, and to gain media attention for gay/lesbian civil rights. The New York chapter's first major action was to stage a march to protest the bombing of a gay bar, Uncle Charlie's; the march drew over a thousand gay and lesbian protesters. Queer Nation conducts self-defense classes for gay and lesbian people to fight back against violence. The New York chapter has paid regular visits to disrupt Life Ministry, a fundamentalist Christian group out to convert gay/lesbian people to heterosexuality. In New York, Queer Nation has staged "kiss-ins" in which gay/lesbian couples invade heterosexual clubs, dance together, and are as equally affectionate as opposite-sex couples.

With chapters in many American cities, Queer Nation has not only begun to fight back against homophobic violence but also has promoted gay/lesbian visibility. Many chapters have formed a Queer Shopping Network that canvasses shopping malls with pamphlets to dispel mistaken stereotypes. Some Queer Nations have staged visibility actions in shopping centers: "We're Here, We're Queer, and We're Going Shopping." Some members have stamped *gay money* on U.S. currency to communicate the economic power of twenty-five million gay/lesbian people. The *Wall Street Journal* has noted the potential economic power of the queer community.

Queer Nation promotes coming out for all gay and lesbian people in society. It seeks to establish an open gay/lesbian presence with highly visible actions. Queer Nation chapters have organized a national campaign against the family owned Cracker Barrel Old Country Store chain of restaurants, ranging from a national action in Nashville to local chapter actions against individual restaurants. Cracker Barrel corporate policy states, "It is inconsistent with our concepts and values ... to continue to employ individuals in our operating units whose sexual preferences fail to demonstrate normal heterosexual values."[34] Cheryl Summerville, a former cook at the Douglasville, Georgia, restaurant, was fired on the basis of sexual orientation and not job performance. Her termination notice read, "This employee was terminated due to Company policy. Employee is Gay." Queer Nation has been able to document Cracker Barrel's firing of a number of gay/lesbian employees since February 1991, after the supposed public rescinding of the policy.[35] Queer Nation chapters have held nonviolent "sip-ins" at Cracker Barrel restaurants, where Queer Nation members take up table space during the busy rush hours on Sunday mornings and early afternoons, ordering only tea or coffee but leaving sizable tips for the "waitrons." Queers were not there to punish employees but to increase visibility on this justice issue: "We're Here, We're Queer, and We're Not Eating Breakfast."

Queer Nation has also taken a clear stance against assimilationist tendencies of many reformist organizations. Many lesbians and gays want only to be assimilated into society; they seek normalization. Queer Nation has challenged the ghettoizing tendencies of these gay and lesbian people, taking gay and lesbian presence from the bars to suburban shopping malls and proclaiming, "We're Here. We're Queer.

Get Used to It." Their vision is not to be assimilated into society. Rather, they want to preserve their difference, continuously informing society of that difference, and transforming society into a pluralistically affirming society.

During the Columbus Day weekend in 1987, seven hundred thousand gay and lesbian people marched on Washington, D.C., to protest the Supreme Court decision *Bowers v. Hardwick.* A coalition of reformist and transgressive groups worked together to express their anger at the decision and its homophobic effects. Thousands of gay/lesbian protesters organized into more than a hundred affinity groups to stage a massive civil disobedience action on October 13. Business at the Supreme Court was closed down for over a half hour. It was the first time in history that the Supreme Court had been closed through civil disobedience. Over 650 gay/lesbian protesters were arrested.

"Outing" has been an issue dividing reformist and transgressive gay/lesbian political activists. Outing is an attempt to break the conspiracy of silence, forcing gays/lesbians out of the closet. It speaks the unspeakable. It unclosets the closeted. The practice of outing demonstrates that there are social outsiders on the inside. Transgressive lesbian/gay activists for some time have argued the need to out public figures like Malcolm Forbes, political figures like Barney Frank before his public coming out, and entertainers like Rock Hudson in Hollywood. "We are everywhere," they claim. The only way to change society's attitudes about being gay and lesbian is to bring everyone out of the closet. They encourage closeted gay and lesbian people to come out on National Coming Out Day in October. Reformists, on the other hand, argue a privacy rights position. Since the privacy rights of gay and lesbian people are not legally protected, many people are forced to remain closeted by necessity or by fear. Their choice to remain closeted belongs to them and to no one else.

The gay philosopher Richard Mohr has persuasively argued that outing does not violate privacy rights. Being in the closet is not a private right, since it is maintained by the homophobic force of society:

> The closet is simply capitulating to society's view about how the gay person should live. Better that they should be dead, but if not, well the closet is the next best [thing]. So, the person who is in the closet, in fact, isn't exercising their right. The person isn't acting free. The person is merely capitulating to social forces.[36]

Unless outing violates an overall dignity value, it does not violate privacy rights. Outing is living truthfully, morally, and politically.

However, when some people claim their right to privacy and at the same time work against the gay/lesbian community, the issue becomes more complex. In 1989, Republicans spread gay rumors about Democratic representative Thomas Foley as he ran for Speaker of the House. Openly gay representative Barney Frank stopped the rumors when he threatened to expose all prominent Republicans in Washington who were gay. The threat of outing stopped a homophobic smear attack. A different situation is the case of Terry Dolan, who was leader of the National Conservative Political Action Committee. The NCPAC carried on a hate campaign against being gay/lesbian in its fund-raising drive targeting the political Right. It was common knowledge within gay circles that Dolan was gay. Transgressive activists claim that people like Dolan need to be outed because they are actively hurting and oppressing the gay/lesbian community. Outing becomes a political weapon against gay/lesbian oppressors; it becomes a cry of anger against those who have betrayed their own.

Transgressive activists also challenge homophobic labels, language, stereotyping, and rules through political parody. They practice "drag," open displays of flagrant sexuality, and the flaunting of the unusual. The public media plays up these displays as bizarre behavior. Often, transgressive actions are described by assimilationist critics as strident, counterproductive, or distasteful in their display. However, assimilationist critics fail to see the political importance of these displays. Drag is both entertainment and a political statement; it is described as "camp" in gayspeak. *Camp* is a theatrical term applied by gay men and lesbians to situations that they poke fun at or burlesque. Theorist Jonathan Dollimore describes drag as "transgressive reinscription," and its principal medium as fantasy. It is an "inherently perverse, transgressive reordering of fantasy's conventional opposite. . . . It has to do with inverting elements of this world, recombining its constitutive features."[37] Drag parodies the worst heterosexist nightmares of women. However, social anger works through the camp parodies. *Drummer* magazine–styled men dressed in leather attire or leather-identified women such as "dykes on bikes" challenge rigid heterosexist notions of gender roles. They caricature those gender stereotypes to extremes.[38] This has led to the emergence of drag activism and leather activism within our community. They are postmodern forms of hostile social eroticism. The rejection of conventional social norms and the parodying of gender roles have a disturbing effect on heterosexist society; they undermine the complex set of political assumptions underlying the social construction of heterosexist gender relations.

Likewise, San Francisco's infamous Sisters of Perpetual Indulgence with their beards, nuns' habits, fishnet stockings and black spiked heels poke fun at and critically parody institutional Catholicism. Their motto is, "Give up the guilt." They perceive institutional Catholicism as oppressor.[39] The Sisters have staged several opportune appearances at the Family Forum sponsored by Phyllis Schlafly. Transgressive art in the forms of posters, cartoons, designs on shirts, songs, chants, and humor become direct forms of political criticism of and antagonism toward heterosexist power relations. No heterosexist power icon remains too sacred for gay/lesbian imaginations. In 1990, *The Advocate's* Sissy Award for oppressor went to Senator Jesse Helms; the 1991 award was conferred on Cardinal John O'Connor.

These transgressive displays are always socially conscious of the network of oppressive power relations and their sacred icons. Transgressive discursive practice provokes and offends homophobic gender norms; it shows contempt in its speech and behavior toward heterosexist power icons. It parodies institutional compulsory heterosexuality. It forms a gay/lesbian political discourse that refuses to conform to heterosexist conventions and refuses to be intimidated by homophobic practices. It criticizes society from the blatantly "sexual" gay and lesbian other; it formulates its political idiom—its "gayspeak" and "lesbianspeak"—from the margins of homophobic power relations. Gay/lesbian language is the communication of an oppressed social minority trying to live with sexual and political difference within a heterosexist society.

"Off the Couches into the Streets"

In his studies, Alfred Kinsey presented startling evidence about the diversity of sexual experience. The studies of psychologist Evelyn Hooker pointed to the social evidence of well-adjusted homosexuals against the prevailing psychiatric clinical practice. Psychiatrists Thomas Szasz and Judd Marmor provided the politically emergent gay/lesbian movement with critical tools for analyzing the homophobic discursive practice of psychiatry.[40] Critical scientific evidence challenged the aggressive reparative therapies of Bergler, Bieber, and Socarides. Furthermore, sociologists moved from a psychoanalytic Freudian model of the cause of homosexuality to a sociological model, viewing homosexuality not as a pathology but rather as a variant of sexual expression. Social scientists had also begun to understand the phenomenon of homosexuality within cross-cultural patterns, noticing that many cultures were tolerant of various forms of homosexual experience while others were intensely hostile. If homosexuality was considered as a variant of human sexual experience, then there was no need to search for its cause and cure. What was significant to social scientists was the social status given to homosexuality; what made homosexuals deviant in a society was when dominant groups differentiated, labeled, stigmatized, and penalized them.

The 1968 convention of the American Medical Association in San Francisco was leafleted by gay/lesbian activists. They interrupted the lecture of Charles Socarides, who was a strong advocate of pathological diagnosis of homosexual behavior. Activists demanded equal representation for those who opposed the pathological diagnosis. That same year at Columbia University, gay and lesbian demonstrators protested a panel on homosexuality convened by Lawrence Kolb, the director of the New York State Psychiatric Institute. Militant activists interrupted the panel, demanding "to be participants in considerations of our condition and in the disposition of our fate. It is time that talk stopped about us and started being with us."[41]

After Stonewall, gay and lesbian activists declared war on the medical and psychiatric practice of treating homosexuals as sick and trying to cure them. At the 1970 American Psychiatric Association convention in San Francisco, gay/lesbian activists and feminists disrupted a panel on homosexuality where Irving Bieber, a longtime advocate of homosexuality as illness, was speaking. Activists heaped abuse upon him; one protester declared, "I've read your book, Dr. Bieber, and if that book talked about black people the way it talks about homosexuals, you'd be drawn and quartered and you'd deserve it."[42] In another panel discussing aversive conditioning techniques to treat sexual deviation, activists shouted out, "torture!" and "Where did you take your residency, Auschwitz?"[43] In October 1970, members of the Los Angeles Gay Liberation Front disrupted the Second Annual Behavior Modification Conference. At a film depicting aversion therapy techniques to control homosexual impulses, GLF activists shouted out, "Barbarism!" and "Medieval torture."[44] One demonstrator announced to the psychiatrists, "We are going to reconstitute this session into small groups with equal numbers of Gay Liberation Front members and members of your profession and we are going to talk as you have probably never talked with homosexuals before, as equals. We are going to talk about such things as homosexuality as an alternative lifestyle."[45] At the 1971 American Psychiatric Association convention, gay and lesbian activists stormed into the convocation, grabbed the microphone, and denounced homophobic psychiatric practice. Frank Kameny announced, "Psychiatry is the enemy incarnate. Psychiatry has waged a relentless war of extermination against us. You may take this as a declaration of war against you."[46] Gay/lesbian activists turned the tables by taking themselves off the psychoanalytic couch and placing psychiatry and its discursive relationship to compulsory heterosexuality on the couch.

The guerrilla tactics of gay and lesbian activists attacked homophobic practices of the psychiatrists and psychoanalysts. Psychiatrists had committed serious human rights violations against homosexuals to change their sexual behavior. The tactics of protest and disruption led to more moderate psychiatrists urging reform of the conservative diagnosis of homosexuality as "sociopathic personality disturbance, sexual deviation, homosexuality" in *the Diagnosis and Statistical Manual II* (DSM II). After several years of intense lobbying and infighting by psychiatrists, the earlier diagnostic classification was removed and replaced with "ego-dystonic homosexuality" from the updated DSM III.[47] The American Psychological Association removed homosexuality from its list of mental disorders and committed itself to removing the stigma of homosexuality within the society.[48] The American Psychoanalytic Association failed to adopt similar measures.

Gay and Lesbian Cultural Space

The Stonewall Rebellion was the catalyst for the creation of a public gay/lesbian subculture. A subculture is a social network that creates a sense of group identity and values distinctive from the dominant culture. The gay and lesbian subculture arose as an alternative form of discourse and practice. Mainstream heterosexist culture spurred what Foucault calls a "reverse discourse." The gay/lesbian subculture initially formed a cultural space around and at the cracks of homophobic violence and oppression. In that space reverse language, reverse symbol system, reverse dress code, particular values and norms of behaviors, lifestyles, and identity were produced and circulated. Gay/lesbian cultural space became a vibrant, dynamic space on the margins of society. The margins were transformed into the creative edge of mainstream culture. The margins generated stylistic trends and cultural innovations that eventually migrated into the mainstream.

Current gay/lesbian aesthetics are both innovative and transgressive. They emerge from our sexual identities and differences. Gay/lesbian aesthetics are born from sexual dissidence and provide mainstream America with cultural confrontation and challenge. Gay/lesbian sexual dissidence, in turn, emerges from the liberation of desire/pleasure. The poet and theorist Audre Lorde wrote, "Our erotic knowledge empowers us, becomes a lens through which we scrutinize all aspects of our existence."[49] The liberation of desire/pleasure is the creative matrix from which gay/lesbian aesthetics are shaped and from which gay/lesbian culture is produced. The liberation of pleasure from homophobic constraint and containment produces a cultural space constructed around a gay/lesbian aesthetics of pleasure. Gay cultural critic Michael Bronski understands gay/lesbian cultural space as a political culture of pleasure:

> Gay [/lesbian] liberation . . . offers a self-affirming vision of sexuality, gender, and personal freedom that is not only a radical critique of the state of culture, but also a signpost to the way out, the road to change. The vision that gay [/lesbian] liberation has to offer goes beyond freedom from sexual repression, escape from the tyranny of gender roles, or movement towards connecting culture and politics. At its most basic, it offers the possibility of freedom of pleasure, for its own sake. Until we accept the role which pleasure must play in all aspects of our lives, we will never be free.[50]

Judy Grahn calls for cultural flaunting: "Without flaunting, there is no culture, there is only the imitation of heterosexual culture and the illusion that only one culture exists."[51]

Gay/lesbian cultural space includes specific associations and social institutions that produced an identifiable gay/lesbian discursive practice. It includes a specific history. These elements are constructed into a gay/lesbian social network that is resistant to and in conflict with mainstream heterosexist culture.

The post-Stonewall period has been characterized by the proliferation of gay and lesbian groups, businesses, and social institutions. Gay and lesbian bars are no longer under Mafia ownership, nor are they the sole institutions constituting gay/lesbian culture. Gay- and lesbian-owned businesses, restaurants, banks, financial services, publishing companies, and vacation resorts have opened. There are gay/lesbian political organizations, legal services, AIDS service groups, hot lines, counseling services, and media watch groups. There are gay/lesbian church groups for almost every denomination as well as the independent Metropolitan Community Church.[52] In every major city there are gay/lesbian neighborhoods, gay/lesbian directories, periodicals, and weekly newspapers.

Gay and lesbian pride marchers chant, "We are everywhere." We are in every profession. There are gay/lesbian associations of social workers, doctors, psychiatrists, therapists, university professors, and lawyers. Other professions create their own social networks for professional support. There are athletic clubs, choruses, and diverse support groups. Every four years the Gay Games (formerly Gay Olympics) are held. Each June Gay and Lesbian Pride celebrations are held all over the nation. The gay/lesbian subculture is rich in its diversity, creativity, and heritage.

What is important is that a visible gay/lesbian community has emerged in every urban center of the United States. It meets a vital social need for many lesbians and gays. The gay/lesbian community has transformed its marginality into cultural practices and institutions. The visible gay/lesbian community provides a lesbian-affirming and gay-affirming social network that counters the prevalent cultural homophobia. Gay and lesbian people want to associate with people who affirm their sexual identity, not denigrate it. From their social network they glimpse the freedom for which they hope and struggle to reach. A visible gay/lesbian community becomes an alternative form of social practice that not only nurtures but also challenges heterosexist social practices.

From the Middle Ages until recently, authoritative forms of discourse have actively falsified or distorted historical accounts of same-sex love. Heterosexist history glossed over the differences and conflicts inherent in their sources, and we read a highly edited history of heterosexual practices. Foucault has drawn the connection between knowledge and power—the exploitation of knowledge by interests of power, the writing of history from the perspective of those in power, and the exclusion of all others from discourse. This has made it difficult to historically retrieve the same-sex discursive practices of Ovid, Shakespeare, Michelangelo, and numerous other men and women.[53] Gay and lesbian historians have opposed the violent heterosexist control over history, its distortions of historical documents and text-books, and its universal claim over history and culture: "Normative texts reflect the views of historical winner."[54] Such heterosexist control and writing promote the silence of same-sex practices in history and sustain the conspiracy of isolation and invisibility. Gay historian Martin Duberman has pointed out that gay/lesbian historical retrieval has focused on biography and the history of repression. Historical retrieval has been "the process of unearthing a tale of oppression."[55] Recent works of John Boswell, David Greenberg, Judith Brown, Allen Berube, Richard Plant, Bret Hinsch, David Halperin, and many others have attempted to retrieve the history of same-sex sexual practices.[56] These works intrude upon the universal constructions of heterosexist histories; they point out how selective and particular are these histories, glossing over documents that preserve aspects of gay/lesbian history. They dismantle heterosexist silence over same-sex sexual historical experience. Not only do these historians of homoerotic discursive practices begin to expose homophobic misconceptions and distortions, but they also retrieve a history of variegated and conflicting sexual practices. Gay and lesbian historians retrieve a cultural history replete with the struggle, suffering, accomplishments, and hope of those whose erotic interests were directed toward the same sex. They reconceptualize history and culture as the product and experience of both women and men with variegated sexual practices. They restore same-sex social practices to history, a history in which gay and lesbian people can find a sense of solidarity and pride for the struggle for freedom. In reclaiming history, they help to forge a communal gay/lesbian identity.

Gay and lesbian cultural visibility has the potential of becoming a means for cultural change. It challenges heterosexist social structures, attacking the foundational practices of heterosexist identity and gender politics. Gay and lesbian subculture becomes a force for cultural change. Its countercultural practices have the potential to change mainstream cultural practices and social institutions.[57] Gay/lesbian cultural visibility in a homophobic and oppressive culture is politically transgressive. It runs counter to the mainstream culture that attempts to control it and to keep it invisible. Gay/lesbian historical retrieval of same-sex practices in history becomes a resource for dismantling cultural stereotypes and misinformation. It attacks the very foundations of a majority culture that is based on the oppression of women, lesbians and gay men, and any social variation. Historical retrieval resurrects those women and men in history who dared to live their sexual differences, and it empowers our struggles for resistance.

The Ravages of HIV Infection

With the first cases of HIV infection and deaths in the United States in 1981 among gay men, the gay/lesbian community faced one of its greatest challenges. Randy Shilts's *And the Band Played On* and Larry Kramer's *Reports from the Holocaust* chronicle the gross insensitivity, irresponsibility, and callousness of the heterosexist political bureaucracy to the deaths of tens of thousands. Shilts notes, "The bitter truth was that AIDS did not just happen to America—it was allowed to happen by an array of institutions, all of which failed to perform their appropriate tasks to safeguard the public health."[58] Larry Kramer, the founder of ACT UP, has also accused political and ecclesial bureaucrats of genocidal indifference.[59]

It is over a decade later and millions are infected by HIV. The gay/lesbian community has been devastated. Many leaders of the gay/lesbian movement and culture have died. Their loss, along with each and every gay man's death through HIV complications, has deeply affected our community. Our community grieves and suffers. It has learned the urgent values of risking love, embodying compassion, care giving, the celebration of life, and justice-doing. Grief has been incorporated into activism and volunteer services. The gay and lesbian community has courageously pulled together in the midst of intense pain and grief. It has been reempowered in the face of tragic loss and the ongoing ravages of HIV infection. It has refused to stop loving and being visible. In fact, it has become more visible, more organized, and more effective in working to change governmental apathy and unresponsiveness to the spread of HIV infection.

The gay and lesbian community discovered that the system of health care delivery was a product of racism, homophobia, sexism, and classism. In response, many gay men and lesbians formed the numerous AIDS service organizations across our country: the Gay Men's Health Crisis in New York City, the Shanti Project in San Francisco, the AIDS Action Committee in Boston, AIDS Project L.A., and many others. They produced and provided compassionate health care alternatives to the social crisis of HIV infection. They pioneered education on HIV transmission and safer sex practices and the development of social and emotional support services for the HIV population. They provided advocacy, buddies, practical services, meals and nutritional supplements, housing, case management, and many other services.

With their heterosexual and bisexual friends, gay and lesbian volunteers have opened their services to heterosexual and bisexual men, women, children, IV drug users, African Americans, the Hispanic community, and all others. The gay/lesbian community transformed gay/lesbian AIDS service organizations into multicultural organizations. Out of compassion, they have reached out to the wider community, a community that has often violently oppressed and hated them. Moreover, the gay/lesbian community has taken up issues from the women's health movement and made those issues their own. Some health concerns, for example, are shared by gay white males and African American women. They press for reform of the health care system and Medicaid; they are lobbying for national health care insurance for every American.

The creation of AIDS service organizations filled a vacuum caused by the social unresponsiveness and lack of public health policy issues of key local and national organizations. People died from AIDS while scientists ignored the pleas of physicians and gay men because AIDS was a homosexual disease. People died from AIDS while scientists competed rather than collaborated in their research efforts. People died from a health care system designed to serve classist, racist, sexist, and homophobic interests. People died from AIDS while the Reagan administration played politics.[60] Thus, people died from human callousness. AIDS service organizations emerged from the grass-roots struggle of the gay/lesbian community to fill the national void created by the unresponsiveness to a major health crisis. They pioneered the practice of compassionate outreach to all infected with the HIV virus.

The Names Project emerged as a national effort to respond to the human tragedy of AIDS. It originated with gay activist Cleve Jones during a 1985 memorial march commemorating the assassinations of Harvey Milk and George Moscone. Mourners covered the walls of San Francisco's old Federal Building with names of people who died from AIDS. They tried to make visible the deaths that mainstream society refused to acknowledge. The idea of commemorating people who died from HIV infection by sewing their names into a quilt was born in the spring of 1987.[61] The Names Project Quilt is composed of over twenty thousand fabric panels, each bearing the name or names of loved ones lost to AIDS. The panels were designed, stitched, and completed in homes and workshops by friends, lovers, and families. For thousands of Americans, creating a quilt panel was an act of love and memorial to celebrate the lives of their loved ones.

The Names Project Quilt began from a grass-roots movement of gay/lesbian and heterosexual people, lovers, spouses, friends, parents, and care providers. It emerged from all segments of the American population that experienced the loss of loved ones. The Project Quilt became an attempt to represent the human face of AIDS, the humanity behind the stereotypic labels and stigmas of HIV infection, and the grief of hundreds of thousands of Americans. Heterosexism inhibited the acknowledgment of loss, and the Names Project became a public ritual performance of loss and grief. In October of 1987 and again in 1988, the ever-growing Names Quilt was displayed in front of the U.S. Capitol in Washington, D.C. It stood as a statement of memorial solidarity, national hope, and compassion in the midst of tragic grief. On both occasions, the Names Quilt was greeted by insensitive silence from the Reagan administration. It was displayed in Washington in 1992 with over twenty thousand panels to an unresponsive Bush administration.

Silence = Death, Action = Life

Many of the gay HIV population, along with gay/lesbian activists and their friends, have formed ACT UP (AIDS Coalition to Unleash Power). ACT UP is a nonpartisan group of diverse individuals united in anger and committed to direct action to end the AIDS crisis. ACT UP brought a new generation of activism into the gay/lesbian movement. For years, many HIV-positive gay men and their friends struggled through attempts at education and advocacy for the formulation of a compassionate national AIDS policy. The gay HIV-positive population fought the gross silence and inactivity of the Reagan administration; the bureaucracy of the Food and Drug Administration, the National Institutes of Health, the Centers for Disease Control, and the medical establishment; the profiteering of the pharmaceutical companies; the discrimination of insurance companies; the unenlightened policies of state governments, educational institutions, and churches. They realized that the connections between the medical and political structures were produced from interlocking racist, heterosexist, classist, and homophobic practices. ACT UP pioneered a consumerist movement in health care that will be the civil rights movement of the 1990s into the twenty-first century. Tens of thousands of gay men, their lovers, friends, and families experienced a social network of intolerance, indifference, and hatred. Most of the gay and lesbian population believes that the federal government did not respond to the spread of AIDS until it perceived a threat to the heterosexual population. Many HIV-positive people perceive the spread of HIV infection and social hostility as genocidal.

ACT UP united people in their anger and committed them to direct action to end the AIDS health crisis. ACT UP incorporated grief, illness, and anger into political activism. At demonstrations, they chant: "ACT UP, Fight Back, Fight AIDS." ACT UP incarnates gay/lesbian transgressive political discourse. It realized that "Silence = Death," "Action = Life," "Ignorance = Fear" (slogans on black ACT UP T-shirts with an inverted pink triangle) for those who lived with HIV infection.[62] Peter Staley from ACT UP/New York admits that he and other HIV-positive gay men joined the direct action movement as a matter of survival: "We shared a crisis mentality. All rules were off, laws were to be ignored and broken; our credo would be 'by any means necessary'."[63] ACT UP now consists of a worldwide network of a hundred chapters, each operating independently. Each chapter prioritizes its actions, chooses its protests, and stages its actions. Large ACT UP chapters break up into a number of specialized affinity groups to build consensus on staged actions and to work as units in nonviolent civil disobedience. ACT UP uses tactics from picketing or zapping legislators in public with direct questions, to more confrontational forms of nonviolent civil disobedience.

One of ACT UP's major targets was the pharmaceutical manufacturer Burroughs Wellcome, which received the patent from the Food and Drug Administration for marketing AZT (retrovir). The company did not expend any funds for research and development. Research on AZT was completed in the public sector. Burroughs Wellcome plundered the HIV community with outrageous pricing, initially charging on the average ten thousand dollars per person per year. The first-year gross sales of AZT amounted to well above two hundred million dollars.[64] Consequently, ACT UP staged several dramatic actions against the pharmaceutical profiteering of Burroughs Wellcome.

On September 14, 1989, Peter Staley and four other New York ACT UP members, sporting conservative business attire and forged identifications, staged a dramatic action against the New York Stock Exchange. They went to the VIP balcony overlooking the exchange and unfurled a banner reading SELL WELLCOME at the opening of the stock market. The five activists chained themselves to the balcony and threw counterfeit one hundred dollar bills, printed with "Fuck your profiteering, we're dying while you play business."[65] The demonstrators were arrested and led out by police as stockbrokers chanted, "Kill the fags!" In an earlier demonstration in the spring of 1989, Peter Staley had led several activists to seize control and seal themselves in some of the offices at the headquarters of Burroughs Wellcome at Research Triangle Park, North Carolina. The publicity generated by their actions forced Burroughs Wellcome to cut the price of AZT by 20 percent (from around ten thousand to eight thousand dollars per year).

The Food and Drug Administration, the National Institutes of Health, and the AIDS Clinical Trials program bureaucracy have been targeted for direct acts of civil disobedience. The massive civil disobedience at the NIH was played to the public media, and many demonstrators were hurt from police with billy clubs charging on horses. The NIH demonstration resulted in the release of more experimental drugs for HIV-positive people and forced the clinical definition of AIDS for women. With media coverage, die-ins, disruptions of medical conferences, angry demonstrations, and other direct action tactics, ACT UP has begun to change the face of medicine in the United States. A measure of ACT UP's successes has been the appointment of two of their members to the Advisory Committee of the FDA.

Another goal for which ACT UP worked was parallel-track testing, which enables experimental drugs to be distributed to people living with AIDS while the drugs are still in clinical trials. This ACT UP strategy has been adopted and implemented by the NIH. ACT UP continues to work on monitoring the efficacy of various drugs for HIV infections and getting drugs through the protocol testing to those who have a desperate need. ACT UP in Boston has been successful in influencing several pharmaceuatical companies and the FDA in the speedy release of new treatments and drugs on a compassionate-use and parallel-track basis.

ACT UP has also targeted the insurance industry and various federal and state agencies. In the fall of 1990, one of the affinity groups of ACT UP/Boston organized a demonstration against a little-known company outside of the insurance industry, Medical Information Bureau. This company collects data on all medical claims to insurance companies and has gathered all claims for the last forty years into a massive data base. Insurance companies have used this information to screen and exclude gay men from insurance coverage. ACT UP/Boston drew attention to the fact that this data base is unregulated by the federal government and used for discrimination. The same Boston chapter targeted the John Hancock Insurance Company, which refused to pay for prophylactic use of aerosol pentamidine for the prevention of pneumocystis carinii pneumonia; their continual pressure forced the Hancock Company to accept insurance coverage of the treatment. ACT UP/St. Louis and ACT UP/Kansas City demonstrated against the Missouri bureaucracy, which has been ineffectual in HIV education, the appropriation of funds, and the delivery of services for HIV-infected people. While some demonstrators picketed in the Capitol rotunda, others disrupted the opening of the House of Representatives with shrill whistles, throwing leaflets from the second-floor gallery and chanting, "We die, you do nothing."

ACT UP/New York staged a dramatic "Stop the Church" protest at St. Patrick's Cathedral against Cardinal John O'Connor, who had long been actively hostile to the gay and lesbian community. He had prevented passage of New York City's gay antidiscrimination bills, evicted Dignity chapters from all Catholic churches, blocked HIV prevention education in the New York school system, and opposed the use of condoms for populations at high risk. His antigay stand had long contributed to the legitimization of violence against the gay and lesbian community. Though he opposed safe-sex education, he was appointed by the Reagan administration to serve on the Presidential AIDS Commission.[66] Five thousand demonstrators from ACT UP and WHAM (Women's Health Action Mobilization) staged the "Stop the Church" demonstration on December 10, 1989. Forty-three ACT UP demonstrators disrupted the cardinal's high mass, chanting slogans, chaining themselves to pews, standing up during the cardinal's homily, throwing condoms, and staging die-ins. They forced the cardinal to abandon his sermon. Outside the cathedral, demonstrators held a huge sign stretched across an entire city block, reading CARDINAL O'CONNNOR: PUBLIC HEALTH MENACE. Protesters chanted, "You say, Don't Fuck; we say, Fuck You."[67] One hundred and eleven protesters were arrested.

ACT UP/Boston has passed out condoms at Catholic high schools in Boston, where Cardinal Bernard Law has used his office to prevent AIDS education and to oppose using condoms to prevent the spread of HIV infection. A couple thousand ACT UP demonstrators surrounded the cathedral at the June ordinations of Catholic priests in a Stop the Church action. Boston riot police cordoned off the cathedral while twenty-five priests locked arms at the entrance to prevent the entry of any demonstrator. "Outlaw Law," the demonstrators cried. "Two, four, six, eight, how do you know your priests are straight?" Cardinal Law has been named the number one public health enemy by ACT UP in the spread of HIV infection in Boston.

Though many from the gay/lesbian community and the heterosexist community have been critical of its confrontational tactics, ACT UP has achieved beneficial results for the HIV-positive community. It has actively fought against a genocidal indifference both in the gay/lesbian community and heterosexist society. Such dramatic acts as the nonviolent closing down of Grand Central Station during rush hour continue to dramatize the need for public action on the AIDS crisis. ACT UP has empowered the gay/lesbian community in the Stonewall legacy of aggressive radical action. It has transformed silence into power/action. HIV truth has become power/action in staged transgressive protests, effecting change in inept HIV policies. ACT UP has declared war on the HIV retrovirus. For many of the ACT UP demonstrators, it has been and continues to be a life-and-death struggle. It is a war against a bureaucracy that has ignored the spread of AIDS and has done little to prevent it. For the militant ACT UP demonstrators, direct action is the only way to effect social change.

Grass-roots Activism for Social Change

Since Stonewall, queer activism has increased its visibility and struggle with socially organized homophobia. Activist groups such as ACT UP, Queer Nation, and various other political organizations have provided the gay/lesbian movement with a specific legacy for change. Gay men came out from the bars and learned from the political experience of lesbian feminists how to organize themselves into nonviolent political groups. Activist groups have organized themselves into affinity groups, which are self-sufficient support groups whose members work together for social/political change, often through nonviolent civil disobedience. These activist groups serve as a source of support, solidarity, and empowerment for their members. They are generally egalitarian, nonsexist, nonracist, nondiscriminating, nonhierarchical decision-making bodies. They work with an open steering committee to plan and facilitate decision making. Each group is autonomous but maintains a communication network of solidarity with other groups across the country. Each decides for itself how it will make decisions, what staged actions it wants to do, and at what level it will participate with other affinity groups.

Frequently, gay/lesbian activist groups such as ACT UP and Queer Nation function on a consensus model of decision making. The voting model makes participants choose between alternatives, leaving some as winners and some as losers. The consensus model however, is a group process for decision making by which an entire group can come to agreement about a direct action. The consensus model works on the fundamental principle that all members of the affinity group can freely express themselves in their own words and with their own differences. The group works through differences to reach a mutually satisfactory decision on a course of action. Without action, consensus decisions are meaningless. This model of decision making within gay/lesbian activist groups promotes gay/lesbian solidarity in a given direct action as well as solidarity with all gay men and lesbians who struggle against oppression. It also enables the affinity group to reflect on planned direct actions, providing means for an ongoing self-critique of methods used to achieve liberation.

Gay/lesbian activist groups have harnessed their queer anger of their own oppression into a practice of solidarity for social change. Staged actions attempt to empower apathetic segments of the gay/lesbian community to become a direct force for sociopolitical change. Most of the gay/lesbian activist groups have espoused nonviolence as a social practice for social change. Nonviolent challenge is not a polite process, particularly since it uses anger as a resource for recognizing injustice and seeking change. Gay/lesbian anger empowers direct action for change. Silence, apathy, and passivity lead to death.

Queer nonviolence renounces violence as a means of social change, but it does not forego conflict. Conflict is inevitable when challenging oppression and violence; it results from acts of queer power. Queer conflict takes place when queers assume the positive forms of produced power/truth and engage in empowering actions that challenge the acceptance of homophobic truth by apathetic segments of the gay/lesbian community. Visible actions and audible voices empower other queers to challenge existing power structures. Queer conflict is confrontational; it is transgressive. It is rude practice. It produces transgressive gay/lesbian bodies and voices to confront, antagonize, disrupt, and overthrow the network of homophobic power relations. Queer power is produced and practiced in civil disobedience against the deployments of homophobic violence. Queer Nation and ACT UP empower the gay/lesbian community by their transgressive actions of challenge and their commitment to fight for social change.

Foucault and the New Politics of Pleasure

Foucault struggled with his sexual orientation for most of his life. It was in the United States that he discovered an open, visible gay/lesbian community and culture.[68] He did not hesitate to act strategically in the political struggles of the gay/lesbian movement. Many critics of Foucault exclude his gay sexual identity from their interrogations of his writings.[69] However, Foucault wrote and practiced as a gay social critic. His discourse was informed by his gay practice, albeit closeted at first and then more openly gay at the end of his life. We will end our discussion of the emergence of gay/lesbian power with a few insights from Foucault's interviews with the gay/lesbian press after he had openly accepted his gay identity.

For Foucault, gay/lesbian sexual identity was a process that must be consciously entered. People have to work at being and becoming gay/lesbian; sexual identity is a matter of their sexual choices: "Sexual choices must be at the same time creators of ways of life. To be gay [/lesbian] signifies that these choices diffuse themselves across the entire life; it is to make a sexual choice the impetus for a change of existence."[70] Gays and lesbians create sexual diversity as well as establish their identity within society through their sexual choices. These choices indicate their political resistance to the operational networks of homophobic/heterosexist power relations. Foucault calls for the politicizing of gay/lesbian sexual practices:

> What the gay [/lesbian] movement needs now is much more the art of life than a science or scientific knowledge (or pseudo-scientific knowledge) of what sexuality is. Sexuality is something we create ourselves—it is our own creation, and much more than the discovery of a secret side of our desire. We have to understand that with our desires, through our desires, go new forms of relationship, new forms of love, new forms of creation. Sex is not fatality; it's a possibility for creative life.[71]

Foucault observed that an aesthetic strategy was introduced into gay/lesbian sexual politics.[72] What he envisioned as the "art of life" is the emergence of new possibilities within the gay/lesbian movement. The "art of life" includes new forms of relationship, new power relations, new forms of language and truth, new forms of love, new forms of pleasure, and new cultural creations. Foucault understood that the gay/lesbian community has the opportunity to create new relational possibilities:

> I think that there is an interesting role [for gay/lesbian culture] to play.... I mean culture in the large sense, a culture which invents ways of relating, types of existence, types of values, types of exchanges between individuals that are really new and are neither the same as, nor superimposed on, existing cultural forms. ... Let's escape as much as possible from the type of relations which society proposes for us and try to create in the empty space where we are new relational possibilities.[73]

Foucault began to articulate a politics of pleasure that emerged within the gay/lesbian community. The politics of pleasure carried challenge, engendered strong opposition from homophobic and antierotic deployments of power, and pointed to a transgressive aesthetics. Gay/lesbian liberation forcefully articulated the significance of the erotic and the pleasurable in modern society.

Gay/lesbian resistance to the deployments of heterosexist/homophobic power relations is not simply "reverse" practice. It is a production of queer power. Lesbians and gay men live their sexual choices and thereby contest homophobic power relations. They transgress homophobic social rules. They produce their power relations on the social margins where they produce their gay/lesbian bodies, affirming, inventing, and creating their gay/lesbian selves. They create a gay/lesbian "asceticism" by working at developing their gay/lesbian selves.[74] Gay/lesbian sexual practices embody new relations of enjoyment, pleasure, mutuality, and creativity. They embody new forms of power relations that contest heterosexist/homophobic deployments of power. Lesbians and gay men create new forms of relating to themselves, to others, to institutions, and to nature.

When lesbians and gay men broke silence, they began to build new alliances in the struggle for freedom. Gay men learned about sexism, feminist issues, justice, and political analysis from lesbians already engaged in the struggles of women for freedom and equality. Both lesbians and gay men formed new coalitions to fight for the politics of pleasure. They began to change the deployments of heterosexist/homophobic power relations as they struggled to assert their sexual diversity by challenging normative practices embedded in familial, legal, medical, sexual, educational, ecclesial, economic, military, political, and cultural structures.[75]

Lesbians and gay men create a gay/lesbian social space that refuses to be assimilated into heterosexist social space. It remains a transgressive space that asserts new positive but defiant forms of gay/lesbian discourse and practice. They create a social space where queers can celebrate their sexuality as life affirming, positive, nurturing, and loving. They are pioneering new ways of being queer; they are pioneering a new nonsexist, nonhomophobic space. In the following chapters, we examine an alternative gay/lesbian theological discourse and practice, its transgressive challenges and contours, and the creation of new queer Christian theology. Many queer Christians are embarking upon a theological discourse that is a transgressive battle for truth. It is no longer a Christian apologetic for being gay/lesbian or being Christian. The battle for truth is not a polite practice; it is a discursive practice that challenges the sacred deployments of homophobic/heterosexist ecclesial power with the power of queer truth. Queer Christians are creating their own empowering theology and practices and their own Christian social space.

From Christ the Oppressor to Jesus the Liberator

It's not a matter of emancipating truth from every system of power (which would be a chimera, for truth is already power) but of detaching the power of truth from the forms of hegemony, social, economic, and cultural, within which it operates at the present.

MICHEL FOUCAULT[1]

Christianity aspires to meaning for all people, at all times. Christian theology, however, is the product of people with power and privilege, influence and wealth. This gives their theology a partisan bias that renders it meaningful to only a limited audience, particular not universal. This partisan bias must be unmasked. The theology of Jesus the Christ must expand to include the reality of gay and lesbian oppression.

My intention in this chapter is not to offer a detailed analysis of the various forms of Christology over the last two thousand years, but rather to focus on the effects of contemporary Christology and its impact on homophobic discourse and practice. I intend to practice genealogical criticism to deconstruct contemporary Christology. Genealogical deconstruction is a way keeping questions radically open, examining heterodoxy rather than orthodoxy. It is a negative hermeneutics or interpretative framework that appears to be lack of piety to orthodox practicing Christians. It is the practice of critically questioning Christologies, their truth claims, and their alignments with power. A queer genealogical criticism attempts to unearth alternatives within christological discourse by investigating the seams, hesitations, contradictions, and resistances in that discourse. Genealogical criticism contests the norm by drawing to the surface oppositions to that norm, exposing the process whereby one of the terms controls or dominates the other. It disrupts traditional Christian theology by an inversion, an overthrowing of the dominant term with its opposite. In other words, it redirects the terms of Christian theology against themselves.

In his essay "Nietzsche, Genealogy, History," Foucault takes a transgressive stance toward social rules; he encourages a genealogical strategy of turning social rules against themselves and their rulers:

> Rules are empty in themselves, violent and unfinalized; they are impersonal and can be bent to any purpose. The successes of history belong to those who are capable of seizing these rules, to replace those who have used them, to disguise themselves so as to pervert them, invert their meaning, and redirect them against those who had initially imposed them; controlling this complex mechanism, they will make it function so as to overcome the rulers through their own rules.[2]

The strategy of genealogical criticism liberates discourse from its former power relations and redeploys it within new formations of truth/power. It contributes to a transgressive or dissident truth. Our disqualified queer knowledge arises out of our experience of homophobic oppression.

Queer criticism deconstructs Christology as universal truth claims, locating it within the shifting cultural systems of which it is a part. It constructs a contextual christological discourse that is born from gay/lesbian social experience. It looks beneath and outside the dominant meaning of christological discourse for absent gay/lesbian voices. Queer criticism uses biblical criticism to discover the dangerous memory of Jesus lost beneath nearly two millennia of patriarchal and ecclesial formulations. Queer criticism considers the alternative meanings, hidden or disqualified, such as sexuality and pleasure. Traditional Christologies usually encode a system of oppositions, divine and human, male and female, asexual and sexual, heterosexual and homosexual. Traditional christological discourse evaluates one term of opposition over another.

Queer criticism is perilous. It intends to exacerbate conflict with institutional ecclesial discursive practices that insist on a particular authoritative reading of christological discourse. By focusing on the challenge of gay/lesbian discursive practice, queer criticism overturns the hierarchical opposition of terms in traditional Christologies. It asserts the the value of the human, the equality of male and female, sexuality, and the queer.

The queer criticism in this chapter and the following chapters will provoke an ecclesial reaction. To deconstruct ecclesial authority in the creation of a queer Christology is to discover how particular ecclesial conceptual discourses restrain gay/lesbian knowledge of Christology. Ecclesial authority is a specific form of heterosexist privilege, which silences queers. For Foucault, authority within a specific discursive field is aligned with a particular set of power relations and deployment of rules. These have a disciplinary and regulating function. Ecclesial authority has power over the discursive field of Christianity. It has the power to silence and exclude; it has exercised its authority in a terroristic fashion to silence critics from speaking and exclude them from teaching. Ecclesial authority over the discursive field of Christianity can affect other fields as well. It can use Jesus the Christ or biblical doctrines to bless homophobic practices, discrimination, or governmental policies. As we noted in chapter 1, it often legitimizes homophobia and homophobic social practices.

Christian churches speak for a certain understanding of historical truth and christological meaning. They claim authority to determine the truthfulness of christological discourse. Our genealogical challenges endanger their ownership of discursive practices and all other connected forms of institutional discourse. Other homophobic institutional practices have depended on homophobic Christian discourse, that is, christological discourse, for their legitimacy. Queer critical practice endangers institutional Christian control and threatens ecclesial authority with what Foucault calls the "insurrection of subjugated knowledges." In this particular context, the subjugated knowledges are queer knowledge, writings, and practices that have been dismissed by mainstream heterosexist/homophobic society. The insurrection of queer knowledge is the foundation of a thoroughly queer theology.

The Deconstruction of Christology

The notion that Jesus was conceived by the Holy Spirit in a virgin was a late tradition in gospel formation.[3] This notion was transformed into an antisexual rhetoric as Christianity evolved in the Hellenistic world. As Christianity became part of the mainstream of the Roman Empire, its discourse and practice were altered. Hostility to pleasure/desire and the body were the Greco-Roman legacies to Christianity. A growing philosophical and Gnostic-ascetic elision of pleasure/desire was accepted into Christian social practices. Classical Hellenistic techniques of self-mastery were transformed into Christian techniques for controlling the self and eliminating pleasure/desire. By the end of the second century C.E., non-Christians and Christians vied with each other in heaping abuse on the body. Non-Christian authors advocated sexual restraint, and Christian asceticism was derived in part from older Hellenistic, Jewish, and Gnostic ascetic practices. Contempt for the human condition and hatred of the body were culturally widespread, and some of the most extreme manifestations were found in Gnostic and Christian religious practices: "Classical techniques of austerity were transformed into techniques whose purpose was the purification of desire and the elimination of pleasure, so that austerity became an end in itself."[4] Christian discursive practice that was once focused on resistance to the Roman state shifted to preoccupation with the control of sexuality. Suffering had earlier been lionized in Christian discursive practice; now ascetical pain and suffering replaced the notion of pleasure.[5]

An emerging Christian sexual discourse accented the negative importance of desire/pleasure in order to exclude it from social practice.[6] Christian discourse emphasized purification or the removal of desire/pleasure rather than mere self-regulation, as in Greco-Roman philosophy. It exalted sexual abstinence as the ideal. Christian discourse, thus, provided social legitimation for its rejection and disapproval of desire/sexual pleasure, celibate practice, and the exclusion of women from Christian ministry: "Christianity did not invent this code of sexual behavior. Christianity accepted it, reinforced it, and gave to it a much larger and more widespread strength than it had before."[7] It is within this crucible of late Greco-Roman ideas of sexual restraint and Stoic self-mastery, neo-Platonism, and conflict with libertarian Gnostic groups that Christian anti-sexual/desire discursive practices were forged.

The elision of pleasure/desire in Christian social practices shaped and accented the image of the celibate Jesus.[8] Christology became an interpretive construction of Jesus and his bodily practices. The more that Jesus the Christ was Hellenized, ontologized, spiritualized, depoliticized, and ecclesialized, the more the human person, Jesus, was neutered. His sexuality diminished into celibate asexuality. In this elision of pleasure/desire, Christian discursive practice incorporated interlocking misogynistic and homophobic power relations.[9]

Christian discursive practice became anti-erotic/anti-pleasure. Pleasure, subsequently, has rarely been successfully integrated into Christian discursive practice.[10]

Along with the elision of pleasure/desire, Christian discourse about God incorporated from Greco-Roman philosophy a similar elision of passion (*patheia*). It accepted the Greek notion of *apatheia*.[11] God became apathetic; that is, without passion, unable to suffer, be affected, or be acted upon. Tertullian's description of God is a virtually Stoic exaltation of *apatheia*. Augustine took the critical Stoic opposition of reason against passion, and he defined passion (*passio*) as a "commotion of the mind and contrary to reason." Thus, he believed that it was an inappropriate attribute for God.[12] The Christian God became apathetic in Christian theological discourse.[13] God became totally other, removed, unchanged. God's love (*agape*) became passionless. This stood contrary to the passionate tribal God of Hebrew Scriptures and the loving parent figure, the God of Jesus, who lives, becomes, changes, speaks, acts, suffers, and dies. It stood in stark contrast to the biblical doctrine of a God who loves or is passionate for justice. A God who is unable to suffer or to feel passion is a loveless God.[14]

Tertullian used Jesus as an example of virginity: "Christ was himself a virgin in the flesh in that he was born of a virgin's flesh."[15] Tertullian's revulsion for sexual passion led him to renounce sexual relations with his wife because sexual desire had no place in the life of a Christian. Christian discourse of the second and third centuries C.E. ranked unbridled sexual passion with idolatry among the gravest offenses. By the time of Jerome and Augustine, a definite antisexual discourse and practice had emerged within Christianity. It reflected three centuries of Christian assimilation into the Greco-Roman world and the struggles with various Gnostic groups. Jerome attacked the British monk Jovinian, who preached that marriage, like the celibate state, could equally be a means for growing in the knowledge of God: "He [Jovinian] put marriage on a level with virginity, while I make it inferior; he declares that there is little or no difference between the two states; I claim that there is a great deal. Finally . . . he has dared to place marriage on an equal level with perpetual chastity."[16] Jerome believed that too much sexual pleasure in marriage was a form of adultery. Other Christian patriarchs such as Gregory of Nazianzus, Gregory of Nyssa, John Chrysostom, and Ambrose praised virginity. They looked with horror at sexual pleasure.[17]

For Augustine, sexual pleasure/desire was what carries original sin from generation to generation. Augustine considered sexual intercourse undertaken for anything but proocreation to be sinful.[18] He codified sexual acts that were necessary in marriage for the preservation of the human race and submitted them to ecclesial control. Such acts were neutral, not sinful, only when they were prompted not by desire/pleasure but for the purpose of procreation. Marriage was good insofar as sexual pleasure was controlled. Augustine connected concupiscence with sexual intercourse: "Everyone who is born of sexual intercourse is in fact sinful flesh."[19] Christ was born without libido or concupiscence since he was born without the intervention of semen. Foucault offers this reading of Augustine:

> The famous gesture of Adam covering his genitals with a fig leaf is, according to Augustine, not due to the simple fact that Adam was ashamed of their presence, but to the fact that his sexual organs were moving by themselves without his consent. Sex in erection is the image of man revolted against God. The arrogance of sex is punishment and consequence of the arrogance of man. His uncontrolled sex is exactly the same as what he has been towards God—a rebel.[20]

Foucault maintains that Augustine read the biblical text of Adam's rebellion against God as the interpretative framework for understanding the relationship of sex and the Christian construction of the ascetical self.[21] The ascetic's task was "perpetually to control one's thoughts, examining them to see if they were pure, whether something dangerous was not hiding in or behind them, if they were not conveying something other than what primarily appeared, if they were not a form of illusion and seduction."[22] This spiritual struggle of the self against rebellious sexual pleasure has continued to remain normative in Christian discourse through recent times.

For Augustine and other church patriarchs, Jesus the Christ embodied the antipleasure principle that generated multiple discursive practices supporting the construction of the ascetical self and the social position of a male celibate clergy. Jesus was born without libido, according to these patriarchs; traditional Christian discourse, therefore, castrated Jesus, making him an asexual eunuch. It absolutized Jesus' maleness. It drew social attention from bodily existence with all its drives, passions, and desires toward the realm of the spiritually constructed self. It glorified the apathetic self, the ascetic self-mastery over passion. It was necrophilic practice, obsessive social preoccupation with what is dead, unfeeling, regulated, controlled, stripped of passion.[23]

Jesus' asexual maleness continued to exercise a normative function, excluding women from full ministerial participation in the church and continuing to legitimize antipleasure and misogynistic practices. The notion of two natures of Jesus the Christ, defined by the Councils of Nicea and Chalcedon, was an unsuccessful attempt to overcome the Christian incorporation of the divine *apatheia*. The Chalcedonian declaration of Jesus as "true God" and "true man" attempted to balance christological discourse within the binary poles of divine and human. However, a close reading of the declaration underscores that Jesus the Christ is the divine apathetic person, who, nevertheless, possessed a human nature. Divine apathy triumphed over the human and the historical. The apathetic divine superseded the sexual human; the asexual male stood above the sexual female. Maleness was assimilated into the the divine essence (*homoousia*), justifying misogynistic and homophobic Christian discourse.

This notion of an apathetic God and "his" asexual Christ was fundamental to the social practices of patriarchy, the family, the church, and politics in Christianity from Constantine through the Reformation. The maleness that had been assimilated into the divine essence became normative for the social construction and legitimation of patriarchal power relations. Maleness was associated with superior rationality, spirituality, and authority, whereas femaleness was considered inferior and associated with emotions, embodiedness, and sensuality. Prohibitions against same-sex practices were grounded in the interests of a hierarchical male, celibate, and clerical church in preserving itself against passion and pleasure. Medieval Christianity was male, hierarchical, clerical, authoritarian, highly discriminatory, and exclusivist. The maleness of God supported male privilege. The maleness of the asexual Christ supported the gender politics of Christianity's subordination of women and their exclusion from social power and from orders. Male celibates used the church just as their secular counterparts used women. Jesus' maleness was used to justify rampant ecclesial and social misogyny.

Throughout the medieval era, Christian discourse centered on an apathetic God and the asexual Christ, but Renaissance artists boldly portrayed Jesus in his full genitality.[24] In his study of Renaissance images of Jesus, art historian Leo Steinberg notes that "the evidence of

Christ's sexual member serves as the pledge of God's humanation."[25]
James Nelson summarizes Steinberg's study:

> In the great cathedrals hung paintings of the Holy Family in which Mary
> herself deliberately spreads the infant's thighs so that the pious might
> gaze at his genitals in wonder. In other paintings the Magi are depicted
> gazing intently at Jesus' uncovered loins as if expecting revelation. In
> still others Jesus' genitals are being touched and fondled by his mother,
> by St. Anne, and by himself. So also in the paintings of the passion and
> crucifixion, the adult Jesus is depicted as thoroughly sexual. In some,
> his hand cups his genitals in death. In others the loincloth of the suffer-
> ing Christ is protruding with an unmistakable erection.[26]

The Renaissance movement to depict Jesus' genitals affirmed not
only his humanity but also his sexuality. The Christ became sexual
within popular imagination, signifying a shift within christological and
sexual discourse.

Reformation discourse affirmed the essential goodness of nature
and salvation by grace. The reformers lifted marriage and, in turn, sexual desire (in marriage) to the level of a more positive affirmation.
Companionship and the restraint of sexual desire, rather than procreation, started to emerge as positive values in the reformers' theologies of marriage. Luther and Calvin did not overcome the spiritualistic
dualism of earlier Christian practice, but they did shift it toward a more
positive understanding. Luther understood the restraint of desire no
longer in terms of religious life, but in marriage. He confined the rag-
ing power of lust/pleasure to lawful expressions within marriage.[27]
John Calvin, on the other hand, stressed the companionship of marriage.[28] The Protestant reformers undermined the celibate ideal of
dominant Christian discourse and practice, and they advanced
Christian discursive practice toward a positive affirmation of human
sexuality. The reformers could not quite accept sexual pleasure as a
complete good; they limited themselves to affirming Jesus' male humanity and erotic feelings. This reinforced the church's emphasis on
family order and marriage and was still used to justify the subordination of women to men and their exclusion from leadership within
churches. The Reformation churches were still in the grip of an antisexual, misogynistic, and homophobic discursive field even though
they made significant modifications.

Reformation discourse effected a shift—albeit a slight shift—in
Roman Catholic discourse on sexuality and the family. Marriage and
family remained in a secondary position to the state of celibacy among

priests and religious. However, Catholic discourse began to recognize in a limited fashion the unitive purpose of sexuality in marriage. It was only with Vatican II and its aftermath that the Roman Catholic church began to shift its discursive focus toward the family. It followed the Protestant vector of discovering Jesus' sexuality and then using his maleness to justify the dominance of a male, celibate clergy.[29] Like most of the Protestant churches, the Catholic church remains in the grip of antisexuality, misogyny, and homophobia.

Sexuality and Christology

Jesus' celibacy has been used by Catholic doctrine and practice to buttress control of the church by celibate men. As a symbol of asexuality, the ecclesial portraits of Jesus promoted a moral/political dualism that subordinated women and denigrated sexual pleasure. Misogyny and homophobia were, therefore, the natural consequences of such asexual readings of the biblical traditions.

There has been some movement to discuss Jesus' sexuality in contemporary theology. Tom Driver observes,

> The absence of all comment in them [the Gospels] about Jesus' sexuality cannot be taken to imply that he had no sexual feelings. . . . It is not shocking, to me at least, to imagine Jesus moved to love according to the flesh. I cannot imagine a human tenderness, which the Gospels show to be characteristic of Jesus, that is not fed in some degree by the springs of passion. The human alternative to sexual tenderness is not asexual tenderness but sexual fear. Jesus lived in his body, as other men do.[30]

Driver's theological comments were preceded by earlier literary attempts at reconstructing a sexual Jesus. D. H. Lawrence, in *The Man Who Died,* originally titled *The Escaped Cock,* attempted to revise the Christian perspective of antisexuality and give an example of sexual integration. Jesus' bodily resurrection provided Lawrence with the symbolism to explore Jesus coming to sexual wholeness through a priestess of Isis. The celibate Jesus who never had an erection comes to full sexual knowledge. Lawrence comments, "If Jesus rose in full flesh, He rose to know the tenderness of a woman, and the great pleasure of her, and to have children by her."[31] Similarly, Nikos Kazantzakis takes up the question of Jesus and sexuality in his *The Last Temptation of Christ.* The movie version of Kazantzakis's novel depicting Jesus' struggle with sexual temptation created an uproar with

Christian fundamentalists when it was released. The asexual image of the Christ prevalent in fundamentalist groups will not entertain even the suggestion of sexual temptation of Jesus.

William Phipps takes up the question of Jesus' sexuality in his book, *Was Jesus Married?* Phipps argues that antisexual rhetoric in early Christianity distorted the picture of Jesus into the celibate Christ. He argues that Jesus was married. Phipps's argument has merit against the strong residual antisexual discourse of Christianity. However, he desperately wants Jesus to be a social construction of heterosexuality.[32] Phipps's unnuanced use of scriptural evidence is not the issue here.[33] The point is that his raising the question indicates a paradigm shift has taken place in the Christian valuation of sexuality.

Within Protestant and more recent Roman Catholic christological discourse, Jesus the Christ becomes a model of heterosexuality, a foundation for legitimizing heterosexist Christian truth and social constructions on marriage and the family.[34] The heterosexual Christ remains, nonetheless, celibate and does not go as far as the fictional reconstructions of Lawrence and Kazantzakis. Jesus the heterosexual male Christ continues the moral/political dualism that subordinates the social position of women in the church and in society and that excludes sexual variation. Jesus the Christ becomes cultural force for legitimizing compulsory heterosexuality.

Contemporary heterosexist Christian theology proclaims a heterosexist Christ; this results in a homophobic creationism. Homophobic creationism is the practice of using the creation accounts in Genesis 1–3 and Genesis 19 to justify heterosexual practice as normative because rooted in creation. Fundamentalist Christian ex-gay/lesbian organizations that convert gay men and lesbians to heterosexuality in order to be saved usually support their homophobic practice by pointing to the creation accounts. Likewise, the Vatican documents on homosexuality promote compulsory heterosexuality as normative of creation. The Vatican notion of homosexual orientation as "intrinsically evil" and "objectively disordered" manifests homophobic creationism.

Heterosexist Christian interpretations of the Genesis creation accounts legitimize a dominant male god, patriarchal power relations of men over women, and gender differentiations. The male God creates man (Gen. 2:7); woman is created as a helpmate to man (2:18–23); woman is created from the rib of man and is dependent upon him (Gen. 2:21–23); man names woman and has power over her (Gen. 2:23); woman's desire for man keeps her submissive (Gen. 3:16); God gives man the right to rule over woman (Gen. 3:16). According to het-erosexist/homophobic creationism, God's creation is distorted by the sin of woman and later the sin of Sodom.[35] These biblical interpreta-tions maintain the normalcy of the domination of male over female and the heterosexual sexual practices over same-sex practices. They contribute to the social organization and legitimation of homophobia.

In *God and the Rhetoric of Sexuality,* Phyllis Trible provides a fresh interpretation of the creation accounts. She tries to deconstruct misogynistic readings by pointing out that metaphors and images for God as masculine are only partial. Trible translates Genesis verses in a way that stresses the notion of the image of God as both male and fe-male: "And God created humankind in his image; / in the image of God created he him; / male and female created he them."[36] For Trible, the deconstruction of biblical misogyny is performed through restoring the balance of the female images of God.[37] It critiques the entrenched patriarchy of biblical criticism.

Recently, feminist theologians have deconstructed the maleness of Christ within christological discourse in a similar manner. They have reconstructed an inclusive christological discourse by not limiting the figure or meaning of Christ exclusively to the male Jesus. They widen the meaning of Christ to include feminine social practice.[38] Elisabeth Schüssler Fiorenza attempts to shift the burden of christo-logical discourse to the *basileia* vision and practice of Jesus.[39] Other feminist theologians have placed Christology in the practices and struggles of women. The term *Christa* refers to the crucifix hanging for a time in the Cathedral of St. John the Divine in New York City where the Christ figure on the cross was female.[40] Rita Nakashima Brock uses the term *Christa* to pioneer a Christology not centered on Jesus but on the community.[41] Brock asserts,

> Jesus participates centrally in this Christa/Community, but he neither brings erotic power into being nor controls it. He is brought into being through it and participates in the cocreation of it. Hence Christa/Com-munity is a lived reality expressed in relational images in which erotic power is made manifest. The reality of erotic power within connected-ness means it cannot be located in a single individual. Hence what is truly christological, that is, truly revealing of divine incarnation and salvific power in human life, must reside in connectedness and not in single individuals. The relational nature of erotic power is as true dur-ing Jesus' life as it is after his death. He neither reveals nor embodies it, but he participates in its revelation and embodiment.[42]

Brock extends Christology beyond the historical Jesus to the feminist community. Likewise, Carter Heyward uses the concept of Christa to embody erotic energy: "In the context of sexist, erotophobic patriarchy, Christa, unlike the male Christ, is controversial because her body signals a crying need for woman-affirming (non-sexist), erotic (non-erotophobic) power that, insofar as we share it, will transform a world that includes our own personal lives in relation."[43] For feminist theologians, Jesus is retrieved in relation to the struggles of women for justice.

Similarly, the practice of a queer criticism radically questions contemporary heterosexual or past asexual constructions of christological discourse. It unpacks sexual oppositions that have been glossed over in totalizing truth claims of Christian discourse. It uses feminist reconstructive practice against misogyny as part of its discourse. It employs its own critical practice against homophobia, but it also constructs queer bodies, queer selves, and queer sexuality. In feminist and queer critical practice, the erotic self is embodied over and against the apathetic self. The recovery of bodily connectedness and the affirmation of the erotic goodness of the body provide a corrective to an Augustinian severity that has long dominated Christian discourse. The contemporary recovery of embodied sexuality as a positive value is important for shaping a Christology sensitive to the struggles of queer Christians.

Queer criticism recognizes christological discourse as historically constructed through misogyny, antisexuality, and homophobia. A queer Christology starts with Jesus' practice and death and reconstructs the claims of Easter within queer critical practice.

The Retrieval of Jesus' Basileia Practice

Jesus used the symbol of God's reign (*basileia*) to speak of liberating activity of God among people.[44] The symbol of God's reign was the organizing symbol of his message and his practices. For Jesus, God's reign was socially provocative and politically explosive.[45] It was socially provocative in that its coming belonged to the least, those like children (Matt. 18:4, Mark 10:15), the destitute (Luke 6:20), the persecuted (Matt. 5:10), and outcasts (Matt. 21:31). God's reign was also politically explosive. Jesus practiced liberation in his siding with the humiliated and oppressed of Jewish society. He gave them hope and the courage to resist the domination politics of first-century C.E. Palestine.

The symbol of God's reign was polymorphous. It could take the metaphorical shape of a physical object (a mustard seed, leaven, a treasure), particular actions (healing, exorcisms, table association, the Temple demonstration), or visionary words. God's reign could be represented in parables, or it could be performed in action. The performed symbol of God's reign could open human communication to new dimensions and possibilities within social and political experience. Jesus and his group of disciples performed toward these social actions as if they represented God's coming reign.[46]

Jesus was a practitioner of God's reign unfolding in first-century Palestine. His *basileia* praxis was social; it had symbolic configurations with definite actions, particular social forms, and specific political goals. In his parables, the image of God's reign is often shocking and provocative: The good Samaritan (Luke 10:29–37), the prodigal son (Luke 15:11–32), the vineyard workers (Matt. 20:1–13), and the great banquet (Luke 14:16–23, Matt. 22:1–10). In the first century, the term *good Samaritan* was as shocking as the term *queer Christians* is to fundamentalist Christians. The image of the father in the parable of the prodigal son breaks patriarchal stereotypes in his surprising actions toward his two sons. The egalitarian vision of God's reign in the parables of the vineyard workers and the great banquet undermines exclusive, privileged, and hierarchical attitudes of social power.

Jesus' *basileia* message and praxis signified the political transformation of his society into a radically egalitarian, new age, where sexual, social, religious, and political distinctions would be irrelevant. Jesus struggled for *basileia* liberation in his siding with the humiliated, the oppressed, and the throw-away people of first-century Jewish society. He welcomed them at table and healed them of their social wounds. Jesus gave instructions on how to invite guests to a dinner (Luke 14:11–14). His meals did not create social distinctions but bridged them by including the outsider. His meals are inclusive metaphors for God's reign and its openness.[47] Jesus emphasized a generalized reciprocity, a giving without expecting a return (Luke 6:35). It is a form of giving that frees other people to give in return.

John Dominic Crossan maintains that the heart of Jesus' ministry was a "shared egalitarianism of spiritual and material resources," an unbrokered reign of God.[48] The discipleship of equals became a form of egalitarian relating between men and women.[49] This discipleship was marked by the sharing of goods, the equality of male and female disciples, an inclusiveness at table, and loving service at the table.[50] Jesus pointed out,

> The kings of the Gentiles exercise lordship over them; and those in authority over them are benefactors. But not so with you; rather let the greatest among you become as the youngest, and the leader as one who serves. For which is the greater, one who sits at table, or one who serves? Is it not the one who sits at table? But I am among you as one who serves. (Luke 22:24)

In his own words, Jesus modeled God's reign as one who serves at table and who washes the feet of his disciples. He asked his disciples to imitate these *basileia* actions. His *basileia* practices at table also criticized domination politics—the politics of Jewish aristocracy and Temple leadership, Herod Antipas, Pilate, and the Roman imperial system.

Jesus' liberative practice of God's coming reign depicted a critical alternative vision of social and political relations. It moved social and political relations in the direction of freedom, justice, and love. What Jesus practiced was meant to communicate to others the social presence of God's reign. God was socially present in *basileia* actions. God was available in the struggles and practices for human liberation.

The critical alternative in Jesus' *basileia* vision was not oppressor and oppressed exchanging roles. The cycle of abusive power, whereby an oppressor is vanquished by a former victim who then becomes oppressor, would come to a halt. God's reign would belong to the poor but not in the counterviolence of the Jewish resistance movement. God's reign would belong to the poor and oppressed who practiced loving service, not dominating power. Service at table would become the political infrastructure of God's new society. Thus, Jesus' basic *basileia* message and practice questioned power that victimized and oppressed people. Without compassion, all religious, economic, social, and political authority became oppressive. The power to dominate was embedded in the motivations behind the extremism of piety, in the inflexibility of fundamentalists and literalists, in economic divisions, and in the legitimations of political control.[51] He gave people hope and the courage to resist domination politics manifested in social and economic inequalities.

Jesus confronted the systemic injustice of the imperial Roman control in which Jewish peasants found themselves. Jewish peasants were squeezed by a religious and political system of economic extraction.

Bread and indebtedness were survival issues they faced every day. In the Abba prayer Jesus addressed these needs: "Give us this day our daily bread, and forgive us our debts as we forgive our debtors," he prayed. As one contemporary theologian puts it, "Indebtedness disrupts the ability of a social order to supply daily bread. God is petitioned to remove the oppressive power of debt in people's lives."[52] Waging conflict and negating the existing structures of socioeconomic and political domination were part of Jesus' liberative praxis. He did not hesitate to criticize, dispute, reject, condemn, and resist power relations and practices that oppressed. These were liberative skills used in fighting for and actualizing God's compassion and justice. Jesus' kingdom praxis fundamentally symbolized and actualized freedom.

The irruption of God's reign into the present called for a new change of direction or a new path. The practice of Jesus made clear the radical freedom from which he acted. His praxis encompassed the political tensions that were realities in first-century Palestine. However, Jesus' praxis contradicted the logic of an oppressive system imposed upon the poor, the socially dysfunctional, the unclean, and the outsider in Palestine. His radical freedom was measured precisely by his ability to participate in their world and point to the innovative social network of God's reign. His *basileia* practice of solidarity was his compassionate identification with the oppressed and his active commitment to social change. The practice of solidarity is what I include in the term *love-making* in later chapters; it is vital to justice-doing. Jesus proclaimed and practiced God's reign, a just and loving society where God would be socially in the midst of human interactions.

Jesus' *basileia* actions were political activities, oriented toward the radical transformation of the Jewish community. Jesus' *basileia* actions presented a critical alternative to the domination politics of the clerical aristocracy and the Roman Imperium. He created a political community that mirrored the social presence and compassion of God. Jesus' *basileia* praxis was performed in specific social situations with specific intention. He engaged his social situation in its entirety with a continuous stream of kingdom action, always trying to perform God's reign within any given social situation.

The Politics of the Cross

It was not God's will that Jesus died to ransom those with sin. This was a Christian interpretation of the death of Jesus. Rather, the cross symbolized the violent and brutal end of Jesus in the context of his political praxis for God's reign. Jesus was executed by the political infrastructure of Jewish Palestine as a political insurgent. The Jewish religious aristocracy and their Roman rulers perceived Jesus' message and practice of God's reign as a threat to the political order. The cross was a political tool, used by Roman landowners to control slaves and by the Roman military to control native populations. It symbolized political terror, the mechanism of social control and oppression. In commitment and trust, Jesus died for God's coming reign. His death embodied his own vision and commitment to practice God's reign to the very end.

Jesus did not accept political legitimacy based on control of the Temple and social exploitation. Nor did he accept the logic of social and political hierarchies built on a foundation of wealth, privilege, status, power, and force. Jesus developed a practice in service to God's reign. The logic of God's reign was the logic of an abundance that is shared. It was characterized by reciprocal sharing of economic, religious, and social resources. The logic of the *basileia* was not the exercise of power to oppress. It was the exercise of power in the form of service, waiting on table and washing guests' feet. Hierarchical relations and social divisions were reduced to unbrokered egalitarian social relations in God's coming reign.

Because of his message and practice of God's coming reign, Jesus came into lethal conflict with the powerful. Jesus died because his *basileia* praxis was politically provocative. It suggested liberation from oppression, poverty, and extremism. God's reign meant liberation from the "Gentile rulers who lord over." It meant liberation from exploitation resulting in indebtedness, slavery, and starvation. It meant liberation from the particular holiness ideologies that excluded people because of illness, sin, or social status from the covenant community.

Jesus' provocation in the Temple demonstration and his active campaign against the Temple aristocracy proved to be lethal.[53] Jesus performed a Stop the Temple action in overturning the money changers' tables, preventing the sale of sacrificial animals and anyone from carrying anything through the Temple precincts. By challenging the Temple leadership, he challenged the Roman imperial system, since the Jewish high priests were appointed by Roman prefects in Jerusalem. It was inevitable that Jesus' revolutionary vision and praxis of God's reign resulted in his political execution. He appeared to the chief priests, the Jerusalem aristocracy, and the Romans as a messianic pretender who threatened the established political order of Palestine. He was murdered by the structures of social control and political repression because he refused to be silent.

Jesus' teachings and practice of the egalitarian, unbrokered reign of God threatened the position of the privileged and the balance of political power that rested in their favor. Wealth was controlled because of the unequal distribution of political power in the hands of less than 2 percent of the population of Jewish Palestine. Jesus spoke of a God who did not side with the wealthy, the privileged, and the powerful but who sided with the poor, the oppressed, the weak, the outsider, and the undesirable. Jesus' practice symbolized God's reign for the poor, a new economics of shared resources and a new politics of service. With his message of God's solidarity with the oppressed and a commitment to justice-doing, Jesus threatened the political order established by the Romans and the co-opted Jewish aristocracy. His action in the Temple was a visible symbol of unbrokered egalitarian relations of God's coming reign. He broke silence and spoke up against the Temple's oppression.

Jesus' sentence of death was handed down and executed by Romans. Jesus was put to death on the cross for political rebellion. The cross symbolized the cruelty of the Roman imperial system, patriarchal violence and privilege, the political infrastructure of the co-opted aristocracy and Temple leadership, a compromised sacerdotal aristocracy, and ultimately ruthless human behavior. Crucifixion awaited both the charismatic prophet and the revolutionary. It was the ultimate deterrent of the Roman political system for keeping revolutionaries and would-be messiahs in check. Crucifixion was the consequence of Jesus' commitment to *basileia* praxis and its conflictual nature.

Easter: The Queer Christ

On Easter, Jesus became God's Christ, that is, God's power of embodied solidarity, justice, love, and freedom. Despite prevalent heterosexist christological discourse, it is not Jesus' maleness that made him the Christ. It is his *basileia* practice of solidarity with the oppressed, his execution, God's identification with his crucifixion, and God's raising him from the dead that made Jesus the Christ. In his *basileia* practice, Jesus asserted God as the saving reality of solidarity and justice for the oppressed. Through the resurrection God affirmed the validity of Jesus' *basileia* message of the end of domination; by raising Jesus, God said no to human oppression. Francis Schüssler Fiorenza asserts, "Belief in Jesus' resurrection is belief in God's justice that vindicated the life and praxis of Jesus and had the effect of affirming that life and that praxis."[54] For queer Christians, the risen Jesus stands in solidarity with oppressed gay men and lesbians. The risen Jesus is the hope for justice.

Easter was God's embodied action of solidarity and justice; God identified with the murdered Jesus' practice of solidarity. The Easter action of God turned Jesus into a parable, a parable about God. God was revealed as the compassionate power of justice that saved Jesus from death. Easter became the event of God's liberative practice, God's truth for justice. God stood in solidarity with the crucified Jesus. God did not negate the brutal death of Jesus; it was real, violent, and cruel. But God identified with the crucified Jesus. God was there in the midst of brutal human violence. God genuinely embraced the total flesh of Jesus in suffering and death. On Easter, God asserted that the oppressive political system would not triumph in the death of Jesus and that the tragedy of Jesus' death in service to God's reign would not be the last action. God asserted that the kingdom would triumph over human oppression.

God's liberative praxis on Easter does not negate the real tragedies of human history, the monstrous cruelties and the forgotten deaths of innocent victims. Rather, the depths of human suffering are met with the solidarity of Jesus. Jesus becomes the Christ. He is a parable of God's strong assertion that human barbarism, political oppression, and dominating power relations will not triumph. This includes the oppressive political systems that have persecuted and executed men and women with same-sex attraction, that murdered gay men and lesbians in the Nazi death camps, that blocked effective and compassionate responses to gay men with HIV infections, and that promote homophobic violence and oppression. God is concealed and murdered; God is there in every death of a gay man or a lesbian woman. God will remember innocent gay and lesbian people, and Easter justice will triumph.

On Easter, God raised Jesus to the level of a discursive symbol and praxis, and Jesus became the Christ, the liberative praxis of God's compassion in the world. God's liberative praxis included the symbolics of Jesus' *basileia* practices. It took the political shapes of Jesus' *basileia* praxis of empowering hope, love, solidarity, and human freedom. It now takes on the form of real solidarity with the suffering and the poor.

God's social praxis is power with the transformative capacity to reach out for freedom, love, and justice. It stands in direct contrast and opposition to the production, circulation, and use of power for domination. The power of God's freedom remains an integral part of the human practice of freedom.

What Easter communicates is the practical correlation of Jesus' *basileia* praxis and God's liberative praxis. Easter empowers the faith that God was configured in Jesus' social activities, in particular, his social practices of solidarity and justice. Easter announces that Jesus' *basileia* praxis actualized God's praxis. The message of Easter is the hope of God's universal solidarity with the oppressed. The hope of resurrection is the faith that God's power will continue to transform the reality of oppression and death into life and freedom. God's Christ continues to be politically configured in solidarity with the poor and the weak, the socially deviant and the outsider. God's Christ is socially in the midst of interactions that empower, that liberate people in the direction of justice, freedom, and love. God's Christ is in the midst of political struggle for liberation. Political liberation is God's insurrection against the political horrors and atrocities of human history, against the misuse and abuse of political power. God's Christ is in the midst of gay and lesbian political struggles; this is the practice of God's justice.

Jesus' *basileia* message is grounded in his political praxis; it provides for alternative, critical, resistant, and conflictual forms of human action. It means that *basileia* praxis is always socially situated, that is, dialectical and symbolic social and political activity. It is political activity that symbolizes the *basileia* interests and is practiced with a critical edge. The growth of God's reign is a historical process of struggle for social and political liberation. *Basileia* liberation requires the communicative idiom of political discourse and practice to present a critical alternative to dominating political relations, networks of oppressive power, and systems of exclusion. It critically engages all oppressive and dominating activity, always very conscious of those who are oppressed and dominated by such activity. *Basileia* liberation expresses and practices novel patterns of nonabusive and nonoppressive power relations. It consciously symbolizes the social alternative of political liberation. It practices solidarity with the poor, the weak, and the vulnerable. *Basileia* activity expands the critical and analogical potential of Jesus' *basileia* symbol system into new economic, social, political, historical, and cultural situations.

God's praxis is not enslaving or oppressive; it is compassionate and liberative. God is "the event of suffering, liberating love."[55] The resurrection of the crucified Jesus constitutes liberating power. God is configured to the suffering and death of Jesus; God dies with Jesus. According to Dorothee Soelle, God's insurrection against human injustice is Jesus' resurrection.[56] God rejects the political sanctioning of injustice, oppression, and exploitation of the innocent. God stands in solidarity with the innocent and the oppressed of history. God's liberative praxis takes the specific contours of justice and the practices of Jesus: healing and exorcism; table fellowship; a Torah of compassion; the foundation of social group to practice the new social relationship of God's reign in advance; solidarity with the poor and the weak; active resistance and critical engagement of domination politics and holiness discourses; reciprocal sharing of goods and mutual service in love; critical challenge, conflict, and martyrdom; the quest for freedom and final liberation. In other words, God takes the role and perspective of Jesus in his solidarity with the oppressed.

What Easter affirms is the total liberative compassion and justice of God in Jesus the Christ. God's creative freedom is the production and circulation of networks of nonoppressive power relations. It is the creative production of power that allows for the novel, new possibilities, and freedom. The oppressed and the oppressor designate concrete political realities. The oppressed are involved in a social relationship of dependence in which their status, power, and economic livelihood are diminished. God's liberative praxis transforms this social reality so that it is no longer characterized by dependence or by negativity. God's liberative praxis becomes specific forms of political interaction, specific forms of nonoppressive power that are oriented toward critical change. These forms of nonoppressive power include strategic forms of social transformation; they include resistance, struggle, reform, conflict, and social transgression.

God's liberative praxis challenges the ideologies that sanction a status quo of oppression, domination, and exploitation. It struggles with the concentration of valued scarce resources—power, wealth, status—in the hands of the few. It moves to an equitable sharing of economic and valued resources. God's social praxis challenges political hierarchies and moves toward a *basileia* egalitarianism. It conflicts with ideologies and practices that absolutize social symbols, interactions, structures, and systems. All "isms" absolutized are shattered by God's liberative praxis.

God's liberative praxis is an ongoing dynamic movement that includes conflict, negation, and the emerging possibilities of the new. In particular, it conflicts with all that is not yet *basileia,* that is, what remains under the politics of homophobic domination and heterosexist exploitation. However, it negates all exploitative human actions, all infrastructures of political domination, and all social stratifications with symbolic and political acts of the emerging reign of God. It negates the social systems and political structures that lead to the executions of Jesus and countless others. It judges those social structures, those discursive and nondiscursive practices as not the *basileia.*

Practical Implications of a Queer Christology

A queer Christology begins with the experience of homophobic oppression and gay/lesbian reverse discursive experience. It is discourse rooted in gay/lesbian practice. This is the practice of Christology, constructed in the midst of human suffering and real oppression; it stands contrary to the practices of ecclesial Christology.

Episcopal priest and writer Malcolm Boyd was not the first to raise the question of Jesus' homoerotic feelings. In the late sixties, Hugh Montefiore, an Anglican canon, suggested that Jesus may have had same-sex inclinations.[57] However, Boyd argues for a gay-sensitive Jesus for queer Christians:

> Gay spirit, as we have come to understand it, fits Jesus easily. He appears to us as an androgynous man. Jesus shared his feelings, empathized with those of others, and was not afraid of intimacy. He was sensitive and vulnerable, consented to his own needs, knew how to receive as well as give to another. Jesus exalts the spiritual dimension inherent in a truly liberated expression of sexuality.[58]

Recently, Robert Williams raises the question of a queer Jesus. He speculates, "Jesus was the passionate lover of Lazarus, a young man who became his disciple. When the two of them met, there was that electricity we have learned to call limerence, or love at first sight."[59] Many queer Christians feel comfortable with the affection that Jesus had for Lazarus, for Mary Magdalene, and for the beloved disciple. They feel at home with the affectional ease of Jesus with both men and women. Jesus broke many of the gender patterns and hierarchies of patriarchal power.[60] Thus, the gay and lesbian community has raised the question of Jesus' sexual intimacy, claiming Jesus as one of their own. This is hardly a strange social phenomenon. African American

Christians have claimed the black Christ for their liberator, and some feminists speak of the Christa.[61] It is only natural for queer Christians to reclaim Jesus as gay/lesbian-sensitive and construct a queer Christ.

Rosemary Ruether calls for restoring sexuality to the traditional image of Jesus. She claims that Jesus "appears to be neither married nor celibate. . . . If there is anything at all to be said about the sexuality of Jesus, it is that it was a sexuality under the control of friendship. He could love John and Mary Magdalene, physically embrace and be embraced by them because first of all he knew them as friends, not as sexual objects."[62]

Jesus' relationships were "controlled not by sexuality, but by friendship." Such attempts by Boyd, Williams, and Ruether to restore the sexuality of Jesus affirms and uplifts the sexually oppressed.[63] However, it says nothing about the historical Jesus' particular sexual practices. That information has been lost to biblical sources and history.[64] Yet we have access to some of Jesus' embodied actions for the *basileia,* and there we glimpse some nonheterosexist and nonhomophobic sexual patterns.

Jesus is liberated from the christological constructions that emerge from Christian homophobic discourse and the oppression of lesbian/gay people. Christology is a matter of proclaiming God's solidarity and justice-doing, which cannot be separated from the reign of God. God's solidarity and justice-doing form the basis of Jesus' *basileia* practice, and with them Jesus is revealed in the Easter event. The churches have made Christ into a symbol of homophobic oppression and violence. Jesus' crucifixion has been transformed into an abstract norm for Christian sexist power relations. Early in Christian history, Jesus' crucifixion was stripped of its political reality, transformed and spiritualized into the event of asexual salvation. It lost its social embeddedness; it was disembodied, abstracted, and spiritualized. A queer reclamation of Jesus retrieves the socially embedded Jesus and the political dimensions of his crucifixion. It was a brutal political death at the hands of a repressive political infrastructure.

It was not God's will that Jesus die. This abstraction of Jesus' crucifixion as God's will forms the basis for the nonsexual practice of power.[65] It legitimizes the construction of the ascetical self, purified of desire/pleasure.

In his message and practice of the coming reign of God, Jesus embodied a preferential option for the oppressed. In his social practices, he modeled a new *basileia* network of social relations that were nonexploitative, nonhierarchical, and nonoppressive. Men and women found hope in new forms of *basileia* relating. Jesus was radical in his practice of solidarity with oppressed men and women. His was a commitment aware of the political risks. Jesus' death is a tragic death at the hands of an oppressive political structure in first-century Palestine. The cross is God's invasive identification with the oppressed. The oppressed now includes the sexual oppressed, those oppressed because of their sexual preference or identity.

Jesus the Christ belongs to queer practice of liberation. We need a Christology that is rooted in gay and lesbian liberative practice, in our struggle for sexual liberation. For centuries, the crucifixion of Jesus represented the death of sexuality. The crucifixion stripped Jesus of his sexuality, his humanity, and the sociopolitical reality of his death. Christian discursive and nondiscursive practices have repeated Jesus' crucifixion. They remain acts of violence against the sexually oppressed. However, God's revelation on Easter aims to bring an end to crucifixions, not perpetuate them in the deployment of oppressive power relations.

The gay and lesbian reclamation of Jesus and his *basileia* practice becomes the generative matrix for reinterpreting Jesus' death and the Christ event in a nonhomophobic, nonheterosexist, and nonoppressive context. For us, the political death of Jesus reveals homophobic/heterosexist power at its fullest. The cross symbolizes the political infrastructure of homophobic practice and oppression. It symbolizes the terror of internalized homophobia that has led to the closeted invisibility of gay and lesbian people. It indicates the brutal silencing, the hate crimes, the systemic violence perpetuated against us. The cross now belongs to us. We have been crucified. We have been martyred. We have been nailed to that cross by most of the Christian churches. They continue to legitimize, bless, and activate violence against us.

Jesus was put to death for his *basileia* solidarity with the poor, the outcast, the sinner, the socially dysfunctional, and the sexually oppressed. Jesus died in solidarity with gay men and lesbians. His death becomes a no to closeted existence, to gay/lesbian invisibility and homophobic violence. The cross has terrorized gay men and lesbians. It has been a symbol of lethal sexual oppression, but Jesus' death shapes the cross into a symbol of struggle for queer liberation. From the perspective of Easter, God takes the place of the oppressed Jesus on the cross. God identifies with the suffering and death of Jesus at the hands of a political system of oppression. For gay and lesbian

Christians, Easter becomes the event at which God says no to homophobic violence and sexual oppression. God says no to the stripping away of Jesus' sexuality by Christian discourses that deny his embodied *basileia* practice. Jesus the Christ symbolizes God's practice of solidarity with us, the sexually oppressed or dissident (*anawim*). The *anawim* represent the biblical poor and powerless, a class of socially oppressed people. In the Hebrew Scriptures, God is partial to the poor (*anawim*), the powerless, and the undesirables. We may expand the meaning of *anawim* to include all those who are oppressed because of the politics of gender or sexual practices. The *anawim* becomes for us all people who were discriminated against, oppressed, tortured, and killed because of their sexual practices or because of their deviation from gender roles. It represents the sexually different or the sexually oppressed.

Easter becomes the hope of queer sexual liberation. The queer struggle for sexual liberation will triumph; this is the promise of Easter. When God raised Jesus from the dead, Jesus became God's Christ, God's practice of compassion, solidarity, and justice in the world. *Christ* is a relational term; it brings together Jesus' *basileia* practice and God's liberative practice. Jesus' *basileia* practice participates in God's liberative actions. To experience Jesus the Christ is to do God's justice; it is to live justice. God's liberative power claims Jesus' *basileia* practice of solidarity with the oppressed; it becomes God's justice for the oppressed.

On Easter, God made Jesus queer in his solidarity with us. In other words, Jesus "came out of the closet" and became the "queer" Christ. Jesus the Christ becomes actively queer through his solidarity with our struggles for liberation. Jesus becomes gay/lesbian rather than gay because of his solidarity with lesbians as well. This is not to deny the maleness of Jesus but to point out the innate human capacity of both men and women to stand in solidarity with one another. It, however, does deny the political gender identifications of Jesus with masculinity and the subsequent ecclesial violence to women in history. Therefore, Jesus the Christ is queer by his solidarity with queers.

The queer Christ is an attempt to construct a christological discourse that interprets Jesus' embodied practices in a positive, queer-affirming theological discourse. To say Jesus the Christ is queer is to say that God identifies with us and our experience of injustice. God experiences the stereotypes, the labeling, the hate crimes, the homophobic violence directed against us:

Three assailants harassed two gay men outside a gay bar and slashed the bar doorman's throat with a knife when he attempted to stop the harassment. Leaving the bar, they approached a gay man waiting for a bus and said to him, "We're going to teach you faggots a lesson." They stabbed the victim, puncturing his lung.[66]

To affirm that Jesus the Christ is queer is to politically identify Christ with the two gay men slashed. Jesus the Christ is "queer-bashed." Here modern Roman soldiers of homophobic violence pierce the gay/lesbian Christ with a knife. The queer Christ is politically identified with all queers—people who have suffered the murders, assaults, hate crime activities, campus violence, police abuse, ecclesial exclusion, denial of ordination and the blessing of same-sex unions, harassment, discrimination, HIV-related violence, defamation, and denial of civil rights and protections. Jesus the queer Christ is crucified repeatedly by homophobic violence. The aim of God's practice of solidarity and justice-doing and our own queer Christian practice is to bring an end to the crucifixions in this world.

If Jesus the Christ is not queer, then his *basileia* message of solidarity and justice is irrelevant. If the Christ is not queer, then the gospel is no longer good news but oppressive news for queers. If the Christ is not queer, then the incarnation has no meaning for our sexuality. It is the particularity of Jesus the Christ, his particular identification with the sexually oppressed, that enables us to understand Christ as black, queer, female, Asian, African, a South American peasant, Jewish, a transsexual, and so forth. It is the scandal of particularity that is the message of Easter, the particular context of struggle where God's solidarity is practiced. God and the struggle for sexual justice are practical correlation in a queer Christology.

Easter becomes God's sociopolitical unfolding of what *basileia* praxis symbolizes. It is a conscious political transformation of the world; it is making God's nearness real in the world. It is the creative transformation of socially embedded men and women in the direction of human and political freedom. God's liberative praxis is necessarily embedded in the social and political situation of gay and lesbian people. It is, thus, impossible to separate the history of God's social praxis from queer social praxis. God's praxis is found socially in the midst of liberative praxis of the gay/lesbian community. It is the heart of our critical and liberative practice for justice and freedom.

4

A Queer Biblical Hermeneutics

Criticism is a matter of flushing out that thought, and trying to change it: to show that things are not as self-evident as one believed, to see what is accepted as self-evident will no longer be accepted as such. Practicing criticism is a matter of making facile gestures difficult.

MICHEL FOUCAULT[1]

What unites gay men and lesbians is their common struggle for justice. Their strength lies in the links forged for justice. Lesbians bear the social burden of same-sex orientation, but they also bear the social burden of being a woman in a sexist society. Gay men share the social burden of same-sex orientation. They also suffer from heterosexist society because they are despised as less than male. However, gay men in their social linkage with lesbians become women-identified not in the heterosexist sense of less than male but rather in the practice of solidarity. They share a common oppressive network of power relations and share in the struggles to free themselves from the destructive effects of those power relations. Women, lesbians, and gay men have been invisible to society. They have suffered many of the same exclusions and erasures in heterosexist histories. Heterosexism tries to erase women and those attracted to the same sex from history. It makes those men and women into other than male, into nonpersons. Therefore, the liberation of gay men is not only linked to the liberation of lesbians but to the liberation of all women.

Feminist liberation theologians have begun to revise Christian biblical and theological discourse. They have applied a hermeneutics of suspicion to all theological and biblical interpretations. Feminist liberation theologians have been critical of biblical writings and ecclesial interpretations as socially constructed within a patriarchal framework. They have begun to deconstruct patriarchal interpretations of biblical texts and have reconstructed an interpretative model for feminist practice.

We can learn from feminist revisions of Christian discourse and from their paradigms of discursive practice. We begin with feminist interpretative models of the biblical texts and then move on to pioneer a queer interpretative model. It shares many of the same deconstructive and reconstructive contours and critical engagements of feminist models because queers share the same oppressive network of power relations. However, the strength of a queer interpretative model is precisely that it is not exclusively gay identified or exclusively lesbian identified. It includes critical feminist hermeneutics and practice. Both feminist and queer interpretative models arise from an interlocking discourse and practice of resistance, conflict, and struggle for liberation. They both try to free biblical discourse from the distortions of heterosexist/homophobic power.

Elisabeth Schüssler Fiorenza has written extensively on the challenge of feminist biblical interpretation.[2] All biblical texts are social constructions of androcentric patriarchal culture and history. The Bible is written in the words of men. It has served and continues to serve to legitimate their clerical, social, and political power. For Schüssler Fiorenza, a critical feminist hermeneutics seeks to develop a critical mode of biblical interpretation and practice that is consistent with experiences of women. The "power of theological naming" was stolen from women by men in the patriarchal constructions of the biblical texts.[3] The feminist challenge recognizes that if the oppressive patriarchal constructions of biblical texts are the word of God, then the God of the Bible is the God of oppression for women.[4] Feminist interpreters must recognize the oppressive social construction of biblical texts in the past and try to find contemporary meaning for women in their struggle for justice, solidarity, and liberation.

Along similar lines, Phyllis Trible investigates four biblical narratives of violence against women in *Texts of Terror:* "Hagar, the slave used, abused and rejected; Tamar, the princess raped and discarded;

an unnamed woman, the concubine raped, murdered, and dismembered; and the daughter of Jephthah, a virgin slain and sacrificed."[5] Trible's approach to each of these stories is to practice theodicy, or the attempt to make sense out of human tragedy, evil, or suffering. It is action that brings the terror of these tales into the present. She does not negate the terrors and patriarchal violence against each of the four women. Rather, she uses these four tales of terror to practice a solidarity, a hermeneutics that "interprets stories of outrage on behalf of their female victims in order to recover a neglected history, to remember a past that the present embodies, and to pray that these terrors shall not come to pass again."[6] Trible's hermeneutics challenges the patriarchal violence of the Scriptures and their misogynistic use in the churches and society by surfacing the reality of violence against women in the biblical text.

The Failure of Biblical Scholarship

Schüssler Fiorenza points out the failure of biblical scholarship in the theological academy, that is, in universities and seminaries. Historically, exegesis of biblical texts has been considered "value neutral." Exegetes reconstruct the meaning of the text within its own historical context but fail to search for contemporary meaning.[7] Schüssler Fiorenza criticizes value-neutral biblical scholarship, for "all theology knowingly or not is by definition always engaged for or against the oppressed."[8] Foucault, likewise, reminds us: "We should abandon a whole tradition that allows us to imagine that knowledge can exist only where the power relations are suspended and that knowledge can develop only outside of its injunctions, its demands, and its interests."[9] Christian biblical discourse is a site of conflict and contestation. Feminist critical reconstructions of the biblical text include not only recovering past meaning of the text but also evaluating it from the power/knowledge perspective of the struggles of women for liberation. Schüssler Fiorenza brings historical reconstruction of biblical texts from the past into the present liberative practice of women. Thus, the Bible becomes an empowering resource for women in their struggle for liberation.

Like most liberation theologians, Schüssler Fiorenza insists that God's revelation is found in the lives of the oppressed. The God of the Bible is the God of the oppressed: "To truly understand the Bible is to read it through the eyes of the oppressed since the God who speaks in the Bible is the God of the oppressed."[10] The Bible is the revelation of God's praxis of compassion, justice, and freedom for the oppressed. It reveals God's preferential option for the poor and the oppressed.[11] It becomes an empowering resource for the critical practice of justice in the struggles of women for liberation from patriarchal (and now heterosexist) Christian discourse.

The Bible is a justice resource in the queer battle for Christian power/truth in two areas: (1) in our dismantling of the Bible as a homophobic/heterosexist and terrorist weapon of oppression; (2) in our reappropriating the Bible as a resource for the critical practice of justice. The texts of the Bible are critically read both as subversive and empowering practice.

"Texts of Terror"

The majority of Christian traditions believe that the Bible opposes homosexuality. The Bible has been used as a weapon of terror against gay men and lesbians. It has been interpreted to legitimize oppression against same-sex practices throughout Christian history. Biblical texts have been used by fundamentalist churches in their homophobic attacks upon gay men and lesbians in hate campaigns and political pressure tactics to exclude queers from ecclesial social practices and impede their civil rights. When we use the term *fundamentalist,* we include not only Protestant ecclesial groups who maintain inerrancy of the Bible as the word of God but also those mainline Christian churches that have been reluctant to introduce biblical criticism into their social practices. For instance, the Roman Catholic hierarchy participates in fundamentalist biblicism and literalist traditionalism when it refuses to accept historical criticism of Scripture to correct and revise its doctrinal positions.[12] This is particularly the case in its public statements on the exclusion of women from the ordained ministry. Cardinal Ratzinger, a trained theologian, distorts the use of Scripture in favor of a literalist, traditional view of natural law in his infamous letter on homosexuality.

Many mainline Protestant churches also share in this failure to apply historical criticism to biblical statements to correct their doctrines. The recent Presbyterian General Assembly overwhelmingly rejected the "Report of the Special Committee on Human Sexuality." The Presbyterian task force report applied the biblical concept of "justice love" to recommend the ordination of openly gay/lesbian ministers and the sanctioning of same-sex unions.[13] Fundamentalist biblicism still exerts strong power in our society. It fails, however, to adequately distinguish between God's revelation and its social construction. It simply identifies the social construction of God's revelation with truth without critically reconstructing past social meaning.

Homophobic/heterosexist biblical interpretation operates within a social context of fundamentalism, authoritarianism, traditionalism, and rigid definitions of social reality.[14] Same-sex practices are not a prominent concern in the biblical traditions. However, fundamentalists base their condemnations of same-sex practices on a few biblical texts: Genesis 19, Leviticus 18:22 and 20:13, and Deuteronomy 23:13 in the Hebrew Scriptures; Romans 1:26–27 and 1 Corinthians 6:9 by Paul; the later first-century C.E. texts of 1 Timothy 1:10, 2 Peter 1:10, and Jude 7 in the Christian Scriptures. These texts have been used to justify homophobic violence against gay and lesbian people and often read from a heterosexist creationist perspective.

Fundamentalist churches and ecclesial hierarchies have subjected the reading of the Bible to a heterosexist and literalist reading of the Bible as one sacred text.[15] They bring uncritical assumptions and prejudices to their textual interpretations. They blur the rapists of Genesis 19 with cultic male prostitution in the Hebrew Scriptures and the ambiguous words *malakoi* (soft) and *arsenokoitai* (lying with males) in 1 Corinthians 6:9. They impose a homophobic interpretation of the texts in the Catholic letters. They equate Sodom with sodomy. We will briefly look at the textual evidence and then return to the production of the biblical truth of Sodom/sodomy.

Genesis 19 must be read with the "texts of terror" that Trible interprets for women.[16] It is a story of phallic violence and aggression against two sojourners or messengers from God. The narrative is an ethnological saga, a fictional composition with perhaps a historical kernel. The story of the destruction of Sodom and Gomorrah stands in contrast to the narrative of Abraham's generous hospitality toward God's messengers (Gen. 18:1–18). Together both chapters form an early literary unit and must be interpreted as a whole. Hospitality toward and protection of sojourners are themes interwoven in the Yahwist tradition in the two chapters.[17] The messengers in Genesis 19 are foreigners within the city, and the male inhabitants demand that Lot bring them out so that they may "know" them. Ancient societies frequently subjected strangers, the conquered, or trespassers to phallic anal penetration as an indication of their subordinate status.[18] What we have in Genesis 19 is that same phallic aggression as in the rape of the concubine in Judges 19. Phallic aggression asserts male dominance over other males and females. This story illustrates a violation of the ancient code of hospitality toward and protection of sojourners; it is a story of oppression.[19] The generalized application of the "rapists" of the Genesis 19 story to modern gay/lesbian sexual practices is an inappropriate reconstruction; there is a fallacy in equating rape with consensual same-sex practices in Christian fundamentalist reading of the text.

The second set of Hebrew texts of terror is found in the Holiness Code (Lev. 18:22, 20:13) and Deuteronomic history (Deut. 23:17) condemning male cultic prostitution. What the Leviticus law prohibits is male prostitution within Canaanite cults. It does not implicate same-sex male relationships outside of the Temple cult. The stress is on the prohibition of cultic prostitution and the idolatry it represented. There are six references to male cultic prostitutes (*qadesh*) in the Hebrew Scriptures.[20] It is not certain or evident that all the references to male cultic prostitutes refer to same-sex practices. The churches' application of the Holiness Code's prohibitions against cultic male prostitution to modern gay/lesbian sexual practices is, likewise, inappropriate.[21]

Two texts in Paul's letters have been used as texts of terror (Rom. 1:26–27, 1 Cor. 6:9). Romans 1:26–27 speaks about a change due to idolatry:[22] "For this reason, God gave them up to dishonorable passions. Their women exchanged natural relations for unnatural (*para physin*), and the men likewise gave up natural relations with women and were consumed with passion for one another. . . ." (RSV) People who formerly desired the opposite sex now practice same-sex actions. It is the only place in the Hebrew and Christian Scriptures that makes reference to female same-sex practices. Paul's use of the phrase "against nature" (*para physin*) links his statement both to contemporary Stoicism and the Pharisaic purity code.[23] "Against nature" has become a code word in traditional and contemporary ecclesial discourse about same-sex practices. Queer Christians have difficulty with the churchs' application of this particular Pauline passage to themselves. Paul, in the first place, does not understand the social construction of modern sexual identity. He has no concept of sexual orientation and has to be read within his own social framework. Paul presupposes a deviation from nature because of idolatry and his Pharisaic purity

code. His statement in Romans 1:26–27 is intertwined with his own
particular sociocultural context, and it does violence to Paul's perspective to apply his linkage of cultic prostitution and idolatry to the
contemporary situation of queers.[24]

1 Corinthians 6:9 presents another set of problems. "Do not be de-
ceived; neither the immoral (*malakoi*), nor idolaters, nor adulterers,
nor sexual perverts (*arsenokoitai*) . . . will inherit the *basileia*." The lin-
guistic meaning of *malakoi* (soft) and *arsenokoitai* (lying with men) remains uncertain. In modern biblical translations, they are translated
as "sexual perverts" (RSV), "catamites and sodomites" (JB), "sodomites"
(NAB), and "who are guilty of homosexual perversion" (NEB). In ecclesial hermeneutics, both words have generated specific social meanings that were directed at same-sex practices.[25] *Malakoi* means "soft";
it was understood by later traditional Christian discourse as referring
to masturbation. Only in the twentieth century has ecclesial discourse
applied *malakoi* as a reference to homosexuality.[26] As for *arsenokoitai*,
its usage is rare in Greek and quite ambiguous. It literally means "lying
with males." John Boswell asserts that it referred to male prostitutes for
Paul and Christians until the fourth century C.E. For John Boswell, the
fourth century represents a dividing line between the Greek-oriented
period of the Western church and its Latin phase. There was a decline
of familiarity with Greek among the aristocracy and the Christian
clergy. Few of the ecclesial writers in the fifth and sixth centuries knew
the precise meanings of unusual Greek words.[27] *Arsenokoitai* then
became confused with a number of other words for disapproved sexual practices and was equated with same-sex practices.[28] At the end
of the first century C.E., the usage of *arsenokoitai* by the author of 1
Timothy (1:10) is linked to adultery (*pornoi*). Boswell's thesis that it
referred to male prostitutes seems to hold firm in the usage in 1 Timothy.[29] There is no evidence that *malakoi* and *arsenokoitai* ever referred to same-sex practices for Paul or for the Christian church for
centuries thereafter.[30]

In the Catholic epistles, the evidence is even more flimsy. Jude 7
speaks of a comparison of Sodom and Gomorrah with those "going
after other flesh" (*apelthousai opiso sarkos heteras*). The interpretation of this passage has been imposed by the later ecclesial homophobic discourse about the Sodom story. The anonymous author of
Jude does not state that they go after the same flesh. The author understands the transgression of the natural order between human beings lusting for angels.[31] The author of 2 Peter virtually reuses and

edits Jude. 2 Peter 2:10 substitutes general language of "unlawful acts" for the sin of Sodom. Neither Jude nor 2 Peter refer to same-sex practices. The Sodom tradition is explicitly used in both letters to condemn false teachers, not same-sex practices.

This biblical literalism of a coded Sodom/sodomy language has dominated Christian political regimes of truth. It has generated blatant mistranslations of key words. Biblical truth has been constructed from inaccurate readings of the text or impositions of political interpretations upon the text, and this truth has been used as a tool of oppression, terrorism, and violence against men and women with same-sex attractions. Biblical notions of male rapists and cultic male prostitutes have been applied to modern gay men and lesbians. The cultural inapplicabilty of this modernization is grossly apparent to the gay/lesbian victims of this oppression.

The Emergence of Biblical Sodomy

There was a hermeneutical shift in interpreting Genesis 19 in the late patristic and early Middle Ages in ecclesial discourse. The shift included a number of interlocking foci of confronting, unstable, and conflicting practices. These led to the formation of Sodom into a coded symbol: "Sodomy is a coded word that encapsulates the moral heritage of those fierce verses that have branded on human remembrance across the centuries the fire and brimstone rained on the disobedient, without respect to age or gender."[32] John Boswell's *Christianity, Social Tolerance, and Homosexuality* and James Brundage's *Law, Sex, and Christian Society in Medieval Europe* reconstruct the historical shift in the discourse about same-sex practices. Boswell documents the social emergence of hostility to same-sex practices with the dissolution of the Roman state. Some of the social factors included the disappearance of urban subcultures, increased legislation to control morality, and increased Christian asceticism toward sexuality.[33] This discursive shift emerged with the symbol of Sodom coded into the word *sodomy* and was completed in Thomas Aquinas's condemnation of sins against nature (*peccata contra naturam*).[34]

Augustine's horror of "unnatural" or nonprocreative sex acts is traceable to his Manichaean past and its basic attitude of disdain for the body. The Sodom story is, thus, linked to his basic philosophical view that same-sex practices (nonprocreative sex acts) are bodily defilements.[35] The development of this view can be traced through medieval writers. In the eighth century, the British missionary monk, Boniface, described "sodomitical lust" without mentioning same-sex practices. He understood sodomy as referring to "despising lawful marriage and preferring incest, promiscuity, adultery, and impious unions with religious and cloistered women."[36] The Carolingian theologian Hincmar of Reims defined sodomy (*sodomia*) as the improper sexual release of semen: "Therefore, let no one claim he has not committed sodomy if he has acted contrary to nature with either man or woman or has deliberately and consciously defiled himself by rubbing, touching, or other improper actions."[37] Albertus Magnus in the thirteenth century attacked carnal unions of persons of the same gender; he declared "sodomy is the sin against nature" (*sodomia est peccatam contra naturam*).[38] Thomas Aquinas adopted the same definitional usage of sodomy as his teacher Albertus Magnus and gave lead to scholastic theological discourse on same-sex practices as sins against nature.[39] Brundage observes that the notion of "natural" is socially constructed: "What is 'natural' means whatever is thought (correctly or not) to be the usual practice of the majority."[40] Aquinas's theological position on sins against nature proved to have normative influence in the subsequent ecclesial discourses of Catholic and Protestant Christianity. It set the pattern of social intolerance and hatred.

While the notion of biblical sodomy emerged in Christian discourse, it also influenced secular legal codes and practices. In his Code of Law, Justinian published two novellae against same-sex practices. The first, novella 77, published in 538 C.E., directly refers to the story of Sodom. The second, novella 141, published in 544 C.E., refers to both Sodom and Paul. For Justinian, same-sex practices endangered the state. The influence of Justinian's legal codes were felt in later codification of laws in western Europe. The early legal codes of medieval Europe varied in severity and enforceability on proscriptions against same-sex practices.[41] In the law code drafted for Alfonso the Wise in the thirteenth century, sodomy is defined as "the sin which men commit by having intercourse with each other, against nature and against custom."[42] It was in the late thirteenth century that same-sex practices incurred the death penalty in most European legal compilations.[43]

Sodomy was an inclusive coded term for all sexual acts deviating from marital intercourse, whether toward the same or opposite sex. It was used frequently in an unqualified and inclusive sense in medieval Christian discourse.[44] However, sodomy/sodomite became associated with a whole range of sociopolitical evils; "socially, sodomy was repeatedly equated with heresy and political treason."[45] The term *buggery* had its origin in the social context of the eleventh-century Bulgars, a Manichaean Christian heretical group that practiced nonprocreative sexuality.[46] Sexual and religious nonconformity were conflated into the term *buggery* which became synonymous with sodomy. *Sodomy* became an encoded word for social threat during the Middle Ages and into the modern era. It was a threat that embodied the notion of foreign infection and was linked to social disorder and economic crisis. Anyone sexually different or socially nonconforming was condemned as a sodomite. Both Boswell and Brundage have demonstrated that during the latter half of the twelfth century, Christian Europe became increasingly conformist and intolerant of difference.[47] Sexual practices became indicators of doctrinal orthodoxy or deviancy. The "other"—Jews, heretics, sexual dissidents, and so forth—were perceived as a threat to the social order. Jonathan Dollimore observes that "the sodomite became the supreme instance of the demonized other."[48]

From the time of colonial America to the present state sodomy laws, sodomy has been legally construed as "unnatural sexual acts" of same- and opposite-sex practices. It has been used as a term for any sexual variation from what is considered normative for marital sex. It was applied to all sexual dissidence. In the more recent twentieth-century production and circulation of biblical truth, sodomy has been exclusively defined as a reference to gay and lesbian sexual practices. Contemporary Christian biblical truth has transformed gay men and lesbians into the "demonized other," as we noted in the discussion of ecclesial homophobia in chapter 1. Queers are a terrifying other to fundamentalists.

The decline of familiarity with Greek and the lack of understanding the precise meanings of unusual Greek words, *malakoi* and *arsenokoitai,* led to the social construction of new meanings. These new meanings were interlocked with the discourse about same-sex practices and the transformation of Sodom into coded sodomy. *Sodomy* became the term for all sexual deviant practices (nonprocreative same-sex and opposite-sex practices). *Malakoi* (soft) and *arsenokoitai* (lying with males) were confused with other words for sexual practices that were considered deviant. *Malakoi* was construed as "masturbation," and twentieth-century construction of sexual morality led to the peculiar interpretation of *malakoi* as referring to homosexual acts.[49]

Likewise, *arsenokoitai* was translated by St. Jerome as "male concubines" (*masculorem concubitores*); he relied on earlier exegetes since the word occurs so rarely in the Scriptures. Hincmar of Reims was the first theologian to use 1 Corinthians 6:9 in writing about same-sex practices. However, he seemed to understand the Vulgate reference to *arsenokoitai* as involving male prostitution.[50] Thomas Aquinas understood 1 Corinthians 6:9 as the scriptural basis for opposing same-sex practices.[51]

Arsenokoitai was translated by the King James Version of the Bible as "abusers of themselves with mankind." Subsequent twentieth-century translations have used "homosexuals," "sodomites," "those who are guilty of homosexual perversion," and "sexual perverts."[52] Boswell comments on the shift of meaning in the twentieth-century translations of the Bible: "Since few people any longer regarded masturbation as the sort of activity which would preclude entrance to heaven, the condemnation has simply been transferred to a group still so widely despised that their exclusion does not trouble translators or theologians."[53] It is evident that the coded sexual discourse of sodomy has affected homophobic mistranslation of this verse. This verse has been used to exclude gay men and lesbians from eccesial participation, for in 1 Corinthians 6:9 Paul lists those who were excluded from the reign of God.

Deconstructing Biblical Terrorism

Ecclesial authorities have appropriated the Bible as their book. The Bible is the center of their discursive field.[54] Biblical discourse is part of the political struggles of power; it has specific social effects in excluding gay/lesbian voices and legitimizing homophobic oppression in other discursive fields: "The power of domination is also the power to fashion, apparently rationally but usually violent, the more truthful narrative."[55] At gay/lesbian pride festivals, fundamentalists wave their Bibles as weapons. They quote the typical Scripture passages to prove that gay men and lesbians are an abomination in the eyes of God. Any attempts at genuine dialogue to reconstruct the social/theological meanings of particular passages prove fruitless. They are closed to historical reconstruction and biblical hermeneutics. The Bible becomes a weapon of condemnation of gay men and lesbians.

Biblical truth is produced and distributed asymmetrically, that is, it is produced, created, and controlled by the churches. Although it is partially shared with biblical scholars, these scholars are inscribed with the church's discourse on the Bible, and they are assigned a given position with the creation of biblical truth. Foucault maintains that the effects of institutionalized practices assign people their discursive position within a given field.[56] In other words, ecclesial practices specify who has control over the interpretation of the Bible.

Biblical scholars are trained in historical/critical reconstructions of the biblical texts, not in raising hermeneutical questions about the present social context. Second, their neutrality is regulated by the fact that they are inscribed into ecclesial production and distribution of biblical truth. When we consider who owns most of the publishing houses that issue biblical discourse and from where most biblical/theological students are recruited, we begin to understand the web of power relations exerted by the churches upon the biblical scholar. If a scholar transgresses ecclesial or canonical discourse, he or she will be removed from the discursive field.[57] This is apparent in the removal of scholars from universities and seminaries, their exclusion from the ecclesial discursive field, and the overt attempts at silencing them. This form of ecclesial terrorism has limited biblical criticism to the task of determining the meaning of biblical texts but failing to apply the meaning to the contemporary social context except with "safe issues."

Modern biblical scholarship has challenged fundamentalist/literalist readings of the Bible, literalist biblical anthropological concepts, creationism, christological discourse, and doctrine. These challenges are limited to education, professional societies, and specific professional publications and are usually outside the reach of public discourse. However, when these challenges circulate more broadly, ecclesial sanctions are applied to them. Fundamentalists will label the applications of historical criticism to the Bible as "godless" and appeal to the inerrancy of the word of God or their own sovereign ecclesial authority.

For the most part, biblical scholars have surrendered their historical-critical efforts to ecclesial sovereignty. They have played it safe with "value-neutral" reconstructions of past meaning. They have failed to unmask the discursive production and distribution of ecclesial power/truth. They have not applied historical criticism to the simplistic or dogmatic correlations of power and fundamentalist biblical truth to unmask their harmful social effects. Uncritical fundamentalist production of biblical truth inevitably leads to serious distortions of the Scriptures with harmful social effects to women, queers, and many others. In addition, biblical scholars have not actively sought to produce a counterdiscourse with engaged applications. Gay and lesbian issues are ignored because of homophobic academic pressures or ecclesial sanctions. Fundamentalist discourse has justified its campaigns of exclusion and hatred against gay men and lesbians with the Bible. Television evangelists, Roman Catholic cardinals and bishops, and other hierarchs have aggressively extended the ecclesial discursive field to city councils, state legislatures, and to Congress to prevent passage of gay/lesbian civil rights bills.[58] Few biblical scholars from the universities and seminaries have challenged Cardinal Law or Jerry Falwell's literalist statements. Their silence has contributed to the homophobic violence committed against gay men and lesbians. ACT UP prophetically reminds us in their transgressive practices, "Silence = Death, Action = Life, Ignorance = Fear." The silence of biblical scholars and theologians has led to death. It has left unchecked homophobic violence.

The Stonewall riots led to the political irruption of gay men and lesbians into American politics. Queers are making their political voices heard; they are openly claiming the right to live and love without homophobic constraints. Their increased queer visibility is manifested in a political movement that struggles for basic human rights and justice. Coming out for many gay and lesbian people overturns the traditional biblical interpretations of same-sex practices. They had been socialized to a Christian homophobia in their particular ecclesial organizations. Many have internalized Christian homophobia and are still vulnerable to the social control practices of the various ex-gay/lesbian organizations or to their own churches. For many other queer Christians, coming out leads to a critical questioning of fundamentalist biblical doctrines on same-sex practices and authoritarianism. Queer Christians refuse to leave the Bible in the hands of the powerful to be used as a weapon against themselves.

Queer Christians use their liberating practice to read the Bible anew. The Bible bursts with claims about a God who is passionately partial to the poor, who enlists people in justice-doing, and who promises a just society for all. Queer Christians can use these scriptural claims as an empowering resource for their liberative practice: they can shape their lives to God's justice-doing. They need to take the battles for truth about queers from the area of biblical and theological ethics to the practice and struggle for justice. The struggle for biblical truth is our struggle for justice and our commitment to theological practice.

This struggle for biblical truth requires ongoing social analysis of the network of homophobic power relations and their oppressive effects. Queer Christians need to present cogent social analyses of societal and ecclesial oppression. They need to name, describe, and analyze their alienation and pain, their oppression and anger. They need to gain more expertise in two areas: the social sciences and the theological disciplines. With the large numbers of gay/lesbian professionals involved in the social sciences, universities, and in the clergy, they have the potential of becoming an articulate social force for change: "Gay people must make a commitment to be a force to be reckoned with in theology, not solely via apologetics, but by claiming and assuming our right to theologize."[59] Queer Christians, clergy, and theologians must first come out and be proud of their sexuality. Then queer Christians can position themselves in the discursive field of ecclesial discourse in a contestatory framework. They can produce a counterbiblical discourse that seeks to challenge, deconstruct, and transform ecclesial discourse. Gay men and lesbians have already established and created publishing houses to distribute and circulate their own productions of queer. Queer theological scholars can utilize them to circulate their biblical production of truth and justice. In this way, they can siphon off ecclesial power/truth by demystifying it, by speaking a different and contradictory discourse, and by critically surfacing its fallacious assumptions.[60]

Social analysis precedes any historical reconstruction of the biblical texts or any other form of theological construction. Latin American liberation and feminist theologians require that practice inform their reconstructions of biblical texts. They have moved from value-neutral historical methods of biblical interpretations of the academy/university/seminary to critically engaged interpretations. In other words, Latin American and feminist liberation theologians politicize biblical interpretation by contextualizing it within their own contemporary social analysis of oppression.[61]

Gay men and lesbians have become a terrifying presence in society to fundamentalist and literalist churches. Queer Christians can become even more terrifying in the battle for biblical truth by magnifying fundamentalist doubts and deconstructing the inaccuracies in fundamentalist creations of biblical truth. The erotic power of queer biblical discursive practices will threaten fundamentalism's fragile grasp of reality with the complexity and ambiguity of human living in a pluralistic world. But the erotic power of queer discursive practices needs to be sharpened. Queer Christians must be educated in the historical and critical methods that biblical scholars have used for the last century to reconstruct and analyze biblical texts. They must not stop with historical criticism of biblical texts but must politicize their reconstructions with their own analysis of homophobic oppression and the struggle for justice. They need to branch out into other theological disciplines to present their production and distribution of queer theological truth. It may mean that they study and practice theology outside the centers of ecclesial social control in seminaries and religiously affiliated universities. It may mean that they will produce and circulate their biblical truth outside ecclesially sanctioned channels,[62] perhaps in nondenominational divinity schools and universities. Gay theologian Michael Clark asserts, "To affirm both our rich diversity and our marginality will require that we make a concerted effort to nurture independent scholars, other disenfranchised thinkers, and those outside of institutional religion, as we shape our theology and spirituality in community."[63] Moreover, the critical practice of a queer biblical discourse from the margins may give biblical scholars and other experts in the theological field the political courage to follow their example in challenging the social deployments and monopolies of ecclesial discourse.

Queer Christians can become a critically engaged presence to fundamentalist churches by producing the truth of their struggle for justice from the biblical texts. They may help rearrange the power deployments of the ecclesial discursive field by their practice of marginalized, critical discourse. Gay/lesbian political discourse will not only transgress canonically produced truth of ecclesial discourse; it will also erode the simplistic interpretations of biblical discourse that legitimize and buttress oppressive homophobic practices. Fundamentalist and literalist Christians traffic in the production and commerce of certain truth, but doubts, ambiguities, pluralities, and complexities will bring their fragile discursive edifice of fundamentalist truth to an end in the area of public discourse and curtail its harmful effect to those who are sexually different.

Reading the Bible as Critical Practice

Is it possible to read the Bible as critical practice so that it becomes a resource for queer power/truth? Foucault observes that the divorce between the practice of criticism and the transformation of culture is inappropriate.[64] Such a gap between criticism and transformation leads to the "value-neutral" reconstructions of past meaning by biblical scholars. These "neutral" reconstructions are partial in the hermeneutical process. They need the practice of critical engagement in the present social context of the interpreter/reader to complete the interpretative process of the Scriptures. These reconstructions need to be appropriated in the lives of their readers. For Foucault, the practice of criticism is a form of discursive activity whose production is an exercise of social power:

> Criticism is a matter of flushing out that thought and trying to change it: to show that things are not as self-evident as one believed, to see that what is accepted as self-evident will no longer be accepted as such. Practicing criticism is a matter of making facile gestures difficult. In these circumstances, criticism (and radical criticism) is absolutely indispensable for any transformation.[65]

Queer Christians are already bringing particular experiences and social truths to their reading of the Bible. Foucault's importance to a queer discourse of the Bible is his postmodern focus upon the power relations between what is defined as truth by the biblical experts and the ecclesial institutions that control and distribute that truth.[66] This means that a queer criticism of biblical truth creates conflicts within "value-neutral" biblical criticism and ecclesial biblical truth, and out of these conflicts, new power relations of truth are generated.[67] Queer criticism surfaces the conflicts, exclusions, and confrontations of homophobic power in institutional discourse with its own subjugated truth, and it generates new forms of action against homophobic power.

A queer critical reading means reading the Bible as our own. The Bible is not the privileged possession of fundamentalist or even mainstream churches. It belongs as well to queer liberative practice for freedom and justice. A queer reading deconstructs the politics of otherness that is inscribed in biblical texts by heterosexist biblical discourse. The politics of otherness is the process of spiritualizing the text—removing a particular text from its original social context and narrowing its application to a personal spiritual quest. In other words, it privatizes a text and removes its material context. It tears the "guts" out of the text and renders it hollow.

For queer Christians, the Bible is read intertextually with their own resistance to homophobic oppression. The truth of a particular text requires an interpretation that includes the social context of the text and the truth of their own queer lives. The lives of queer Christians become another text from which they interpret the biblical text. Queer Christians refigure the meaning of the text by interpreting and applying it to their lives. They realize that for change in ecclesial biblical discourse to take place, they must start to reject the traditional ecclesial constructions of the text. In fact, they reject all readings that either depoliticize or spiritualize the text. Their commitments to their queer identities, practices, and the struggle for justice become a framework for interpreting a particular biblical text.

The ecclesial guardians of biblical truth participate in a ruthless struggle for authority to maintain their homophobic power/truth. They suppress, censor, condemn, exclude, and battle dangerous hermeneutical discourses around the Bible. If a queer critical practice of biblical truth is less than resolute in its "will to truth," that is, in its commitment to produce a gay/lesbian biblical truth, then queer Christians surrender power to the authoritarian and fundamentalistic churches. The political effects of such a surrender can be lethal to the gay/lesbian movement. Fundamentalist churches are actively extending their discursive production of power into other fields of discursive relations of power. They have lobbied and blocked appropriations for AIDS education during the Reagan administration; they have blocked entry of HIV-positive people into the United States. There are dangerous genocidal fantasies in ecclesial discourse against gay men and lesbians, and we have witnessed two major genocidal persecutions of lesbians and gay men within this century: one, the Nazi holocaust, without ecclesial intervention, and the other, mass death from AIDS, with implicit and often explicit ecclesial approval.[68]

A critical queer biblical hermeneutics seeks to develop a critical mode of interpretation that can do justice to the queer experience of resisting the ecclesial production and circulation of biblical truth. Queer hermeneutics means critically reading the Bible as a subversive text. It means accepting the work of subverting fundamentalist assumptions of truth with historical criticism of biblical texts. It means deconstructing the ecclesial monopolization of power/truth with an alternative production of power/truth. It means deconstructing inherent inequalities within ecclesial authority over the production of biblical truth. A critical queer reading of the biblical texts is engaged in "pointing out on what kinds of assumptions, what kind of familiar, unchallenged, unconsidered modes of thoughts the practices that we accept rest."[69] It activates and enlists the Bible in the particular

struggles of queer resistance against homophobia and liberative practice. Queer Christians engage in a battle for biblical truth with consciousness of their own oppression and of the biblical God's
preference for the oppressed.

Thus, a critical queer reading means engaging queer social struggle
with the biblical text. This includes their experience of the social organization of homophobia, their coming out, and their commitment to
struggling for justice. Their social engagement as gay men and lesbians
creates many critical questions about the techniques, tacit assumptions,
and the power deployments in the ecclesial production of biblical truth.
Their social engagement involves their critical production and practice
of the biblical truth of God's justice for the oppressed.[70]

The Privilege of the Nonperson

Feminist and other liberation theologies have reclaimed the privileged position of the nonperson in the biblical texts.[71] The nonperson is the other, the poor (*anawim*), the one without power, privilege,
or status within social structures. The nonperson in the Scriptures includes the poor, the ill, the socially dysfunctional, the prostitute, the
tax collector, the woman without social status, the outcast, the social
deviant labeled sinner. The importance of the nonperson to a gay and
lesbian liberation theology is that it provides a means for dismantling
heterosexist/homophobic biblical interpretations. Lesbians and gay
men have been made into the "demonized other" by homophobic/
heterosexist biblical discourse.

However, their exclusion not only empowers their critique but also
empowers their own interpretative practice. Despite its androcentric
trappings, the God of the Bible is the God of the oppressed. Heterosexist biblical interpretations tend to either legitimize the status quo or
be actively employed in homophobic hate campaigns. To recover the
nonperson is to surface the oppositional tensions and conflicts that
are inherent in the biblical text. The historical Jesus embodied God's
preferential practice of solidarity with the oppressed. In his *basileia*
message and practice, Jesus modeled a new network of *basileia* social
relations. The Jesus material contains a political edge that is often read
out of or ignored in heterosexist/homophobic reconstructions.

A critical gay and lesbian interpretation seeks to make the reading of
the text an experience of liberation. It becomes a practice of solidar-

ity with the nonperson in the text, surfacing the oppositional conflict between religious-political power and the nonperson. It deconstructs heterosexist/homophobic biblical interpretations. A queer hermeneutics of critical social engagement becomes a hermeneutics of solidarity in appropriating the past meaning of the biblical texts. Solidarity is the compassionate identification with the oppressed and the active commitment to social change, the creation of God's reign in their midst. Gay men and lesbians can identify with the nonperson in first-century Palestine. They can reclaim identity with the leper, the homeless Jewish peasant displaced by a privileged economic system, the woman caught in adultery, the Samaritan, the prostitute, the poor, the hungry, and the shunned. The nonperson becomes a powerful symbol for our own oppression and the need for God's practice of justice. The nonperson becomes the sexually oppressed (*anawim*).

As the sexually oppressed, queer Christians claim the epistemological privilege of the oppressed. This means that a critical queer interpretative practice uses a hermeneutics of solidarity to transform the Scriptures into narratives of resistance. They can retrieve, for instance, the Jesus material, reading, interpreting, and transforming it into political practice. When it becomes socially embedded in the texts of their own life struggles, the Jesus material becomes transformed into an empowering resistance narrative. It becomes a critical challenge to the "master narratives" of Christian discourse, the homophobic/heterosexist reconstructions of biblical texts.[72] Their own struggles against homophobia open the past Jesus material to new possibilities that empower their own present practice of resistance. They attack the symbolic foundations of homophobic ecclesial discursive practice and erect the symbolic foundations of their own Christian discursive practice.

Through a hermeneutics of solidarity, queer Christians can stand with the band of fugitive Israelite slaves that escaped Egyptian oppression, with the heroes and heroines of the Hebrew Scriptures, the hopes of liberation of the conquered Jewish people, and the liberated hopes of the nascent Jesus movement against the background of Jewish nationalism and Roman politics of domination. A hermeneutics of solidarity challenges queer Christians to articulate their social and theological commitment to practice the justice of God's liberation. In solidarity with the biblical oppressed, God's justice shapes their lives as they practice God's compassion. It transforms their political practice for justice into God's liberative practice.[73] The Scriptures become symbolic of their own history of political resistance, conflict, and struggle for the sexual justice of God's reign. Jesus' *basileia* parables, his preferential solidarity with the oppressed, his table association, his healings and exorcisms, his practice of God's reign in advance, and his political challenges to the religious-political infrastructure become for queer Christians a political idiom of their resistance against homophobic oppression and their struggle for *basileia* liberation. They remember the *basileia* practice of Jesus and employ it as a powerful resource for their contemporary political struggle. They remember that the God of the oppressed has not abandoned them to homophobic violence and hatred. God remains active in the queer Christ; Christ is identified with the justice practices of their struggle.

Queer Biblical Criticism

It is not enough to dismantle homophobic biblical interpretations. Biblical texts can enhance the queer battle for truth and the struggle for liberation. A queer critical reading of the Scriptures transforms texts into narratives of resistance, releasing powerful motivational elements in our struggle against homophobic oppression. For example, the exorcism stories in Mark's Gospel dramatize Jesus' direct struggle and conflict with antihuman social forces that control people's lives. Jesus associated his practice of exorcisms with the reign of God; they represented a confrontation over power and control. In the exorcism stories, the forces that possess are the focus of Jesus' symbolic interactions rather than the people possessed. The possessed people are the battlefields for Jesus and dominating political forces. They are the reason for the narrative, the prize to be captured or liberated.

Three stories are constructed around exorcisms in Mark (Mark 1:21–28, 5:1–20, 9:14–24).[74] They tell of Jesus' overthrow of oppressive restrictions upon human life that dominate and enslave people. Jesus defeats the demon and liberates the afflicted from domination. He symbolizes the sociopolitical freedom of God's reign.

In Mark 1:21–28, Jesus enters the synagogue of Capernaum and begins to teach. The demon-possessed man challenges Jesus' authority to teach. The demon in the synagogue represents the scribal religious establishment. Jesus asserts an alternate authority and a new teaching. His attack upon the legitimacy of the prevailing religious order begins his campaign to preach God's reign. This is also apparent in his interaction with the Gerasene demoniac (Mark 5:1–20). The Gerasene demoniac has been psychologically taken over by Roman militarism, for his name is now "Legion." Jesus in his interactions with the demoniac struggles against all those sociopolitical forces that were the direct consequences of the Roman imperial system which fractured the Jewish social system. Demonic power is socially and politically structured within Jewish society. It is an idiom for comprehending the political struggles of Roman domination. Satan appears in the tradition as a military commander (Luke 10:19); he rules over a *basileia* (Matt. 12:26; Luke 11:18). Demons are his Roman legionnaires. He is the "master of the house," and the implication in the saying in Mark 3:27 is that Jesus is the "stronger one," who enters his house and binds him. Jesus' saying highlights the political nature of his practice of exorcism. It is a struggle between Satan's current reign and God's coming reign.

Biblical scholar Paul Hollenbach provides an innovative sociological glimpse into demonic possession in the first century C.E. in Palestine. Mental illness is both personal and social. For Hollenbach, mental illness was often caused or precipitated by sociopolitical tensions in first-century Palestine. These tensions were "class antagonisms rooted in economic exploitation, conflicts between traditions where revered traditions are eroded, colonial domination and revolution."[75] Roman domination, political conflicts, and intense economic pressures were present in Jesus' day; they contributed to the social disruption and uprooting of thousands of Jewish peasants. Political oppression generates an "oppression sickness" that fractures personal and social structures of meaning. Frequently, "mental illness can be seen as a socially acceptable form of oblique protest against, or escape from, oppressions."[76] Through classifying persons as mentally ill, society dehumanizes people. It gains control over them by destroying them or by degrading their social status with labels of demonic possession. They are discredited by dominant groups that maintain social control.

A queer reading of the Marcan exorcism stories can take the interpretative track of understanding the political implications of mental illness. For years, the Christian church has labeled those who practiced their same-sex attractions as sinners. It rendered mute those men and women attracted to the same sex, like the boy in Mark 9:14–24, who was possessed by a spirit that rendered him dumb and threw him into fire and water to destroy him. Likewise, gay men and lesbians for a hundred years have been defined as pathological or clinically ill by psychiatrists, who have used their authoritative positions to act as partisans for heterosexual norms. Fundamentalist churches have contributed to the social definitions of gay men and lesbians with stereotypes of child molesters, abominations, sinners, or sickness. The web of homophobic discursive practices in society has been employed to dehumanize gay men and lesbians. Gay men and lesbians have been portrayed in fundamentalist discursive practice as the "demonized other."

Jesus' exorcisms disrupted the Jewish social accommodation that allowed people to be labeled as demon possessed. He countered the Roman and Jewish social systems that discounted people unable to cope with the intense social pressures and political tensions arising from Roman domination. He fought the displacement process of demonizing the other. For lesbians and gay men, the labels, stereotypes, pressures of compulsory heterosexuality, and institutional violence have led to antihuman forces controlling their lives. Homophobic control over gay and lesbian people has been demonic. For Jesus, something was demonic when it stood against God's *basileia*. It stood against God's preferential option and solidarity with the oppressed. It was by God's coming that Jesus bound antihuman forces and released people from personal and social domination. He released them from their internalized social pain and welcomed them into the *basileia* social network of relations where God's justice and compassion would be practiced in advance.

For Jesus, God was now present and active in the liberation of people from the social forces of antihuman domination. The portrait of Jesus in these exorcism stories is one of the fighter or combatant, who lays siege and drives out the antihuman forces. Jesus' exorcism can be read as public symbolic actions directed against the political and religious order that produced oppressive sickness. The oppression found in these stories can be read in light of gay/lesbian struggles against homophobia/heterosexism and its damaging effects. Jesus the Queer Christ fights for gay men and lesbians who are dominated by homophobic power relations, and he struggles to liberate them from the effects of homophobic oppression and from antihuman possession of internalized homophobia. He overthrows violent social forces that prevent queer people from experiencing themselves as free and loving human beings. He challenges the religious authority that main-

tains the social system of violence. Jesus wages conflict against homophobia. He becomes a liberating force of sexual grace and salvation for queers. He models liberative activity, dissidence, struggle,
and the freedom of God's reign, and he calls gay and lesbian Christians to imitate his *basileia* practice. The real negativity of the "demonized other" and internalized homophobia is transcended when
people are capable of receiving God's reign, that is, accepting the gift of
their sexual identity and practicing God's justice.

"Dangerous Memories"

Gay and lesbian theology is not a "value-neutral" academic creation;
it is born from the pain of homophobic oppression and queer struggles for freedom. It is a practical or perhaps strategic theology, based
upon our experience of resistance, solidarity, struggle, and the hope
for liberation. The truth of gay and lesbian liberation is to practice
liberation. Sin, redemption, grace, Christology, sacraments, and other
Christian doctrines and practices are real to queer Christians insofar
as they are practiced strategically from the perspective of or in our
struggles. Abstracted and universalized, these dogmatic discourses
and practices have frequently become instruments for ecclesial oppression. Jesus' *basileia* discourse and critical practice were political
and transgressive. Queer *basileia* discourse and critical practice are,
likewise, political and transgressive.

For queer Christians, God is the justice-doer in raising Jesus to the
queer Christ. God identified with Jesus' practices, his conflict, and his
execution on the cross. God embodied justice-doing in Jesus' *basileia*
practices. God transformed Jesus' *basileia* practice and death into
liberating power. God transformed the lethal silencing of Jesus into
the liberating word of the risen Christ, God's practice of compassion
and justice in the social world. God empowered Jesus as the Christ
at Easter. Jesus' message and practice were no longer muted. The
Christian Scriptures become the voice of God's promise of liberated
practice.

As queer Christians retrieve the Jesus material as a source for their
critical practice, they discover a powerful, subversive memory of
Jesus.[77] It is a dangerous memory of God's insurrection against
human oppression. The God Jesus preached is the God of the sexually
oppressed. God's coming is experienced in this world in the social

practices that overcome poverty, disease, injustice, and oppression. What Jesus preached is God's insurrection against human cruelty and oppression. The subversive memory of Jesus' death and the event of God's solidarity with Jesus keeps alive not only Jesus' suffering (*memoria passionis*) but also solidarity with the oppressed. Queer Christians remember that God gave the murdered Jesus a voice for justice beyond the cross. God broke the silence and spoke against human oppression and atrocity. God transformed the wood of the cross into the tree of life, justice, and liberation.

The narrative story of Jesus' death becomes a powerful cipher for unpacking other biblical stories and discourses. Queer Christians enter any particular gospel story or biblical discourse with their memory of God's practice of justice and solidarity with Jesus. With the help of historical criticism and the primacy of their own struggles as lesbians and gay men, they transform any particular story into a narrative amplification of their own struggles. They imaginatively release the elements of struggle and resistance within the text into their lives. They transform what was the disinterested past into the interested actualization of their own struggle, resistance, and emancipatory *basileia* practice. In other words, gay/lesbian practice leads to active reflection on the text, and their reflection is verified in their liberative practice. Queer Christians actualize God's practice of justice and solidarity. They retrieve and practice the subversive *basileia* practice of Jesus.

God's word of justice becomes visible in Jesus the queer Christ. Jesus the queer Christ symbolizes God's solidarity with the sexually oppressed (*anawim*) in the midst of their resistance, conflict, and the struggle for justice. God lives in the practice of justice and, in particular, in their critical struggle for justice and liberation. A queer critical hermeneutics includes the textual reconstruction, their social involvement in the present struggle for freedom, and their solidarity with the oppressed.

A queer hermeneutics of solidarity includes the subversive memory of those who have suffered and died from oppression. Queer Christians focus on the Jesus material, remembering the nonperson and the story of God's liberation from social negativity, oppression, disease, and possession. They remember the resistance narrative of Jesus, his struggles, death, and God's liberative practice. In a hermeneutics of solidarity, gay men and lesbians become the bearers of a "dangerous memory," activating and empowering their struggle for the practice of justice. The subversive memory of the Jesus material keeps alive their own suffering and the suffering of the sexually oppressed (*anawim*). It allows for a universal practice of solidarity with the oppressed Jesus. This solidarity is concretized in justice actions for the oppressed. Queer Christians reclaim their suffering through the subversive power of the memory of Jesus' oppression, the persecution of those who were attracted to same-sex practices, and their own gay/lesbian experience of oppression. They remember the hundreds of thousands of gay men and lesbians murdered in the Nazi death camps; the hundreds of thousands of gay men who have died from HIV infection; the millions of men and women in history who loved members of the same-sex and who were tortured, murdered, oppressed, or rendered invisible; the tens of thousands of gay men and lesbians who are victims each year of hate crimes; the twenty-five million gay and lesbian Americans who suffer from the network of homophobic power relations. The memory of their sufferings does not mitigate the atrocities, nor does it lessen the reality of human pain and homophobic violence. Queer Christians practice a solidarity with the risen Christ that challenges crucifixion. They practice resistance and struggle with the hope of ending crucifixion once and for all. Their memory is shaped with the Easter hope that God will do justice to all those men and women who lived their sexual difference and suffered. Their memory shapes and sharpens their present justice actions. If they are unable to end the crucifixion, God will remember them and do justice.

Embracing the Exile

*It is a question of making conflicts more visible, of making
them more essential than, mere confrontations of interests or
mere institutional immobility. Out of these conflicts, these
confrontations, a new power relation must emerge, whose first,
temporary expression will be a reform. If at the base there has
not been the work of thought upon itself and if, in fact, modes
of thought, that is to say modes of action, have not been
altered, whatever the project for reform, we know that it will
be swamped, digested by modes of behavior and institutions
that always will be the same.*

MICHEL FOUCAULT[1]

The very nature of Christian practice is God's practice of liberation.
Christian practice is organized socially into institutions whose function is to re-present God's reign in human society. The Christian task is
to present the liberating images of God in the Bible, to live Jesus'
basileia practice of solidarity with the oppressed, and to actualize
God's liberating practice in human society. Christian social practices
try to produce God's truth for justice by remembering (*anamnesis*) and
imitating (*mimesis*) God's practice of justice within their own practices. Too often, many churches confuse themselves, their social practices, and their authority with God's reign. God is God and cannot be
limited by ecclesial institutions. God's reign is not identifiable with any
particular institution; it is identifiable with the human practice of social justice, the struggle for liberation and freedom. God's reign can

only be correlated with Christian power relations. There are too many modern examples of ecclesial institutions knowing the "will of God" but not knowing, or not practicing, God's preferential option for the oppressed. The quest for God's reign has been eroded by churches; the project of human liberation has been abandoned in favor of obtaining and maintaining social power. Churches have not been immune to the social organization of oppression.

Jesus' practice of solidarity in the Gospels can be limited, narrowly defined, or distorted to legitimize ecclesial social practices. Christian churches have become asymmetrically structured networks of homophobic power relations. These asymmetrical social networks focus their attention on preserving, extending, and deepening their control over the production and the circulation of homophobic biblical truth. They produce social practices of exclusions, oppression, and violence against gay men and lesbians. The churches remain in the grips of heterosexism and homophobia.

As soon as ecclesial power is centrally organized and hierarchically deployed, there is the possibility of resistance. Foucault's analysis of power relations suggests the possibility of multiple forms of resistance for people in their own specific places within the field of ecclesial discourse and power relations. Local gay/lesbian resistance to ecclesial production of power/truth about sexuality can take many forms. Gay and lesbian Christians can modify the ecclesial grip over themselves. Some have tried to covertly subvert its grip over their lives within institutions. They have remained closeted, segmenting their sexual identities from their public identities.[2] Other queer Christians find themselves in varying degrees excluded from the ecclesial field of discourse and power relations by coming out. They can begin to modify the ecclesial grip over homophobic society from the vantage point of their exclusion. They can change ecclesial fields of discourse and power relations with precise transgressive strategies. What has been produced in and by ecclesial discourse can be overthrown and replaced with their own theological practice. What has been produced by ecclesial deployment of power can be dismantled by queer power/truth.

Faith praxis for openly queer Christians is a specific kind of action in the world; it has the contours of resistance, struggle, solidarity, and hope. Queer faith practice is committed to actualizing God's reign within the social world. Queer Christians are the bearers of a dangerous memory of *basileia* insurrection. Gay and lesbian faith practice is the direct action of reproducing God's justice for the oppressed. Gay men and lesbians have been forced to live outside the value structures of society and to establish their own values. They have been marginalized, hated, despised. It is the oppressed gay/lesbian community in the situation of struggle for liberation that determines the meaning and scope of Jesus the queer Christ. Those Christians who have discovered themselves gay or lesbian must learn to come to love themselves despite church discourse and practice.

Critical confrontation of ecclesial oppression is an essential strategy in queer Christian practice. In general, confrontation is essential to political communication. It makes conflicts visible and presents alternative possibilities. Homophobic people and ecclesial institutions are not likely to hear what we are saying unless they are challenged, unless conflict is made visible and struggle intensified. Critical confrontation is not an end but a means to a political end; it can contribute to real gains only when it leads to dialogue, change, or both. If it succeeds in getting public attention and if dialogue begins, then new power relations emerge, and change becomes possible.

However, confrontation must be supplemented with dialogue or at least the openness to engage in true dialogue. Dialogue with the churches on the issue of gay/lesbian sexuality is generally monological; it is a polemic aimed at winning lesbians and gay men to the side of sexual orthopraxis (correct sexual practice). There is no genuine attempt to listen or to understand. In confrontational practices, queer Christians must try to the best of their ability to be open to the possibility of dialogue. Gay men and lesbians do not want to reproduce the cycles of ecclesial oppression with counteroppressive action. Their actions must be balanced with love-making and justice-doing. They, however, must not remain silent.

The Failure of Justice

Christian definitions of correct sexual practices are not only founded on a misreading of the biblical traditions but are also based on a supposed "natural law." Natural law is rooted in classical Greek philosophy and the Stoicism of the Roman Empire. Popular and philosophical forms of Stoicism influenced Christian writers of the first several centuries. Natural law construction of sexuality emerged from such a philosophical milieu and a deep Christian horror of the body and sexuality.[3] Christian views of natural law remain based on the premise that the sexual instinct is lower and bestial while rationality is the highest function of human nature. It originates in mind/body and spirit/body dualism. Much of the earlier Christian fear of the body and the need to restrain sexuality still colors the positions of Christian ethicists.

For Christian ethicists, the basic premise of natural law is the conviction that human nature serves as a ground for judging what is right and wrong. Conservative ethicists become obsessed with the act of sex, while more progressive ethicists focus on the intention or the social circumstances of sexual activity.[4] Conservative ethicists seldom venture beyond the biological argument for the purposes of human sexuality, whereas the more progressive ethicists will incorporate the understanding of the biological sciences as well as the social sciences.

Conservative Christian ethicists judge gay and lesbian sexuality from a reductionistic or literalist perspective. They reduce human sexuality to marital sexuality and further narrow it to reproductive sexuality. All sexuality outside of this reduction is construed as sinful, unnatural, deviant, disordered, or pathological. Natural law arguments are buttressed with biblical texts of terror or the Genesis creation accounts to uphold compulsory heterosexuality as God's purpose for sexuality. Conservative ethicists argue for the reproductive purpose of the genital organs. They will state that the anus is not a vagina and not a proper receptacle for the male penis. This form of natural law argument is founded on a biological literalism of the fit of male and female sexual organs; it maintains a one-dimensional view of human sexuality. God intended heterosexuality because God made the male and female sex organs to fit. Moderate and progressive ethicists acknowledge that there is more than one purpose for human sexuality. The notion of human sexuality is broadened to include human communication, intimacy, love, pleasure, creativity, fecundity, and spirituality. However, many moderate ethicists will argue that heterosexual marriage and sexuality are the norm or the ideal for humanity.

The problem of conservative and moderate ethicists is that they are not cultural historians of natural law and the Christian constructions of human sexuality. They overlook the diverse social meanings and cultural constructions of human sexuality throughout history.[5] Conservative advocates of the natural law perspective fail to understand the comment of James Brundage, a historian of the Christian construction of human sexuality: "What is natural often means whatever is thought to be the usual practice of the majority."[6] A second failure of natural law is that it is a male-defined endeavor. The constructions of the natural law perspective of human sexuality are aligned with male power, heterosexism, and homophobia. Male voices have been valued over female voices; celibate voices over noncelibate voices. Natural law is based on the construction of compulsory heterosexuality but a heterosexuality with male dominance and female subordination. Little or no space has been given in the natural law constructions of Christian ethicists to female voices or queer voices from the margins.[7]

Many Christian ethicists and churches fail not only to revise their natural law constructions of human sexuality with the social sciences but also to listen to voices from the margins. They do not take seriously the testimony of gay and lesbian Christians on their sexuality and their unions. They are threatened by nonreproductive same-sex practices and condemn them. Their positions are grounded on a lack of common decency and a lack of justice. Christian ethicist Marvin Ellison calls for genuine solidarity of the churches with gay and lesbian people. He writes, "Our problem is not homosexuality or non-marital sex but conformity to the unjust norm of compulsory heterosexuality and gender inequality. This unjust norm must be altered, not those who question it."[8] A Catholic theologian, Xavier Seubert, echoes a similar sentiment when he says, "Until the homosexual experience is truthfully spoken and truthfully heard, the disorder will not be homosexuality, but the inability of the church to stand in truth, endure it and live from it."[9] The demands of justice and the gospel require that Christian ethicists and churches listen to gay and lesbian voices before constructing their natural laws. Justice requires natural law proponents to listen to sexual and gendered diversity.

The final point that I will make about natural law is its need to be reconstructed with a positive perspective of human sexuality and justice. Natural law proponents need to change their heritage of sexual phobia, misogyny, and homophobia. It is ridiculous to argue against condom usage as an "intrinsically evil means" when it stops the transmission of death. Natural law proponents need to embrace the erotic and the body as naturally good and move beyond literalist

constructions of procreative sexuality. Christians know God through
their embodied selves and sexuality. Sexuality needs to be reconstructed within new metaphorical constructions that embody the
mystery of human sexuality, creativity, love, and justice. A creative
dislocation of natural law from the hands of heterosexist and homophobic male ethicists to the voices at the margins will correct the injustices. The Presbyterian Task Force on Human Sexuality
reconstructed sexuality within the context of "justice-love":

> To do justice-love means seeking right-relatedness with others and
> work to set right all wrong relations, especially distorted dynamics of
> domination and subordination. Embracing the goodness of our sexu-
> ality, of our erotic desire for wholeness and connectedness is, there-
> fore, a godly gift to us. Erotic power, rightly ordered, grounds and
> moves on, gently yet persistently, to engage in creating justice with
> love for ourselves and all others.[10]

Love-making and justice-doing are metaphorical and revelational
bases for reconstituting human sexuality on nonliteral levels. Such a
hermeneutical framework includes biblical revelation, the social sciences, and the voices of the marginalized. I will build on queer and
feminist voices to discuss the sacramentality of queer sexual experience in this chapter and, in the last chapter, the introduction of eros
into the model of God. It provides a creative dislocation of the impoverished ecclesial natural law theology and reclaims the symbolic
power of erotic love, relationality, creativity, and justice. Love-making
and justice-doing are the interpretative framework for a gay and lesbian Christian view of sexuality.

Why Stay in the Church?

Queer Christians have listened and continue to listen to the empty
rhetoric about God's justice in our churches. What are the churches
doing about the increased homophobic violence against us? Why are
they perpetuating a Christian discourse that legitimizes homophobia and violence? Why do they continue to exclude gay men and lesbians from ordination, ministry, and service? Why do they refuse to
recognize and bless gay/lesbian unions? What are they doing for
people living with HIV infection besides burdening them with condemnations and guilt? What are they doing to affirm us as a people
"gifted" from God? Why do they not take seriously the social sciences

and biblical scholarship to revise their homophobic doctrines and practices? Why do they engage in abusive monologue, refusing to engage in genuine dialogue? The failure of the churches to do God's justice to lesbians and gay men raises the complex issue of gay/lesbian participation in the churches. Why stay?

Those who choose to stay within their churches must examine their reasons closely. They need to begin a discernment process. It is obvious to gay men and lesbians that the churches have made significant contributions to their oppression. Churches produce and distribute homophobic discourses. They engage in exclusionary and hierarchical practices of power. For many queers, Christianity has become an alienating experience or rather the experience of negative *basileia*. Christian homophobic discourse contributed to the final solution for gay men and lesbians in the Nazi death camps.[11] The churches continue to contribute to homophobic hate campaigns and violence, often taking a leading role. They have contributed to the spread of HIV infection in their attempt to prevent the distribution of safe-sex information.[12] The churches exclude gay and lesbian people from the promises of salvation. These facts undercut the biblical message of God's solidarity with the oppressed and the churches' credibility in the practice of solidarity. Credibility, witness, and the practice of biblical truth are serious issues to queer Christians.

Many closeted gay men and lesbians have highly visible positions within their churches. There is a high percentage of lesbians and gay men in ministry, religious life, and administrative positions. Many gay men and lesbians feel called to ministry within their churches; they have a strong desire to serve God's people. They do not find gay/lesbian identity an impediment to ministry. One gay Catholic priest wrote,

> I love the priesthood and work by the Church; to leave would be the hardest thing in my life. I have been in love and when in love have been sexually active with my lover. Church structure brings a lot of tension to a love relationship. I don't think I can survive as a human without a lover. If the Church authorities force the issue with me, I'll leave the priesthood to keep my freedom to be in a loving relationship.[13]

The conflicts of remaining in a homophobic church, remaining closeted with a lover, living a double life, or even remaining celibate place incredible strain on many gay/lesbian Christians within their churches. Often they have to conceal their sexual identities, assuming

both a public and a private persona, or struggle with internalized homophobic feelings and guilt. The experience of church is far from
being liberating; it is restrictive, oppressive, and even terrorist.

Fear is not an appropriate reason for remaining in a church. Living
and practicing faith as a closeted Christian does not practice God's justice, nor does closeted ministry reform the church. A closeted minister
commented to me, "At least, I do not get up in the pulpit and preach
against gay people." Closeted Christian leaders cooperate in their own
oppression and the oppression of other gay men and lesbians. They
cooperate in perpetuating antieroticism that sustains homophobic exclusion and the subordination of women. They remain silent against
ecclesial homophobic discourse and homophobic oppression; this
silence is not God's preferential option for oppressed queers. Ecclesial terrorism is still a very real threat to many closeted clergy.

Ministers who come out to affirm their gay/lesbian identity are silenced, defrocked, suspended, or voted out of their churches. Those
who speak for justice are excluded from ministry.[14] The Jesuit priest
John McNeill had silence imposed upon him by the Vatican Congregation for the Defense of the Faith for his publication of *The Church and
the Homosexual*. When he broke the silence to speak out against Cardinal Ratzinger's pastoral letter on homosexuality to the Catholic bishops, McNeill was expelled from the Society of Jesus. The Pennsylvania
western regional conference of United Methodist Church voted to de-
frock James Hawk, who came out after ordination. Hawk disclosed
his gay sexual preference when he realized that "who we are is so very
good and our way of loving is a good gift from God and nothing to be
ashamed of."[15] The Evangelical Lutheran Church of America pres-
sured Paul Johnson, the assistant to the bishop of La Crosse, Wiscon-
sin, to resign when church officials discovered that he was gay. These
are a few of the forms of ecclesial terrorism practiced to discipline
clergy who speak up against oppression or who come out and declare
themselves gay/lesbian.[16] Craig O'Neill, a Catholic priest and coauthor
of *Coming Out Within*, was suspended by Bishop John Steinbock of
the Fresno diocese for his publication of a pastorally sensitive book
helping gay and lesbian people transform the losses of homophobic
oppression into a gay and lesbian spirituality.[17] Silencing, exclusion,
expulsion, condemnation, and other forms of ecclesial terrorism are
the rewards for God's solidarity with the oppressed: "Blessed are those
who stand for God's justice with the sexually oppressed, for theirs is
the reign of God."

Reform cannot take place through closetedness in the churches. It is critical that those who remain in the church challenge homophobic Christian discourse and practice. Closeted Christians claim to follow Jesus the Christ, who was persecuted and murdered for the sake of *basileia* solidarity. If they do not stand up for themselves or for other gay men and lesbians who suffer at the hands of Christian homophobic oppression, how can they effectively witness to primary biblical revelation of God's solidarity with the oppressed? They cannot pick and choose the "socially safe" oppressed? They cannot represent one group of oppressed people, for example, the homeless, and ignore another group. Christian solidarity does not work like that. If closeted clergy and Christian leaders do not speak up for us, they are guilty of the homophobic violence that their church commits against us.

It is time for queer Christians to examine their involvement of staying in the churches in light of the biblical God's preferential option for the oppressed. Facing the truth of their gay/lesbian identities will be painful for closeted clergy and leaders as it has been for many of us. The truth of their gay/lesbian sexual identities is part of their Christian proclamation of God's truth for the oppressed. If they are not publicly able to come out, then the very least is to admit publicly that they participate in an oppressive structure and commit themselves to change ecclesial homophobia. It is a humble admission that they are both oppressor and oppressed. Personally, I espouse a national coming-out day for religious, clergy, bishops, and cardinals; administrators of universities and seminaries; pastors, theologians, biblical scholars, church elders, religious educators, choir directors, and musicians. It would surprise all denominations how deeply involved are gay men and lesbians in the ministries of churches and how dependent those churches have become upon them.

It makes no sense to remain in an oppressive structure unless one publicly admits that he or she participates in institutional oppression and is committed to changing that structure to conform with God's justice-doing. Unless the grip of homophobia/heterosexism upon the ministry of churches is broken, the churches cannot become locations for the practice of justice. They remain the locus of negative *basileia*.

The Exile

The question "Why stay?" reframes the reformist versus transgressive debate that divides the gay/lesbian community. Ostensibly, it is a division of strategy, yet the question has larger ramifications for our community. Christian activists point out that reformist Christians are too apologetic in their discourse and surrender too much to cultural patterns of the churches. Reformist efforts seem, at best, to yield mediocre, conditional acceptance with some churches. This acceptance, however, is purchased at the cost of denying their unique sexual differences, the development of a queer spirituality, and the lack of a whole-hearted commitment to justice-doing for our community. It avoids a queer revisioning of Christian discursive practices.

The articulation of a queer Christian liberation theology in this book is wholly unapologetic. Reformist efforts have lacked critical practice to engage the churches or the courage to embrace exile from the churches.[18] They are failing in their struggles to develop inclusive, egalitarian communities within the churches. To many gay/lesbian people, they are failing to undo the sexual injustices of the churches. Many gay and lesbian people have already abandoned organized Christianity. They have found reformist attempts too apologetic and too assimilationist in trying to soften the antagonisms of ecclesial homophobia. Like ACT UP, Queer Nation, the Radical Fairies, and various lesbian and queer activist groups, Christian exiles have sought to create alternative social space for the radical process of coming out and self-discovery. The exiles have had to first withdraw their support of ecclesial structures that negated their self-affirmations as gay men and lesbians. The exiles have tried to create an alternative community that affirms lesbian/gay identity, values, and beliefs. Unlike the separatists within the gay/lesbian community, Christian exiles, however, have begun to maximize their sexual differences with society. They have refused to compromise their hard-fought self-affirmations of their sexuality as life giving; they have refused to stop loving or stop practicing their faith. Christian exiles have created an alternative social space. It is an experimental social space where gay/lesbian sexual differences and *basileia* practices are creatively brought together into new queer Christian practices. Queer Christians can articulate and discover the sacramentality of their experience of coming out.

Reformist efforts have created halfway stops for those journeying into the exile. They have created a number of denominational support organizations in the post-Stonewall period such as Dignity for Catholics, Integrity for Episcopalians, Affirmation for Methodists, and so forth. These are local communities of resistance that have chosen not to separate themselves totally from their churches but to continue to be visible and struggle for justice. These local communities of resistance have created a social space on the margins of their churches. Their visibility has kept gay/lesbian issues in the forefront of their churches with often unfortunate official responses.[19]

Many of these local communities of resistance remain at the margins of their churches but have not embraced the exile. They try to keep the lines of communication open with their churches but find an ecclesial unwillingness to dialogue. These local communities have sustained gay men and lesbians in their struggles against ecclesial homophobia and against internalized homophobia. More often than not, these local communities of resistance have duplicated the structures of their own churches to find self-acceptance. They have not yet progressed and taken an active role in becoming a change community, that is, a base community in exile. They have not created an unapologetic social space that affirms gay and lesbian experience and allows them to critique and to critically engage the homophobia/heterosexism of the churches.

Creating Queer Christian Base Communities

A Christian change or base community is a local community of resistance made up of disenfranchised exiles or oppressed people who are committed to actively and politically changing oppressive structures.[20] Some of the unofficial local denominational communities of resistance and some of the gay/lesbian-affirming churches such as Metropolitan Community Church have become Christian base communities.

Local communities of resistance, however, too often simply replicate the past experience of church and are not sufficiently oriented to becoming a change community with new alternative forms of religious practice. They practice church in a traditional manner but do not provide a critical alternative for *basileia* liberation. For instance, Dignity has been officially proscribed by Cardinal Ratzinger and the Catholic bishops.[21] Some of the chapters, like Dignity/New York, have taken the political offensive against Cardinal O'Connor; they have staged protests at St. Patrick's Cathedral. Members of the social justice committee of the New York chapter have stood up in protest and remained silent during the cardinal's homily. They have been arrested for disturbing the peace. They have prophetically embodied their exclusion in dramatic justice-doing actions. Some members of Dignity/

New York have formed the Cathedral Project to challenge the Roman Catholic church and Cardinal O'Connor's homophobic hatred. On the other hand, other Dignity chapters have chosen to remain silent and safe on the margins of official unrecognition. Their resistance has been confined to the celebration of their sexual lifestyle. Dignity/New York and the Cathedral Project are base communities, whereas many other Dignity chapters remain at the level of practice of local communities of resistance.

The difference in practice between a Christian base community and resistance community is measured by the degree of political commitment to critically engaging ecclesial homophobia. Critical engagement is not merely resistance; it is proactive struggle for political change. It is radical engagement of Christian practice, acting in public as a witness to God's reign. It is the practice of resurrection, God's uprising against the political death of Jesus.[22] It is a new way of practicing church, a new way of envisioning and expressing a Christian presence among oppressed exiles. Base communities become nurturing alternative forms of community practice that challenge homophobic power relations in churches and in society as a whole on an operational level of power production. They challenge the truth of oppression with their social resistance and commitment to direct action. Base communities are biblically centered affinity groups, reflecting on biblical truth in the midst of social oppression. By witnessing to the gospel of God's preferential option for the oppressed, they replicate Jesus' *basileia* action and indicate God's saving initiative. Base communities work on concrete problems of oppression and specific goals for liberation.

It is time to create hundreds and thousands of gay/lesbian-affirming base communities of faith that practice God's justice.[23] It is time to break the grip that homophobia/heterosexism exercises upon the discourse and practice of the churches. It is our moment to radically challenge churches to practice God's solidarity with the oppressed. Gay and lesbian Christians must fight back for justice. Justice is the reality of our same-sex love, equal to opposite-sex love. Gay and lesbian believers must no longer submit to the belief that their relationships do not reflect God's love and justice. Making love and doing justice have become synonymous for gay and lesbian people. Queer erotic connectedness empowers us to justice-doing. Queer erotic connectedness begins with love-making with lover, expands in solidarity with other oppressed queers, and moves with queers to fight for justice. A queer practice of justice needs to turn churches upside down, open the eyes of the blind, and assist Christians to do justice.[24] This can only be done through the formation of Christian change or base communities.

Liberation is not otherworldly; it is concretely social and political. Liberated action is the organization of gay men and lesbians into a community to struggle for and practice justice. It is like the direct action groups, ACT UP and Queer Nation, in their struggles to practice justice against homophobia, heterosexism, and oppressive HIV policies. Both organizations are affinity groups that operate out of egalitarian, non-sexist principles in deciding and staging a political action. A queer Christian base community differs from ACT UP and Queer Nation in using the Bible as an additional justice resource for its critical practice of liberation. Group prayer and reflection on God's word from a gay/lesbian perspective strengthen their commitment to doing God's justice. This appears to be the situation of a Presbyterian ACT UP chapter.

A queer Christian base community is a change community in exile; it is shaped by *basileia* practice. Such a base community has the social space to allow the emergence of new forms of *basileia* practice and new sacraments that embody gay/lesbian experience. *Basileia* practice is egalitarian; within a base community, there is a discipleship of equals between lesbians and gay men in facilitating prayer and direct action. It is a nonhierarchical community, sensitive to the needs of the full inclusion of women in Christian social practice, the use of inclusionary language in its reshaping of biblical truth, and the practice of God's reign in advance. A queer base community works by a consensus model for decision making, not by authoritarian and hierarchical models of church. It is a community that pools its economic resources for the poor, those who have been made poor by the ravages of HIV infection. It is a community that refuses to accept or participate in the network of homophobic power relations and other networks of oppressive relations. It engages in direct actions that transgress the network of homophobic power relations and present a critical alternative.

Preaching to a Queer Base Community

Preaching to a queer base community is a communal task of reflection, education on past reconstructed meaning of the biblical text, and application to the specific task of homophobic oppression and liberation. It is the production and circulation of queer biblical truth;

it is a discursive practice that affects the social formation of gay/lesbian Christian base communities. Preaching is an interpretative communal activity that reconstructs past biblical meaning within the concrete situation of the homophobic society in which we live. It requires facilitators specializing in biblical reconstructions, basic community members, and concrete situations of homophobic oppression. Preaching in a queer base community is a mutual process between colearners who share biblical reflections within the social horizon of oppression and critically engaged political activity. Sharing, listening, and mutual learning are the social ingredients for social formation, conscientization, and the practice of freedom.

Preaching is vital to the formation of a queer basic community. Preaching evokes the meaning, memory, and power of Jesus' resistance to oppressive power and his *basileia* solidarity with the oppressed. Preaching to a queer basic community is a dangerous practice. It activates the dangerous memories of Jesus' resistance and God's insurrection against human injustice. It challenges the traditional homophobic interpretations of the biblical text as belonging to powerful vested interests of the churches. Past biblical meaning becomes reconstructed from our discursive practice and within our social practice. Past meaning and present gay/lesbian social experience become the contextual horizon for generating queer biblical truth and critical practice.

The activation of dangerous memories within the present social context challenges the gay/lesbian community to critically rethink and reperceive Jesus' *basileia* practice within its own context of social oppression. Preaching communicates and envisions the alternative social reality of God's reign. Preaching may focus on the particular struggles and strategies of the gay/lesbian community. However, as queer Christian groups become more self-critical and recognize their own contributions to oppressive structures, they show greater concern for the issues of women, for justice and solidarity with the poor, for the environment, and for other global issues. The critical practice of solidarity with the oppressed leads to expanding the practice of solidarity.

Sacramentalizing Queer Experience

It is essential for a queer Christian base community to ritualize its political/spiritual experience of exile. Mary Hunt affirms, "To sacramentalize is to pay attention. It is what a community does when it names and claims ordinary human experience as holy, connecting them with history and propelling them into the future."[25] What I mean by sacrament is the symbolic representation of *basileia* actions that focus the orientation of the community's action as striving toward God's love and justice in the world. Sacramental actions implicitly represent the social reality of oppression and the need for transformation by God's liberating presence. Sacraments are not institutional actions of power. They are often practiced in an exclusionary manner by churches, contradicting the very purpose of the sacraments as they have been developed in the church's history. They are empowered *basileia* actions, actualizing the *basileia* in our midst and engaging all that is not *basileia* in our world. Gay and lesbian Christians in a base community need to sacramentalize God's reign in an oppressively homophobic/heterosexist society.

Sacraments are intense moments of *basileia* action; they are *basileia* love-making and justice-doing. They embody lesbian bodies and gay bodies; they embody lesbian love-making and gay love-making. Ecclesial sacraments frequently eclipse gay men and lesbians as human beings. They disembody or ritually abuse queers. Ecclesial sacraments have often become a means of social regulation or political control. They exclude those who openly dissent and those who dare to be sexually different. Ecclesial sacraments have been used to demand obedience, sanction a hierarchical deployment of misogynistic/homophobic power, and punish infractions. Instead of ritual representations of love-making and justice-doing, they are reenactments of injustice.

Basileia love-making refers to the erotic connectedness of gay men and lesbians to their own sexuality. It is embodied in erotic connectedness to lover, community, the oppressed, and nature. Carter Heyward aptly connects love-making to justice-doing: "Our sexuality is our desire to participate in making love, making justice, in the world; our drive towards one another; our movement in love; our expression of our sense of being bonded together in life and death."[26] Gay/lesbian erotic connectedness starts with self and lover; it radiates its embodied love to the oppressed gay/lesbian community and other oppressed peoples. Gay/lesbian erotic connectedness is embodied in justice-doing. The Christian base community itself becomes a sacrament of liberation when it proclaims the values of God's reign by discourse and practice. Sacraments are symbolic ways of re-presenting God's reign in queer social practices. Sacraments do not legitimize power relations;

in fact, they destabilize power relations, including gay/lesbian relations, by disclosing God's liberating practice.

Through base community, queer Christians have the power to define themselves as gay/lesbian and as Christian with one another in opposition to the definitions of heterosexist churches. To liberate the churches and society from the grips of homophobia, queer Christians must first liberate themselves. They must experience themselves and their sexuality as graced. Despite the network of homophobic oppression and violence deployed against them, they struggle to understand God's partiality for lesbians and gay men, God's love and compassion for them. Queer Christian base communities form a *basileia* network of new relations and practices. They need to sacramentalize their gay/lesbian experience, to transform their embodied sexuality into a performance of God's reign.

Initiation Practices

During the last decade, there has been a movement within the gay/lesbian community to discover its own spirituality. The retrieval of the Native American berdache, or shaman, and the Goddess have been powerful images for re-visioning the spiritual dimensions of being gay or lesbian.[27] In re-visioning their spirituality as shamanistic, queers have attempted to integrate their spirituality and their sexuality. The vocation of being queer has also been a vocation to sexual transcendence, to including the erotic dimensions of human relating within the experience of God. It may range from trying to re-vision sexuality and spirituality as an integrated whole to practicing the vision quest of the shaman, the creativity of the berdache, or the inclusiveness of the Goddess.

At the core of the Gospel traditions, Jesus is depicted as a shaman. He is portrayed as a spirit-filled charismatic, an exorcist, a magician, and a visionary.[28] He is labeled a sorcerer by his opponents.[29] At his baptism, Jesus is depicted in the Gospels as receiving a vision from the heavens. The descent of the Spirit and the revelatory voices in the stories about Jesus' baptism are arguably a post-Easter portrayal. The evangelists interpreted what was undoubtedly a significant event in the life of Jesus but from the horizon of his ministry, death, and the community's experience of Easter. They interpreted Jesus' baptism as an event of disclosure and a rite of initiation.

Jesus underwent an initiation into God's reign. He went into the desert on a vision quest, separating himself from his society and journeying into a liminal space.[30] Upon his return, he proclaimed God's coming reign: "The Spirit of the Lord is upon me." Jesus had a new sense of identity. He saw things differently, perceiving God's reign as new social space, as a new age. As a spirit-filled shaman, he remained a liminal figure throughout the Gospels. He lived in liminal spaces, those in-between boundaries and categories of first-century Jewish Palestine. Jesus invited the outcasts, the undesirables, and the nobodies of his society to share his vision quest for God's reign. He was a boundary breaker, threatening the social boundaries constructed to privilege some and exclude others. He understood that God's reign could only be perceived from the margins of his society and that it would be created from the liminal spaces.

Theologian Tom Driver notes that "the shaman perceives himself or herself as an agent of transformative power."[31] The shaman performs public rituals for their transforming effects; the shaman creates an exile space, a liminal or marginal space that challenges the boundaries created by society. Driver identifies Jesus as a shaman who invoked God's Spirit for personal and social transformation.[32] Jesus lived as if God's reign was already present, shattering the Jewish theologies that sharply separated sacred and profane with particular activities and particular places. For Jesus, God's reign was intimately present in love-making and justice-doing. God was present in Jesus' identification with the poor and the oppressed and present in his commitment to justice. His exorcisms, meals, and practice of God's reign became ritual enactments of God's love-making and justice-doing. These rituals were precisely the instruments used by Jesus to effect change of the social situation from oppression to freedom.

Baptism and the confirmation of the risen Lord's Spirit are traditionally symbols of vocation to God's reign. They may be reappropriated or modified or discarded for new rituals that embody the solidification of queer Christian identities within a liminal community of companionship. My personal preference is for reappropriating the traditional ritual of baptism. Its symbolism of immersion in water embodies eroticism, purification, liminality, death, and rebirth. Robert Williams observes,

> Queers are by nature a highly liminal people. We live our daily lives in the liminal spaces between society's perceptions of "masculinity" and

"femininity." In our homophobic culture, we also inhabit the liminal spaces between respectability and criminality.[33]

Baptism initiates Christians into the struggle for God's justice. It is a sign for queer Christians of their commitment and service to the reign of God; it is also a recognition of their liminality. Lesbians and gay men are invited to imitate Jesus' practices by living in the liminal spaces of society and creating God's reign in companionship.

Queer Christians are called to be shamans like Jesus and embark upon a vision quest to integrate their vocation to be queer and serve God's reign. Baptism becomes an initiation rite that creates new social boundaries from the margins. It symbolizes an entry into a new life, a new identity. The baptismal symbolism includes queer sexual identities. Coming out of the closet is a pivotal event for many queer Christians. It initiates them into a certain course of action after struggling with self-acceptance issues, and it confirms their sexual identity as a gift. Coming out needs to be ritualized and celebrated by queer Christians, for coming out initiates them into *basileia* resistance. It opens them to their political identities as embodied gay men and lesbians. Gay men and lesbians relate to God's reign with their bodies and their sexuality and, thus, can become agents of *basileia* change.

Matthew Fox describes the "sacrament of coming out" as a "kind of letting go: a letting go of the images of personhood, sexuality, and selfhood that society has put on one in favor of trusting oneself enough to let oneself be oneself."[34] Coming out is always relational; it is relational to other lesbians and other gay men. Gay men and lesbians find traditional gender roles too restrictive and pioneer new egalitarian roles between men and women. They reject the homophobic stereotypes and hatred into which they have been socialized. Together they live new models of gender relationship in liminal spaces.

Tom Driver describes gay/lesbian coming out as a "confessional performance." He claims, "Confessional performance is an early, necessary step in the liberation of any oppressed people. I am speaking of acts in which people openly proclaim their identity as members of an oppressed group, and confessing loyalty to the cause of liberation."[35] In coming out, queer Christians learn to accept same-sex attraction, tenderness, and love as good, holy, and just. Carter Heyward affirms, "Coming out is a way of coming into our Yes."[36] Coming out ideally means that they relate with other women and other men without gender politics. However, the reality is that gay men and lesbians have to unlearn cultural gender politics. They will no longer pass as heterosexual, moving from passing to an open resistance to coercive heterosexism. As Heyward says,

> Coming out is a protest against social structures that are built on alienation between men and women, women and women, and men and men. Coming out is the most radical, deeply personal and con- sciously political affirmation I can make on behalf of the possibilities of love and justice in the social order. Coming out is moving into rela- tion with peers. It is not simply a way of being in bed, but rather a way of being in the world. To the extent that it invites voyeurism, coming out is an invitation to look and see and consider the value of mutual- ity in human life. Coming out is simultaneously a political movement and the mighty rush of God's Spirit carrying us on.[37]

Coming out for queer Christians is not just coming into their sexual identities but into their own liberating spirituality.[38] It is a perilous faith practice full of risk and hope. They hope that their families and friends will come to understand and celebrate their sexual identity. The risk of rejection was all too real and painful in their closeted strug- gles for self-acceptance. In coming out, queer Christians recognize that Christian maturity is now a genuine possibility. Closeted lives did not allow them to witness in a public fashion, nor did it provide them with healthy models of Christian maturity. Queer Christians can re-envision God no longer as parent but as lover, a sexual intimate and erotic power that beckons them to discipleship—to practicing God's reign. They embark on the path of love-making, making erotic con- nections to lover and embodying the erotic connectedness to com- munity, the oppressed, nature, and God. They create God's reign together with other out and liminal companions. They embody in themselves the erotic practice of a *basileia* community.

The ritualizing of coming out within a Christian practice of God's reign means that queer Christians can move into a shared erotic power for justice with other gay/lesbian Christians. They come out as queer Christians; they celebrate the giftedness of their sexual identity. Their sexual praxis becomes *basileia* praxis when they recognize it as critical committed action. Queer Christians assert their erotic blessedness be- fore God and the community. They can now tell their stories of struggle, commitment, and grace to other queer Christians. They move from the resistance of coming out into the direct action of embodied erotic power for justice. Queer Christians claim their collective power to seek out liberation. They are aware that God's Spirit is the liberating power and erotic practice of justice. They do justice to one another in the base community; they do God's justice for each other and extend that justice beyond the reach of the community. In their base communities, they are introduced to Jesus' *basileia* practices and practice a discipleship of gender equality. They share their resources for the struggle for justice and practice nondominating service to one another. God's justice is love in action for each other, the practice of solidarity with the oppressed, and the transformation of oppressive social relations into *basileia* relations.

Breaking Bread and Sharing the Cup

Most ecclesial celebrations of the Eucharist have lost sight of their symbolic roots. They have become overritualized actions that have lost the symbolism of the meal. The earliest Christian Eucharists were celebrated in homes and around real meals. They were celebrations of hope and liberation, intimacy and commitment in a hostile Roman Empire. As Christianity became respectable, it institutionalized its celebrations in church buildings. It traded liminality of the house assemblies for social respectability. Queer Christian basic communities, however, need to recapture the empowering symbolism of the communal meal and the liminal dynamism of the earliest house communities. Eating togther as equals envisions a new political order of God's reign.

Breaking bread and sharing the cup are empowering actions of *basileia* liberation. Table companionship around a shared meal is the location where the Bible and politics, God and society, faith and erotic practice creatively interact. Queer table companionship is the ritual practice of *basileia* thanksgiving of social outsiders or liminal people who become *basileia* insiders. The eucharistic meal becomes an act of defiance against homophobic oppression.[39] Eating together speaks of the new egalitarian relations between gay men and lesbians in the *basileia* society without oppressive hierarchies and gender politics. It also points to the joy of celebrating human sexuality, the intimacy of community, and the shared commitment to justice-doing. Queer house gatherings around the table nourish committed relationships, provide the liminal space for lesbians and gay men to relate as equals, and strengthen their commitment to love-making and justice-doing on behalf of God's coming reign.

The Eucharist meal represents Jesus' mission to transform the world into God's reign. It animates and motivates gay men and lesbians to work for justice—their own liberation and the liberation of others. It stirs up queer imaginations and hopes for liberation. Queer Christians envision critical alternative possibilities to homophobic/heterosexist oppression. The shared meal changes them by activating the dangerous practices of Jesus, his resistance to political oppression, and God's availability to overturn injustice. It changes society by changing queer Christians who, in turn, work for social change. Empowered, they stand up for themselves and for the powerless.

Breaking bread symbolizes their willingness to commit themselves to God's practice of liberation. Jesus surrendered his life in service to God's reign and practice of justice. Likewise, queer Christians commit themselves to breaking their bodies in loving service to each other and to the struggle for God's justice-doing. Sharing the cup symbolizes their participation in Jesus' *basileia* practice of solidarity and liberation. They share both in the fate and destiny of Jesus: "Whenever you do this, remember me." They practice theodicy by remembering those lesbians and gay men who have given their lives for God's justice. They remember that God will do Easter justice to them as it had been done to Jesus. They remember those in their community who have died of HIV infection; they celebrate their lives and giftedness.[40] The community has been graced by their lives. The practice of theodicy places queer Christians in an ecosphere of God's love-making and justice-doing.

The shared meal provides queer Christians with an important political orientation for their actions for justice in the world and for solidarity with other oppressed people. They grow in opposition to the institutional practices of homophobic churches and society. They grow as a *basileia* affinity group, struggling for change. The eucharistic meal becomes the prayerful nourishment that inspires and empowers their direct actions for political change. God is not neutral to injustice; God is active in the irruption of justice-doing into society. The Eucharist fosters freedom; it inspires rebellion against unjust homophobic/misogynistic structures.

The shared meal of God's reign inspires the base community to build coalitions with other gay/lesbian affinity groups. It motivates the base community to participate, create, and activate performances of justice-doing. Staged actions of nonviolent civil disobedience are not merely public demonstrations; they ritually enact the death of Jesus and God's insurrection against human injustice. Nonviolent staged actions remember the transgressive *basileia* practice of Jesus, his political execution, and God's promise of justice on Easter. Nonviolent staged actions are performances of Eucharist. They celebrate and continue the justice-doing of Easter.

Healing and Reconciliation

As queer Christians become aware of their own internalized homophobia, they acknowledge their own woundedness, their own oppression and sinfulness, and the need for healing. They are oppressed as lesbians and gay men; however, they are also oppressor, perpetuating cycles of violence and oppression. They have damaged their own bodies with drug and alcohol abuse, abusive relationships and behaviors. They have internalized homophobia, damaging their own self-esteem; it is a form of "oppression sickness." Gay men and lesbians also oppress other people, directly and indirectly. They have perpetuated the social cycles of abuse, violence, and hatred in their own lives. Queer Christians do justice by healing and changing themselves. They transform their exile into grace.[41] As they become aware of how they contribute to social oppression of other peoples, queer Christians can understand that homophobic people are not only oppressors but also children of God. Oppressors are caught in homophobic social processes and practices; they also need healing and liberation.

Jesus' *basileia* practice of healing and exorcisms represents the end of social isolation, brokenness, suffering, and oppressive behaviors. Jesus' practice indicates the new social order of God's coming reign of connectedness and wholeness. Queer Christians embody or sacramentalize their need for *basileia* healing within their base community. Their prayers and rituals keep them self-critical of their patterns of destructive behavior and centered on their practice of love-making and justice-doing. In community, they acknowledge and symbolize their woundedness, their broken connectedness to themselves, other people, and the natural world. They embody their change and commitment to self-critical practice. Queer Christians recognize that they are healed when they take responsibility for their behaviors and change them. They are healed in compassionate outreach.[42]

Healing has been experienced in their community's outreach to HIV-positive gay men and to HIV-positive people beyond the gay community. In fact, the queer community has become a model of the suffering servant as in Deutero-Isaiah (Isaiah 42:1–7, 52:2–12). It has become a community tempered by intense pain, suffering, and activism. The gay/lesbian community also practices theodicy in its outreach to its HIV-positive brothers and sisters.[43] The practice of theodicy is its love embodied in pain, compassion, anger, questioning, transgressive protests, and continual risk taking for its HIV-positive brothers and sisters. Non-gay/lesbian Christians have only to visit the display of the memorial quilt to experience the depth of theodicy, grief, pain, and life affirmation of the gay/lesbian community. Love-making and justice-doing are embodied in the thousands of quilt panels.

For queer Christians, the face of God is imaged in the many faces of people living with HIV illness within their own community and outside it. They have practiced faith in the midst of the ravages of HIV illness. They discover a God who is deeply embodied in their social world, a God who suffers when they suffer. God is not the "unmoved mover" of patriarchal models of God. God really suffers with HIV people, their illness, and their social afflictions. A leather jacket of an HIV-positive individual reads "God is HIV+." The inscription asserts God's solidarity with HIV-infected people, their marginalization and suffering. Queer Christians witness in their love-making: "To reject people living with HIV illness is to reject God." The ecclesial responses to people living with HIV illness with a few exceptions have been morally bankrupt. The witness of gay/lesbian compassion toward HIV illness has become an opportunity for heterosexist society and churches to become liberated. They can find salvation, forgiveness for their oppression by reaching out to people living with HIV illness and thus practicing God's justice-doing. They need to repent and change their social practices of denial, hostility, and condemnation. The churches must humbly admit HIV-infected people to their congregations without judgment and with compassion.[44] They need to stop stereotyping HIV-positive people into the categories of innocent and guilty.

Reconciliation is a dimension of *basileia* healing; it is the work of God. Liberation and reconciliation presuppose each other. For queer Christians, there can be no reconciliation unless they are truly free. This means that they cannot be reconciled to society and churches on terms of heterosexist oppression. Ecclesial language for reconciliation is used to mute their critical practice, their transgressive outbursts, and to stop their journey into the exile. Heterosexist freedom is oppression, violence, and death for them. It is based on their lack of freedom and their conforming to compulsory heterosexuality.

Gay/lesbian freedom is not a freedom won at the expense of heterosexual people; it is the liberation of heterosexist society from its own
hierarchical, exclusivist, and authoritative deployments of sexist
power to more egalitarian power relations. Queer Christians can only
be reconciled from the strength of their practice of solidarity and God's
liberating justice. They can only be reconciled from the strength of
their love-making and justice-doing.

God's liberating presence is a disturbing presence. Queer Christians
need to be critical of heterosexist deployments of power relations but
also must be critical of their own participation in those deployments.
When God ceases to be a disturbing presence for them, it is a clear indication that they have become oppressor and have compromised
their practice of solidarity. Their struggle for justice does not stop with
the liberation of the gay/lesbian community. The practice of solidarity
and justice extends to all the other nonpeople on our planet. Reconciliation can be possible only with their liberation as well. Reconciliation cannot take place without the creation of a liberated and just
basileia society.

The Blessing of Same-Sex Unions

The idea of gay/lesbian marriages, domestic partnerships, or unions
is a difficult issue for heterosexist Christians and churches. It is ab-
horrent to a heterosexist society that equates marriage with its procreative function. All attempts to separate procreation from sexuality
have met with resistance and hostility from patriarchal forms of Christianity, which have had difficulty in locating or integrating pleasure in
marriage. Marriage has become the rallying political symbol of traditional family values of the Christian Right and fundamentalist
churches because they identify queer relationships with unadulterated pleasure. Unadulterated pleasure is both sinful and dangerous
from their perspective; it threatens traditional family structure and
opens the social construction of sexuality to innovative meanings and
values. Christian discourse has in the past interpreted and continues
to define marriage as both heterosexual and procreative.[45] It has leveled the charge that same-sex unions are nonprocreative and pleasure
seeking. If Christian discourse understands marriage as pleasurable, it
is so narrowly construed as to exclude gay/lesbian relationships. Thus,
most churches will not bless same-sex unions; they fear constructing
human sexuality in new ways.

The blessing of a gay/lesbian union recognizes that union; it affirms it as a value to the base community, the churches, and heterosexist society.[46] The question of blessing same-sex unions begins the queer reconstruction of traditional family from its exclusive social boundaries to more inclusive forms of family. In this book, I am addressing only the blessing of unions and not the many forms of family within the queer community. Gay/lesbian unions have neither ecclesial and civil recognition nor the protections afforded opposite-sex couples. To charge that same-sex unions are unable to transmit life does not mean that they are not life-giving. Catholic theologian Andre Guindon speaks of a gay/lesbian "fecundity" within their sexual partnerships.[47] Gay/lesbian unions can be life-giving, loving, tender, sensual, nurturing, cooperative, and creative. Moreover, the power of God's just love is more likely, but not exclusively, expressed in gay/lesbian unions. Guindon asserts that gay/lesbian couples "who remain in a partnership generally do so by the strength of their mutual love and dedication and because of a highly qualitative, relational sexual fidelity."[48] Gay/lesbian unions are "gratuitous celebrations of love"; they become models of Christian love or Christian sexual praxis in their ability to signify God's gratuity. Guindon asserts,

> Gay [lesbian] persons whose sexual language is fruitful in faithfulness to a partner, in forgiveness towards their enemies, and in compassion for the oppressed have indeed mastered the art of sexual love in a way which can only build the Christian community. They celebrate love with a gratuity which testifies to the fact that their love is indeed Christian love.[49]

Same-sex unions are frequently without heterosexist power relations or conjugal stereotypes that are socially incorporated into the institution of marriage. That is, the dominance/submission patterns and gender roles found in patriarchal patterns are frequently absent. Same-sex unions are often more egalitarian, with more mutuality, creativity, and care. All of these components form the basis for life-giving and life-affirming relationships; they are the components of *basileia* praxis.

Queer relationships have flourished in recent years despite the lack of social and institutional supports. More often than not, same-sex couples stay together because of their voluntary commitment. Healthy long-term relationships have emerged within the gay/lesbian community, and they have begun to model new forms of coupling. Such long-term unions have diffused the psychiatric myth that healthy and emotionally satisfying same-sex relationships were impossible. Gay/lesbian unions, nevertheless, become dysfunctional when they ape heterosexual marriage models and incorporate the structures of domination and submission into those unions. Heterosexist models work for increasingly fewer opposite-sex couples and are not applicable to same-sex couples.[50] They carry with them unequal power relations, leading to dysfunctional communication and abusive interactions. Healthy, functional gay/lesbian unions tend to be egalitarian, cooperative, creatively mutual, sensual, and communicative. Gay/lesbian unions are pioneering new models of nongenderized relationships without the stereotypical roles.[51]

Gay/lesbian unions form a prophetic model of relating for the Christian community. The blessing of same-sex unions represents the *basileia* practice of solidarity; it recognizes the union as sexual praxis, sexual action committed to God's reign. *Basileia* practice starts with the couple's commitment to love, solidarity, and God's justice-doing, and it extends outward to the base community and those in need of God's justice. *Basileia* practice accents the creative mutual love that is the primary focus of coupling. Their love-making becomes erotic power sharing in service of God's reign. It attempts to integrate pleasure as a positive component of erotic union. Their love-making also represents the practice of God's reign in an inclusive discipleship of equals, shared resources, and service at table. It practices an oppositional *basileia* model of relationship, contrary to the hierarchical political model of heterosexist marriage. It challenges the inequalities and lack of mutuality found in opposite-sex coupling based on such biblical and cultural injunctions as, "Wives be submissive to your husbands as to the Lord" (Ephesians 5:22).

Recognition of Queer Ministry

Ministry is service directed to changing the world into God's reign. It is action in service of human freedom and God's practice of justice. Priests and ministers, bishops and deacons, pastors and leaders in queer base communities must be men and women who are community facilitators. They must be deeply committed to love-making and justice-doing. In a Christian base community, ministry is not exercised within a matrix of authoritarian power relations. *Basileia* leadership is service, not being served as ecclesial "rulers who lord over." *Basileia* power in ministerial practice is neither centralized nor dominating power. Community facilitators are not interested in preserving, extending, and deepening their own power over other members. Rather, they are invested in shared power, the immanent, productive power of God's Spirit within nondominating and egalitarian practices of justice-doing.[52]

The gay/lesbian priests, ministers, and facilitators in a base community lead by example. They are willing to do more than symbolically wash the feet of a "few men" on Holy Thursday. They are prepared to bathe a person with Kaposi's sarcoma and to feed, be with, and care for that person. The facilitators of our base communities empower gay and lesbian Christians to develop their own creative ideas and practices. They assist the community in imagining the alternative reign of God and in practicing that alternative. They empower *basileia* change, building and shaping their own actions into God's coming reign. Facilitators act as bridges, reconstructing past biblical truth in the present. Facilitators train community members in the skills of reading and interpreting the biblical text within their own lives. Together they produce biblical truth; they make God's reign, circulating and distributing biblical truth as community practice.

Gay/lesbian priests, ministers, and leaders are characterized neither by their ecclesial authority nor by permanent office nor by dominating power. They are characterized by love-making and by justice-doing. Authority not shared in symmetrical and egalitarian relations leads to basic inequalities. Base community facilitators have authority only to preach biblical truth, facilitate worship, organize the community, and build consensus in the project of creating God's reign. They assist the community in creating a gay/lesbian space where we can explore, develop, celebrate, and produce a gay/lesbian Christian practice. They lead by example of service, taking a back seat to the development of other members in facilitating the practice of the church. Community leaders keep gay/lesbian Christians focused on their battle for sexual justice. Base communities are places where they can begin to construct a genuine gay/lesbian theological hermeneutics of the Bible and the Christian tradition. Base communities are places where gay/lesbian Christians can begin their practice of justice.

Queer Basic Community: Sacrament of God's Reign

A queer Christian base community attempts to live God's reign in advance. Queer Christians reappropriate what has been expropriated from them: Christianity, Christ, the Bible, sacraments, their sexuality as sacrament, and a community of love-making and justice-doing. The queer base community tries to make present God's justice within its own struggle for justice, or what Mary Hunt calls the "ekklesia of justice." It is a sacrament of *basileia* liberation, God's power at work for liberation in their social midst. Faith in God's reign poses the demand for actualizing it within social practice. It presents a new map of social relations, a visible restructuring of society and a deployment of new power relations. The queer base community is a reverse community whose egalitarian production and circulation of queer biblical truth challenges the asymmetrical organization of ecclesial power. It is a challenge community where gay/lesbian Christians can mutually grow in love, justice, and freedom. From their exilic space, they become determined to change society and churches into God's reign by extending their practices of love, justice, and freedom into heterosexist/homophobic social space.

A queer Christian base community aligns itself with other gay/lesbian affinity groups such as ACT UP, Queer Nation, and others who are committed to justice. It participates in their staged actions against AIDS-phobic and homophobic organizations that contribute to the systemic exclusion of gay men and lesbians. The difference between a queer Christian base community and Queer Nation is not in their commitment to justice or in their staged actions. It is in the faith practice that informs a base community's inclusive vision of *basileia* liberation and motivates it to justice-doing.

A queer base community is a place where Christians can celebrate the joy of being lesbians and gay men. It is a place where they can experience creative mutual love, their own giftedness, and healing. The community fosters self-esteem, gay and lesbian pride, and hope. It is a foretaste of liberation, where the diversity of God's reign is respected and celebrated. The hospitality of the base community helps to heal the damaging effects of internalized homophobia. The queer base community welcomes queer Christians rejected by their churches and HIV-positive gay men who need emotional support, love, and care. The base community is also a haven for the many gay/lesbian HIV care givers. Together the members of the community grieve, remember, and celebrate the lives of those who have been dear to them. Their strength comes from the shared hope of the Easter promise that God will do justice for their loved ones. It strengthens their outreach to their own gay brothers and other nongay groups with HIV infection.

A queer Christian base community becomes a visible sign of the failure of the churches. Churches have failed in their pastoral outreach to queer Christians and to people living with HIV infection. The rejection experienced by queer Christians and people living with HIV infection is an experience of the churches' sinfulness. The churches have not been immune to oppressive behaviors and practices; they have failed to extend God's reign to lesbians and gay men. Queer Christians have watched churches lose credibility in their practices toward gay men and lesbians. Queer base communities will challenge the assumptions underlying Christian discourse and practice. They will embody a new Christian practice of gay/lesbian sexuality as creative, empowering, and symbolic of God's reign. They provide a critical *basileia* alternative to that experienced within the churches.

The power of queer Christian base communities is the power of solidarity. It is not only solidarity with their own oppression and their own oppressed community, but also solidarity with other oppressed—the disabled, women, people of color, the elderly, the disenfranchised, the homeless, the poor, the Third World poor and oppressed, and all others suffering injustices. Queer Christians cannot be free until all are liberated from oppression, until homophobic oppressors and other oppressors are liberated from themselves. The practice of solidarity keeps queer Christians from reifying social practices as God's reign; it keeps them aware that their social practices for liberation are only tentative albeit important actions in God's project of human liberation.

6

The Struggle for Sexual Justice

*The Holy Spirit is the revolutionary power which comes to an
exploited people as they struggle to escape from powerlessness
and to end the institutional oppression forced upon them by
an enemy. . . . And in our kind of world the language of
the Holy Spirit cannot but be the language of revolt.*

ALBERT CLEAGE[1]

Inequalities initiate social conflict. Conflict becomes a social fact of
liberated practice. The conflict with institutional Christianity is a life-
and-death struggle. Christianity is not the enemy; Christianity presents us with a revolutionary discourse and practice for social change.
Nor is Jesus the enemy; Jesus, undomesticated and freed from ecclesial
discourse, radically confronts queer Christians with the critical practice of God's reign. He is executed for his service to God's reign and
his practice of justice-doing.

The enemy consists of those ecclesial institutions, their discourses, and their practices that foster homophobia and legitimize
social violence against the gay and lesbian community. The churches
have excluded and marginalized gay men and lesbians. The churches
proclaim salvation doctrines linked to their own exclusionary practices, whereas God's compassion and justice-doing are incompatible
with the exclusion of any people. The churches have ignored the
scholarly publications of biblical scholars, social scientists, and
theologians that is sympathetic to gay men and lesbians. In some
cases they have silenced legitimate theological research and biblical

investigation. Biblical scholars and theologians are fearful to speak out for justice for gay men and lesbians.

The churches refuse to engage in a dialogue with active listening; they engage in monologue, an unequal distribution of power in dialogue.[2] Ecclesial resources for changing homophobia are blocked by the churches' refusal to listen to what they are doing to gay men and lesbians. Therefore, many lesbians and gay men have withdrawn from the churches when channels for redressing their grievances are insufficient or when their grievances are categorized as sin or illness. Reconciliation does not seem possible when there is a refusal to dialogue. Moderate voices for reconciliation within the churches encourage gay men and lesbians to be patient and work within the legitimate structures for change. At a symposium sponsored by New Ways Ministry, a Catholic education and research organization on homosexuality, Bishop Gumbleton stated, "The Church should affirm and bless the gay community for teaching what it means to love." He also urged the assembled participants to "wait with the church until more and more bishops, priests and pastoral ministers come to a better point of compassion, understanding, love and care."[3] Patience is unacceptable to many queer Catholics/Christians. Their voices have been too long muted by ecclesial homophobia and violence. Queers and queer Christians remain in a state of homophobic siege from the pulpits.

Queer Christians have the power to define themselves. They can define themselves as an empowered *basileia* community on the way toward liberation. They can practice God's justice-doing and solidarity with the oppressed to the best of their finite abilities. They can practice God's insurrection against human oppression with their own insurrection against homophobia inside the churches and in society. They have begun to produce a queer theology that is only in its infancy and have begun to organize themselves against ecclesial oppression.[4] They present a critical alternative to the social practices of the churches. Their experiences of Christ's Spirit outside the social practices and theological definitions of churches have forced them to see that salvation is found outside the churches; the Spirit of the queer Christ has been excluded from the churches.

The Spirit of the risen Lord is at work within the struggles for gay/lesbian liberation; the Spirit is engaged in a new and critical practice of God's reign within queer base communities. The Spirit is present in gay/lesbian holy anger, their coming out and political opposition to institutional and homophobic churches. Beverly Harrison observes,

"Anger is a mode of connectedness to others, and is a vivid form of caring."[5] Anger is not the opposite of love. Rather, anger is a form of lovemaking that fuels queer justice-doing. Gay/lesbian Christians must not avoid the power of their anger. It is the energy from which they forge Christian base communities and affinity groups that struggle for justice. The Spirit is practiced in the midst of their waging conflict and staging transgressive actions against homophobic churches and society. Their collective outbursts of holy anger and justified rage are precipitated by an impatience not to accept any longer homophobic violence and oppression.

Jesus and the "Stop the Temple" Disturbance

It is reasonable to see the Temple as the real focus of Jesus' journey to Jerusalem. He came to Jerusalem with the intention of challenging the Temple with its encoded values and bringing down the privileged social group that controlled the Temple. Jesus' disturbance in the Temple signaled the new social arrangements of God's reign. His statements and threats against the Temple, his attacks on the Temple priesthood, and the implicit authority in those claims threatened the control of Jerusalem and the people by the priests of the Temple. The political infrastructure would be dismantled with the coming of God's reign.

The Gospel accounts narrate that Jesus caused a disturbance by driving out those who sold sacrificial animals, overturning tables of money changers, and stopping workers from working on the Temple. Liberation theologian and political activist Ched Myers applies the term *messianic theater* to Jesus' farewell meal.[6] The term might apply also to Jesus' actions in the Temple. The symbolics of God's reign could be understood as a form of street theater.

Any real effort to stop the trade in the Temple would have required an army. Jesus' action did not bring all buying and selling in the Temple to a halt. It was not substantial enough to interfere with daily routine. If it had not been limited in scope and rather was an attempt at seizing control of the Temple, the Temple police and the Roman soldiers looking down from the Antonia Fortress would have arrested Jesus on the spot.[7]

In anger, Jesus overturned some tables to make a point; it was a demonstrative action and not a cleansing as traditionally interpreted.[8] By this act of overturning tables, Jesus symbolized the destruction of the Temple. His action was premeditated and carefully orchestrated and staged. There are three components to Jesus' symbolic action or messianic theater: the overturning of the money changers' tables, the driving out of those selling sacrificial animals, and the stopping of those working on the rebuilding of the Temple.

On Passover, it was incumbent on pious Jews to offer a sacrifice and payment of the half-shekel Temple tax. It was not permissible for Jews to use the coins of everyday commerce; they were required to obtain Tyrian half-shekel coins for the purpose.[9] By overturning the tables of the money changers, Jesus symbolized the destruction of the Temple, its revenue system, and the socioeconomic exploitation of the Jewish peasant. His action was a provocative assault on the priesthood and aristocracy, who made a living off the Temple. In the coming reign of God, there would not be a religious or priestly elite. Religious and economic privilege would be abolished in God's reign. Jesus demonstrated his own Galilean resistance to paying taxes and the resulting social burdens of taxation. No one could serve God and money (*mammom*) in the new reign of God, he preached. The Temple was at the center of the Jewish economic system in which Jewish peasants supported the priests and the priestly aristocracy through their tithes. The poor would no longer be financially burdened with service to God through the Temple taxation and tithing system. Exploitation of people's devotion and piety would come to an end. Nor would the lame, the blind, and the outcast be any longer excluded from God's reign as they had been in the Temple (Matt. 21:14–16).

Jesus stopped the selling of sacrificial animals. In Mark 12:15 and Matthew 21:12, he stopped the selling of pigeons; in John 2:14–15, he stopped the selling of sheep, oxen, and pigeons. The disruption of trade represented both an attack on the divinely ordained sacrificial system and the economic exploitation of the Temple by the Jerusalem elites. This gesture pointedly attacked the priesthood. In the new age, there would be no need for priesthood, for cult, or for mediating God's presence. God would be accessible to all; God would be present within the *basileia* social network. In addition, Jesus challenged the economic exploitation over and control of the Temple by the Jerusalem elites. In God's reign, the new social order would belong to God and the people.

Jesus stopped anyone from carrying anything through the Temple (Mark 12:16). The Temple was a building of great beauty; it was the central national institution of Israel, the locus of Jewish religious and political life. During the reign of Herod the Great, the Temple was vastly expanded. The building program burdened the Jewish peasant with heavy taxes. Work on the Temple was still continuing a half-century later on Jesus' final visit to Jerusalem. The Temple was the largest employer in Jerusalem; it was central to the economic life of the city, and merchants prospered from its trade. Jesus' stopping workers and work on the Temple was not only an affront to the Jewish religious life but also a challenge to the economic benefactor of the city, for the entire population of Jerusalem had some financial interest in the Temple.[10] His demonstration was a blatant attack against the Temple and the financial interests of Jerusalem citizens.

Jesus' arrest resulted from his angry demonstration in the Temple.[11] He disrupted the Jewish political order at its heart. His demonstration signaled the total disruption of the Jewish political order with God's coming reign. His demonstration was directed against the wealthy priestly aristocracy and Jerusalem elites, their exploitation of the poor, and their exclusion of "throw-away" people. He antagonized the guardians of Jewish religious and political values with his transgressive actions. The chief priests and the Jerusalem elites took the initiative in arresting Jesus and bringing him before Pilate. They perceived Jesus' action as threatening to and contemptuous of the Temple. Such a challenge to the Temple clergy and the Jerusalem elites had to be decisively met. From one perspective, Jesus' demonstration within the sacred space of the Temple failed and directly led to his arrest, legal proceedings, and execution. Jesus' staged demonstration models transgressive practice for queer Christians.

Jesus: The Model for Transgressive Practice

Jesus waged conflict with the clerical aristocracy controlling the Temple and challenged Roman power.[12] Jesus' action in the Temple is the model for the transgressive "Stop the Church" actions at St. Patrick's Cathedral, for which ACT UP/New York has been accused of sacrilege. The Stop the Church action, like Jesus' demonstration, violated sacred space, transgressed sacred ritual, and offended sensibilities. It was viewed as strident, blasphemous, and counterproductive. One particular incident in the cathedral drew media attention. An individual took it upon himself to go up and receive communion; he crumbled the communion wafer. This action was the individual's responsibility. ACT UP/New York had neither planned, discussed, nor reached consensus on such an action. The media focused on this one instance of individual rage. The action alienated segments of both the gay/lesbian community and the general public.

I do not condone such an action. I believe that the crumbling of the communion wafer was counterproductive to the goals of the demonstration. The media fallout was extremely negative. However, I want to examine the incident a little more closely, for it raises a potential issue of sacred contempt. The crumbling of the communion wafer was an act of personal rage against Cardinal O'Connor. The protester drew attention to the cardinal's policy of interfering with both safe-sex education in the New York school system and the advocacy of condom use to protect against the spread of HIV. The cardinal frequently had used the pulpit and the Eucharist as opportunities to push for his position. He denied life-saving information to counter the spread of HIV and continued to endanger lives. Cardinal O'Connor also had used his influence with the national conference of U.S. bishops to force the withdrawal of a pastoral letter, *The Many Faces of AIDS*. In that document, the use of condoms was viewed as a medical issue that prevented the spread of HIV, not as a sexual issue.[13] The Catholic hierarchical position has continued to allow the spread of HIV by limiting education about safer sex practices. Cardinal O'Connor has contributed from the pulpit at St. Patrick's Cathedral to the genocidal spread of HIV. The holy rage of the ACT UP protester was justified, but the means of expression were unfortunate.

The charges of blasphemy, sacred contempt, and sacrilege were also leveled at Jesus for his "Stop the Temple" disturbance at the so-called trial scene (Mark 14:53–65).[14] He violated sacred space just prior to a religious festival. Enraged, he attempted to disrupt the sacralized commerce and activity in the Temple courtyard during a pilgrimage festival time. He offended the Temple clergy and clerical aristocracy by challenging their authority. He upset the general public of Jerusalem who had a financial interest in the Temple. He was criticized, arrested, beaten, and eventually executed for his staged action in the Temple.

Too often, this action of Jesus is misidentified in ecclesial interpretation as the cleansing of the Temple. Such an interpretation manifests either anti-Jewish polemics—attempting at supersessionary statements placing Christianity over legalistic Judaism—or an idealization of Jesus' actions as a metaphor for the spiritual path. The Gospel narratives portray a staged political action that challenged social practices controlled by the Temple aristocracy and manipulated to their own financial and political advantage. It was a staged direct action in which Jesus criticized and presented the *basileia* alternative to the oppressive social practices of the Temple clerical aristocracy. Ecclesial tradition has domesticated the Jesus tradition; it spiritualizes the dangerous elements of the Jesus narrative to legitimize its own social practices. The Jesus tradition within the biblical sources is far more conflict-laden and open to queer political hermeneutics.

Conflict is inevitable for a disciple of God's reign. There are no manners or polite courtesies in the struggle for justice.[15] It is a lethal struggle. It may contain a contempt for sacred icons, discourse, and practices that have become oppressive to gay men and lesbians. The experience of ecclesial injustice and terrorism opens queer Christians to their full participation in the organization of heterosexist power relations. We need to pierce the armor of heterosexist rationalization; only then can the problem of injustice be faced. The erotic power of justice-doing and love-making takes the idiom of transgressive discourses and practices. Various Stop the Church actions have emerged all across the country. Their principal target has been the institutional Catholic hierarchy. Unfortunately, these actions constitute the only language that grabs public and ecclesial attention.

"Stop the Church" Actions

Queer Christian basic communities need to retrieve Jesus' *basileia* practice of staging transgressive actions. Jesus' *basileia* practice subverted the power relations of the political infrastructure of first-century Palestine. He did not hesitate to challenge the ecclesial control of the chief priests over the Temple and Jewish society. When critics focus on the transgressive actions of ACT UP/New York at St. Patrick's Cathedral, have they not forgotten that Jesus intruded upon sacred space? He disrupted the commerce in the Temple courtyard during a major Jewish festival. He challenged clerical and institutional control that oppressed the poor, that led to a spiraling economic indebtedness of Jewish peasants, that sanctioned Roman political control.[16] He reminded the clerical aristocracy that their social practices were exploitative and oppressive. Jesus waged conflict against the Temple system that had become the negative *basileia* experience of earthly rule and domination. The biblical but lethal precedent of the ACT UP demonstration at St. Patrick's Cathedral was practiced by Jesus in his disturbance in the

Temple. As in Jesus' day, sacred space has become oppressive space—oppressive to people living with HIV infection, to lesbians and straight women, and to gay men. Where is the real sacrilege?

ACT UP, Queer Nation, and activist Dignity chapters point to the transgressive path of challenge when no dialogue is possible. Queer Nation has disrupted the meetings of Christian aversive groups that try to convert gay men and lesbians to heterosexuality. ACT UP and Queer Nation have staged actions in the ecclesial centers of homophobic oppression, disrupting services, protesting ordinations, and intruding upon homophobic sacred space. Dignity chapters in New York and San Francisco have staged protests during services at cathedrals. They have been accused of having a contempt for the sacred.[17] Their contempt for the sacred is like Jesus' messianic theater in the Temple; it is, in fact, a profound reverence for the sacred based on God's justice-doing.

A Stop the Church Coalition in St. Louis, consisting of ACT UP, Queer Nation, and other concerned people, staged a Stop the Church protest on Easter Sunday in 1992. The coalition claimed Easter as its day of liberation and indicted the Catholic church hierarchy for crucifying women, gay and lesbian people, and people living with AIDS. The demonstrators used street theater to liturgize their specific message. The street liturgy occurred in three phases: silence, rage, and celebration. In its press packet, the coalition explained its actions:

> SILENCE: We stand before the cathedral, a people oppressed and held silent by the oppressive policies of the Catholic hierarchy. Our stance symbolizes our crucifixion as "evil" by the church; our mouths are covered to enforce our silence. The three crosses dragged before the cathedral symbolize the church's trinity of oppression: that of lesbians and gays, of women, and of people living with AIDS. But today, we join—proud, united, and strong—to officially inform the church: "We will never be silent again." We hold the church accountable for its past actions, accountable for its shame, and demand a change.

> RAGE: Our demand for change takes the form of controlled rage, a strength born of our common oppression. We will lift our voices, speaking truth to power in the tradition of nonviolent resistance, and call upon people of conscience to stand with us. Though we daily confront death at the hands of the church's policies and actions, symbolized by the chalked outlines of fallen bodies on the sidewalk, we draw strength from the courage and dignity of those who have left us.

. CELEBRATION: We end our struggle with freedom, dignity, and celebration. We stand confident that we will someday see a time of true
celebration, and we embrace that vision as we embrace each other:
lovingly, compassionately, with courage to live according to the dictates of our conscience, not the doctrines of the oppressor.[18]

Queer Christian base communities must practice queer visibility actions that are transgressive and nonviolent acts of civil disobedience.
If queer Christian base communities do not participate in nonviolent
civil disobedience and staged actions, they will never have freedom.
The imperative of queer Christian base communities is "to shift the
language game, to speak, demonstrate and demand in ways that are
seen as inappropriate to the game when that game erases them or excludes them from its continual reformulation."[19] In staging direct actions or transgressions, queer Christians remind the churches that
their social practices are remembrances (*anamnesis*) of God's reign.

Queer Christians have reconfigured the biblical narrative of Jesus'
Stop the Temple action into a new narrative. Through guerrilla street
theater and transgressive actions, Jesus' Stop the Temple actions have
become Stop the Church actions. The churches have become Temple
oppressors of God's *anawim*, the sexually different. Queer Christians
make the churches and their leaders uncomfortable with the practices
that now crucify queer Christs in their midst. The churches and their
leaders are now the clerical bureaucrats, the Temple hierarchy, and the
privileged who stand against God's partisan love for the oppressed.

The intrusion upon homophobic space by queer Christian base
communities may take many shapes and forms. The scope is limited
only by gay/lesbian imaginations and transgressive ingenuity. Here are
some strategies for waging a transgressive campaign against homophobic churches and leaders. Some of these suggestions have been
adopted from specific actions that already were staged by transgressive queer groups. Each base community must discern its own focus of
struggle and what actions are appropriate to itself.

Queer Christians might stage celebrations and blessing of same-
sex unions on the steps of cathedrals and central denominational
churches to increase the sacramental visibility of their relations and
the ecclesial failures to recognize them. Queer Nation/Boston recently
performed such a prophetic action, when a dozen gay and lesbian
couples exchanged commitment vows on the steps of the Holy Cross
Cathedral. It was a prophetic statement of anger at Cardinal Law's

lobbying efforts to defeat Boston's Family Protection Act, which would have extended insurance benefits to the spouses of same-sex couples who worked for the city. Danielle Mavronicles presided over the service. She said, "Queers, like heterosexuals, have loving, lasting relationships. But we are not given the same rights under law. Cardinal Law was one of the primary opponents of the Family Protection Act, and therefore, to our love."[20] The Catholic archdiocese condemned Queer Nation for its intent to parody and ridicule marriage.

Queer Christians may protest ordinations, stage kiss-ins at the exchange of peace, or distribute HIV educational material and condoms to parishioners after services. For example, three thousand gay/lesbian and feminist demonstrators surrounded Holy Cross Cathedral in Boston while Cardinal Law ordained deacons to the office of priesthood. The demonstrators chanted, "Two, four, six, eight, how do you know your priests are straight?"

Queer Christians may hold silent vigils on the steps of fundamentalist churches to remember those lesbians and gay men who have suffered violence or those people who have died from complications of HIV infection. They may stage mock trials of ecclesial and civil leaders for their complicity in legitimizing homophobic violence and the spread of HIV infection. They might disrupt ordinations or consecrations of bishops and other hierarchs with nonviolent civil disobedience actions.

Queer Christians may choose to out closeted church leaders who have taken active roles in leading homophobic hate campaigns. This is an action that takes some discernment, prayer, reflection, and dialogue. The following are several real situations that demonstrate the complexity of such an action. The first is an excerpt from a letter of a gay priest, written to Robert Williams:

> Robert, I have slept with so many closeted clergy, including three closeted bishops. Plus, I have a very good memory for detail. Do you have any thoughts on outing in the Church? Is it too violent an act? Is it time for retaliation and fighting back? I believe that it is.[21]

Williams' response is worth quoting:

> I wrote him my usual line—if they are doing something to actively harm us, then yes, I think that outing is in order. If they are simply living their lives quietly, it is not. In [the] next letter, he asked pointedly, "How can anyone who's in the closet be seen as not causing the community any harm? The very fact of being closeted, rather than out and

proud, is harmful." And you know, I believe he is right. Everyone who remains in the closet helps sustain the atmosphere of homophobia in which you must live your life.[22]

Outing can be equally as violent as homophobic oppression. It brings ecclesial sanctions and terrorism against the outed individual. Does closetedness constitute sufficient reason for the violence of outing? There would be no question of outing Jerry Falwell or Cardinal O'Connor if it could ever be proven that they were gay. The amount of pain, violence, and oppression suffered by the gay/lesbian and HIV-positive communities because of these two religious leaders outweighs the proportionality of any violence of outing these two individuals. They need to be blocked; they have produced an atmosphere of religious homophobia that has sanctioned and blessed homophobic violence. They have contributed to the genocide of AIDS by blocking educational information on safer sex practices and condom usage.

A second instance is that of a bishop who has been apprehended by the state police three times at rest stops for soliciting male sex but not prosecuted because of his ecclesial office. This bishop has failed to speak up against the ecclesial and social violence against gay men and lesbians. He has the ability to affect a compassionate response from the parishes within his diocese. What does a queer Christian base community do? Does it meet with the bishop and ask for a more sensitive response to gay/lesbian issues? If dialogue fails to elicit a more compassionate response, the base community may discern that it is time to publicly out this bishop. However, again outing must be weighed against the proportionality of the violence contributed by the bishop.

The third case is a priest who is president of a major religious-affiliated university. He is known by queer Christians to be gay. However, he has not declared himself publicly for fear of ecclesial repercussions. He has persuaded the board of trustees to adopt a gay/lesbian antidiscrimination employment policy. Do queer Christians out him because his high visibility would challenge the church? The greater proportionality of violence may swing more directly toward the outing group. Outing is an issue of proportional violence, and this course of action must be taken only when homophobic violence overwhelms the personal violence of placing an individual in the gay/lesbian community.

Outing is just one tactic a base community may employ. Christian base communities may also distribute printed materials on HIV infection and condoms to young churchgoers. They may want to use guerrilla theater tactics against church leaders who have impeded educational efforts on safe-sex practices to prevent the spread of HIV infection. Queer Christians might build coalitions with other groups to stage protests against the churches. On Easter, they may erect a cross with names attached of particular groups such as HIV-positive people from all walks of life, queers, and women who have suffered from violence perpetrated by the churches. Queer Christians may attempt to retrieve Easter as the feast of the queer Christ and the feast of gay/lesbian liberation. Gay/lesbian base communities might sponsor coming-out days for visible church leaders, ministers/priests, and members.

Boycotts, picketing, leafleting, demonstrations, freedom marches, civil disobedience, rallies, and prayer vigils are all means for exerting "queer" power. Since all churches are nonprofit organizations, it may be useful to scrutinize fund-raising efforts and the use and abuse of church funds for political purposes, and to work to revoke churches' tax-exempt status.

Gay/lesbian communities like Dignity lost an opportunity to protest and provide emotional support to John McNeill when he was silenced and expelled from the Society of Jesus. John McNeill spoke up for queer Christians, but where were queer Catholics? Queer alumni represent 10 percent of the alumni of Jesuit colleges and universities; they could have held Jesuits accountable for their commitment and statements on justice. The Jesuits have claimed that "the promotion of justice should be the concern of our whole life and a dimension of all our apostolic efforts".[23] The expulsion of John McNeill from the Jesuits, forced by Cardinal Ratzinger, is a solidarity and justice issue.

Gay/lesbian base communities may discern that nonviolent civil disobedience is the most effective means in challenging ecclesial structures. It has been used effectively by activists from Jesus to Emmeline Pankhurst of the English women's suffrage movement, to Mahatma Gandhi, Rosa Parks, and Martin Luther King.[24] Base communities may escalate their campaign to bring the nonviolent battle for queer truth to the churches. They may stage prophetic actions to challenge and disrupt churches of television evangelists. They may interrupt church services, chain themselves to the altar rails, practice die ins, or chant slogans or blow whistles during homophobic homilies. They may stage visibility actions at social events such as church fairs. Open queer Christians can participate with specific groups in reaching out to the homeless. Queer Christian activism may range from polite involvement in certain church activities to more disruptive staged kiss-ins during church services. Queer civil disobedience carries a misdemeanor charge with it, but arrests receive media coverage. Media coverage is an important means for campaigning against the ecclesial organization of homophobic violence. It keeps the public pressure on ecclesial organizations to begin dialogue with queer Christians.

Gay/lesbian Christians need to practice a critical strategy of transgressively challenging public ecclesial statements. This means that they need to challenge church leaders on their specific contributions to homophobic oppression and the incompatibility of their actions with God's preferential option for the oppressed. They may target church leaders with zapping questions at public affairs and use the public media to underscore the contradictions in their positions. They need to engage church leaders in confrontational debates, pointing out that their homophobia is a "reaction conversion" response, masking their own deep-seated same-sex attractions and the need to stamp out their own same-sex feelings by stamping out those feelings in other people.[25]

Whatever course of transgressive action a queer Christian base community chooses, its members need to be clear on their long-range and short-range goals. Liberation will probably not be achieved in their life, but they will contribute to the total project of human liberation. The project of liberation is their present responsibility and the responsibility of other groups in the future. Their responsible action to human liberation creates alternative social conditions for re-visioning human liberation:

> Responsible action does not mean one individual resolving the problems of others. It is, rather, participation in a communal work laying the groundwork for the creative response of people in the present. Responsible action means changing what can be altered in the present even though a problem is not completely resolved. Responsible action provides partial solutions and the inspiration and conditions for further partial resolutions by others.[26]

Christian base communities need to work on consensus building, discernment, and decision making to commit themselves to responsible action. Commitment to consensus building and direct action enables them to plan and sustain their campaigns against homophobic injustice within the churches and society. Queer Christians need to harness the power of their prayer and their anger in companionship, the power of the Christ's Spirit to nurture and sustain their revolutionary struggle for liberation. It will allow them to be honest in their own self-critical analysis and evaluations of staged actions.

Critical Practice in the Queer Community

There is much that is good, holy, creative, alternative, and liberative about the gay/lesbian community. This book has affirmed only a fraction of the many positive gay/lesbian community developments, cultural contributions, and political actions. There are many queer political saints; there are many gifted people in the gay/lesbian community. If gay/lesbian Christians practice criticism of homophobic/ heterosexist society and churches, they must be prepared to criticize their own community. Self-criticism is painful. We must look inward to surface destructive and oppressive patterns of social behavior. White, middle-class queers must be sensitive to exclusions of people of color. Many Dignity chapters, for instance, are dominated by white males and perpetuate exclusions. Many gay/lesbian organizations suffer from a false inclusionism. Many gay men must examine their misogynistic attitudes while some lesbians must shed their radical separatism. Self-criticism is an attempt to break the repetitive cycles of abusive power patterns that gay men and lesbians perpetuate. It is healing ourselves of the residual effects of internalized homophobia and internalized patterns of social violence.

There is much that lesbians and gay men need to be critical of within their own community. The gay/lesbian community can at times be cannibalistic. Internalized homophobia can be directed against those who are out of the closet. In turn, anger can be directed by out gay men and lesbians against those who are still closeted. Cannibalistic tendencies are also directed against those members of our community who are successful, for some gay men and lesbians act out some self-fulfilling need to punish themselves and trash others.[27] Torie Osborn, former executive director of the Gay and Lesbian Services Center in Los Angeles and now the executive director of the National Gay and Lesbian Task Force, observes, "Next to the right wing and their ideological determination to obliterate us, I think our own oppression sickness is the most dangerous force around."[28] For many oppressed and angry queers, it is easier to trash members of the gay/lesbian community than to face their real homophobic oppressors. Oppression sickness stems from the gay/lesbian inability to effectively deal with their own internalized homophobia. The destructive patterns of cannibalistic tendencies, drug and alcohol abuse, sexual addiction, codependence, battery, and abusive relationships are produced from low self-esteem. Queer Christians must be critical yet compassionate of these destructive social behaviors, examining their own behaviors and seeking out means to heal themselves. They also need to encourage their brothers and sisters to seek appropriate therapeutic treatments to heal low self-esteem. They need to assist themselves and and others in healing and learning to appreciate the joy of being/gay lesbian.

Related to oppression sickness is "horizontal hostility,"[29] the hostility directed by the gay/lesbian community against itself. What makes the queer community unique is its diversity and plurality, but this diversity also threatens to pull it apart. Diversity is found in competing strategies for social transformation and sexual practice. Tolerance is espoused as a value, but at what cost is tolerance preserved? Any disapproval or criticism is viewed as oppression, impinging on privacy rights or freedom. Name calling between groups is an attempt to discredit criticism; it also tends to control others and deflect genuine dialogue. Name calling, according to Julia Penelope, trivializes the real dangers to the gay/lesbian community, obscures the issues, serves as divide-and-conquer strategy, and is substituted for critical dialogue.[30] This is apparent, for example, in the intense and often vitriolic debate about sadomasochism in the gay/lesbian community.[31] Intolerance and name calling have failed to create a genuine dialogue over sadomasochism.

In addition, gay men and lesbians suffer from sexism, ageism, classism, consumerism, racism, able-body-ism, selfishness, and apathy. These issues are not particular to the gay/lesbian community; they are complex, confronting large segments of society. Gay men and lesbians are not immune to the consumer trends of their society. Their consumer lifestyle is at the expense of other people around the globe. They need to be critical of their own consumer habits, become aware of how they affect other people and the delicate ecological balance of the planet, and begin to effect microchanges within their own lifestyles.

Gay men are often sexist, and lesbians have sensitized gay men to feminist issues. Many gay men and lesbians also practice a reverse sexism to heterosexual, bisexual, and transsexual people. They repeat the violence and oppression done to themselves by directing it toward those different from themselves. They proclaim not merely that queer is good but that queer is best. Some take the slogans too seriously and their separateness to the extremes. Slogans and separateness are effective only if they are used against homophobic oppression. Lesbians and gay men are suspicious that bisexual people are only going through a "phase" and that they are really gay/lesbian. Gay men and lesbians are slowly starting to understand the bisexual community as it organizes and affiliates itself with their struggles for liberation. Some lesbian establishments have advertised themselves as only for female-born lesbians, against the growing social phenomena of transsexual MTFs (male-to-females) who have identified themselves as lesbians.[32] Some gay men who dress in leather want no association with men dressed in female drag. They are caught in rigid "macho" male stereotypes. Some lesbians are critical of gay drag because it demeans women, while drag queens may use drag as political satire on sex roles and societal pressures. Gay men and lesbians are not free from their own gender stereotyping and restrictions.

Separateness from heterosexist society is formative for gay/lesbian political identity and is effective for political struggle and change. However, intrasegregation of gay men and lesbians is not an end unto itself; it is harmful to the solidarity of the gay/lesbian community. It reproduces the abusive sexual politics of the heterosexist society. The social segregation of gay men and lesbian women indicates the direction of their sexual interest. They socialize separately in all-male bars or female bars. Lesbians and gay men have to be careful that intrasegregation is not carried to extremes. The gay/lesbian community needs more social organizations for women and men together to counter the intrasegregational forces within their own community. More social intermixing will correct any latent sexism and restrictive gender stereotypes within their community. The strength of the movement is the interaction of lesbians and gay men with one another. Lesbians have been in the forefront of the civil rights movements for African Americans and for women; they have held leadership roles in the peace and justice movement for decades. Lesbians have sensitized gay men to political issues and feminist concerns. Gay men have been politicized by the ravages of HIV and have learned from lesbian experience in the peace and justice movement and their struggle for the reproductive rights of women. Lesbians and gay men continue to learn from each other, and they voluntarily unite to fight in a common struggle for justice. Their communication provides them with the opportunity of experiencing new forms of nonsexist relationship.

The gay/lesbian community also reproduces the same exclusions as general society does. Gay men and lesbians do not just rank their social interest in people according to their sex, but according to their economic status, education, and profession. They also stereotype other gay men and lesbian women by their appearance. Their stereotypes are just as much social degradation rituals as homophobic stereotypes of themselves. Moreover, classism is similar to racism, the social mistreatment of and prejudice against people of color. Both are prejudicial and prevent gay men and lesbians from experiencing other people in their social diversity. Likewise, lesbians and gay men discriminate against those with physical disabilities and exclude them from their social circles. They fail to get to know people for who they are. They are also an age-segregated community. Ageism intensifies all the preceding discriminations. All exclusions within the gay/lesbian community impoverish the community; they limit gay men and lesbians from experiencing the diversity and richness of community. Gay men and lesbians can become like their homophobic oppressors.

A queer Christian base community begins with self-criticism. Its members first change themselves from the role of oppressor, criticizing all the exclusionary behaviors and oppressive practices. They practice inclusionary language and commit themselves to practicing nonoppressive social interactions. They must end the cycle of social oppression within themselves and try to change the cycle within their network of social relations. Queer Christians form a discourse community with specific Christian and gay/lesbian values. This means that they take a critical stance against the prevalent sexism, consumerism, classism, racism, ageism, able-body-ism, and abusive relations in the gay/lesbian community. Queer Christians take responsibility for their own behaviors and commit themselves to live in a nonoppressive fashion. Queer Christians empower the gay/lesbian community to practice freedom by ending intraviolence and oppression. They start by practicing liberation within their base communities to effectively change homophobic oppression and extend the struggle to heterosexist society. As *basileia* communities listening to God's justice-doing, they confront, criticize, and fight all forms of exclusionary violence within themselves, around them, and between them. Only in this way can their communities be committed to love-making and justice-doing.

God as Love-Making and Justice-Doing

God is experienced, known, and celebrated—through presence and solitude—as the power for justice and friendship among all human and other creatures in great and small places of our life together. By this power, we god. Godding, we experience our personal lives as profoundly connected at the root of who we are, rather than as separate and disconnected from our professional lives and from one another's places of deepest meaning. Godding, we share how we really feel about our body selves-in-relation, in our living and working, our living and dying. We share, we act, we are together.

CARTER HEYWARD[1]

A queer liberation theology refuses to accept a God who is not identified with the liberation goals of its community. God identifies with our erotic practice and struggle for justice as long as we are self-critical and open to the practice of solidarity. The threads of queer liberation theology come together in our *basileia* reflections and practices. The reign of God is the political reality of their erotic power, justice, solidarity, and freedom.

Images of God, however, can become oppressive. God has to be liberated from ecclesial practice. God is neither heterosexist nor homophobic. Feminist critics have challenged patriarchal constructions of God: "If God is male, then the male is God."[2] Feminist critics have introduced the image of the Goddess to show that "traditional language for God is not non-sexual; on the contrary, it is male."[3] Sexuality, God, and power have formed a trinity of social truth: Male Sexuality, Male God, and Male Power.

Mary Daly angrily protests the oppression of male trinitarian models of God:

> "The Processions of the Divine Persons" is the most sensational one-act play of the centuries, the original *Love Story*, performed by the Supreme All Male Cast. Here we have the epitome of male bonding. . . . It is "sublime" (and therefore disguised) erotic male homosexual *mythos*, the perfect all-male marriage, the ideal all-male family, the best boys' club, the model monastery, the supreme Men's Association, the mold for all varieties of male monogender mating.[4]

Mary Daly rightly asserts that a feminist theism moves beyond classical male notions of fixity of being. She proposes that God be re-envisioned in process terms as "Be-ing," a verb rather than a noun.[5] What is lacking in Daly's model is the passion for struggle. Rather, it is a passion for separation. Her anger at traditional theistic models and practices leads to woman-identified separatist practices, not to active struggle for social change. Her transgressive practice is her separatist creation of a woman-identified space. "Womanspace" challenges heterosexist deployments of power relations by its sociopolitical independence. It is an exile space similar to gay/lesbian marginalization. "Womanspace" is separatist but not transgressive enough. It needs to lessen its otherworldly tendencies and replace those tendencies with this-worldly political practice of struggle, challenge, transgression, and confrontation. "Womanspace" needs to engage heterosexist power relations not by escaping heterosexist space but challenging it. Daly needs to create "womanspace" within heterosexist deployments of power relations so that "womanspace" becomes the revolutionary practice of nonviolent fighting, critical engagement, the refusal to be invisible, and the overthrow of heterosexist power relations.

Recent trends within feminist theology have moved beyond Daly by recognizing this need to incorporate human resistance and struggle into understanding God. Daly's reconstruction of religion is too Catholic in its leap into "otherworldly Womanspace."[6] This-worldly feminist practice attempts to transform the apathetic theistic metaphors of God into socially involved and erotic metaphors of God.[7] Sallie McFague speaks of the erotic involvement of God as lover: "We speak of God as love but are afraid to call God lover. But a God who relates to all that is, not distantly and bloodlessly, but intimately and passionately, is appropriately called lover."[8] God is opened to the erotic power of human action.

Like feminist critics, the queer battle for truth includes the liberation of the Liberator, the Justice-Doer, the Lover. God has been used as a heterosexist and homophobic weapon to repress women, gay men and lesbian women, and other minorities. The apathetic God has rendered them socially and politically invisible. However, the biblical God does not sustain the current political order or the deployment of homophobic/heterosexist power relations. God is neither a homophobic oppressor nor an ecclesial super-ego, constraining us from integrating our own gay/lesbian sexual identities. This imaging God as passionless is ecclesial idolatry.[9] It is biblical heterosexism and homophobia that culturally constructs God as apathetic, failing to understand the Hebrew theological statement that we, female and male, lesbian and gay, bisexual, transsexual, and heterosexual, were created in the image of God. The biblical God is a God of erotic and human diversity.[10]

The Hebrew and Christian Scriptures are clear that God chooses those who have been made to feel powerless or like outcasts. God is passionately involved; God is socially in the midst of human practices for liberation and conflict. What is at the heart of the many parenting or nurturing images of God in the Hebrew Scriptures is God's compassion. God turns to the weak in solidarity. God rescues from Egypt a band of Hebrew slaves who had been excluded from the Egyptian social system and forms them into a community that was defined by justice and compassion. God gives the Hebrews a new self-worth defined by their imitation of God's justice and compassion. God's irruption into human society is liberative and conflictive. This theme carries on into the Christian Scriptures. Jesus' message and practice of the *basileia* constructs God's social presence. For Jesus, God is not neutral to the oppressed. In fact, God is passionately partial, choosing the oppressed, the weak, and the powerless. God is actively working within their struggles for liberation.

God was conceived as love (*agape*) by Augustine and later Christian theologians. It was the love of the "unmoved mover," the "gracious absolute monarch," and "the gracious father." Implicit in this notion is God's generalized reciprocity, the parental loving without expecting any return. It was this spiritualized love around which the Christian technology of the perfected self was ideally and socially constructed. Love was disembodied, losing an important aspect of its symbology.

The notion of love (*agape*) was one-sided, abstract, and passionless. It lacked the dimension of erotic love and friendship. It legitimized an eclipsed notion of male sexuality and male heterosexist power. Yet God is *eros* as well as *agape*. McFague suggests that both erotic passion (*eros*) and friendship (*philia*) be introduced into the conceptual model of divine love that gives with no thought of return (*agape*). Her suggestion forms a corrective to the one-dimensional model of divine love. Divine love cannot be reduced to the erotic, nor can it exist apart from it. *Agape, eros,* and *philia* are unified in love and are part of God's relating to us.[11] To eclipse one aspect of love in God is to eclipse the image of God.

Queer Christians refuse to leave Jesus the Christ, the Bible, and the social practices of church under ecclesial fundamentalistic control. Queer theological practice refuses to leave God in the hands of the homophobic or misogynistic power class of clerics. God belongs neither to the privileged nor to heterosexist or homophobic power relations. God belongs to the powerless and the sexually oppressed in need of liberation. God is neither abstract nor male nor apathetic. Gay/lesbian sexual liberation and the liberation of God from heterosexism/homophobia are intimately interconnected. Queer practice battles for the liberation of God when gay men and lesbians battle for their sexuality as life-affirming and life-giving. The more self-affirming they are of their sexual praxis, the more they need to re-vision God as erotic power and as companionship. At stake now is God's eroticism and their own eroticism.

Re-Visioning God as Erotic Power

Important contributions to sexual theological discourse have been made by people in the feminist and the gay/lesbian movements.[12] Their analyses of sexual oppression have underscored the need for sexual liberation and open discussion of the erotic. Being spiritual does not consist in eliminating the erotic. Pleasureless sex operates out of an Augustinian dualism and an eclipsed notion of God. The reintroduction of eroticism and pleasure into the discourse of sexuality leads to a profound change in the discourse about God.

Human sexuality is part of the human experience of God.[13] Sexuality and God are directly related. An eclipsed view of sexuality leads to an eclipsed concept of God as apathetic. Queer and feminist theologians need to reenvision human sexuality, its love-making capabilities, its erotic potentialities, its pleasure, and its connectedness to the world. As queer and feminist critics begin to reexperience and reenvision their own sexuality, they may reenvision God. The liberation of human sexuality and the liberation of our God are interconnected.

For queer Christians, sexual liberation is neither about promiscuity nor about monogamy. Sexual liberation is about the cultural, social, and political liberation of desire from oppression. Sex is our most basic physical symbol for human unity, interrelatedness, and community. Like speech acts, sexuality is a form of physiological human interaction. Like speech acts, it also conveys meanings that are socially constructed and communicated. Human sexuality embodies all sorts of personal, social, and culturally constructed meanings. Gay men and lesbians embody sexual communication, and they give expression to sexual meaning or truth in their interactions. Sexuality is the means for harnessing human erotic energies, pleasures, the desire for union, and the communication that produces sexual truth.[14] Sexuality is a definitive mode of human truth. Sexuality is the language of intimate communication. It includes genital expression but also includes sensuality, pleasure, tenderness, and intimacy. It is integrative, creative, life affirming, mutual, and loving.

Sex is a process of making erotic connections. Gay and lesbian lovers produce an abundance of pleasure (as opposed to the scarcity of pleasure in the ascetic construction of the self). This pleasure has been opposed by homophobic/heterosexist discourse. Nevertheless, our sexual liberation is not merely freedom from heterosexist and homophobic deployments of power relations. It is also the freedom of lesbian women and gay men for sexual and pleasurable/passionate interrelatedness with lover, with gay/lesbian community, and with society and planet: "The pleasure of sex is in its capacity to enhance sensuality; the full-body orgasm feels good because it increases a sense of well-being, of integrated bodily integrity. The pleasure in making love comes from experiencing one's own sensuous empowerment while being present to that of one's lover."[15]

Though pleasure producing, our eroticism is not self-indulgent. It is a way of being open to life. Our sexual liberation affirms gay/lesbian sexuality as God's creative design for sexual creatures. Erotic power is about inclusive love-making and justice-doing. Erotic power opens queer lovers beyond themselves to a network of erotic relatedness and embodied interactions.

Feminists have used the notion of erotic power as a form of feminist power/truth.[16] In the first place, eros is not lust: "Eros is power and love."[17] It stands in contrast to the patriarchal usage of *agape,* which is a-pathetic (without passion) and rational. The erotic is the human ability to feel passion in relatedness; it seeks wholeness through interconnectedness: "Erotic power is the power of primal relatedness."[18] It is nondualistic relational power; it is shared power or mutually generative relational power. This erotic power is a lesbian/gay "fecundity."[19] It involves the whole person in mutual relatedness, self-awareness, openness, vulnerability, and caring. Rita Nakashima Brock poetically describes it as creating and connecting hearts.[20] Eros is the power of embodied connectedness. Eros is "passionate attraction to the valuable and a desire to be united with it."[21] In contrast to homophobic and heterosexist power relations, erotic power is inclusive, mutually produced and shared. It is "love as the power to act-each-other-into-well-being."[22] It is the energy that empowers queers to affirm themselves in the face of an antierotic society.

The erotic is gay/lesbian embodied selves yearning for mutuality. The erotic represents the most intense connectedness of lesbian women and gay men with the world, and it can embody their most intense experience of connectedness to God.[23] It is their capacity to make love, make connections of mutuality with other people and with God, and to do justice. It opens them to loving with no thought of a return and friendship: "To speak of the erotic or of God is to speak of power in right relation."[24] God's erotic power is embedded within gay/lesbian passion for connectedness. God is the power of their mutual relatedness. It is a shared power that nurtures love-making, fosters justice doing, embodies relationality, and stages transgressive actions. It is coempowering passion. In imaging God as "mother," "lover," and "friend," we make connections to the practices of love-making and justice-doing.[25] God's erotic love empowers queer love-making and justice-doing. It is the creative source of change and transformation. Queer love-making coempowers God's presence in the world; God's presence is found in queer justice-doing.

Implicit in this model of God as lover is the notion that "God needs." It has been difficult for patriarchal Christianity to perceive an absolutely perfect God needing anything or anyone. However, an absolutely perfect God is too constraining and too abstract a social construct for the biblical God: "The model of God as lover, then, implies that God needs us to help save the world."[26] God as lover passionately needs us to help make whole the entire beloved cosmos, including gay and lesbian selves.

The denial of erotic passion removes Christians from God, and it removes them from justice-doing. There is a strong correlation between despising the body and apathy:

> Many religious people still learn to fear, despise, trivialize, and be ashamed of their bodies. But if we do not know the good news of God in our bodies, we may never know it. When we find bodily life an embarrassment to so-called high-minded spiritualized religion, we lose our capacity for passionate caring and justice. We lose the sense of the holiness of bodies of starving children and the bodies of women and men torn by violence and torture.[27]

The feminist and the queer reclamation of the erotic as a moral good opens queer Christians to the revelation of God's own passion for connectedness. It opens them to God's love and justice. Their passionate reclamation of love-making as the basis for their justice-doing moves closer to a reclamation of the biblical God who is passionate for justice.

Love-making and justice-doing are interdependent responses to God's call to *basileia* practice. Love-making is the practice of solidarity, compassionate identification (*hesed*) with the sexually powerless and oppressed (*anawim*). Love-making connects queer Christians to their lesbian sisters and gay brothers. Together they make love by building up mutual and egalitarian relations, minimizing the distortions of social deployments of dominant and abusive power relations. They live in solidarity with one another's sufferings, struggles, and hopes. Justice-doing becomes the social shape and form of their love-making. Love-making and justice-doing practice God's coming reign, the central political event for which Jesus preached, lived, and died.

God is neither male nor female, but God is not androgynous. God has erotic capacities to create, make connections, and do justice. The erotic element in God is creativity, the dynamic capacity for union and community. God is the erotic power of sexuality, embodied interrelatedness. God is transgenderal and panerotic. The biblical God is not characterized by apathy but by erotic passion for the oppressed. The biblical God manifests a preferential option for the powerless and the poor (*anawim*).

Only within Christian constructions of God influenced by Greco-Roman philosophy do we find an apathetic God, a God without erotic power, a God lacking the social dynamism for change, a God who ratifies misogyny and homophobia. God has too long been constructed as heterosexist dominating power; it is power without passion, power without a heart or without erotic connectedness. An apathetic, dominating God is conceived within a discursive field of sexual dualism, a practice having a long history in Christianity. It formed binary constructions of logos/eros, good/evil, light/dark, rational/passionate, spirit/body, male/female, and subject/object. Sexual dualism alienates; it breaks mutual connectedness through its polarized categories. Sexual dualism distorts love-making; it breaks queer connectedness by producing conceptual and lived dualities that are arranged in asymmetric patterns of dominating power.[28]

The creation of asymmetric and dualist sexual power relations has shaped homophobic/misogynistic understandings of sexuality, social reality, and nature. Domination becomes the displaced focus of alienated erotic power; it connects gay men and lesbians to an alienated social reality and nature through patterns of power domination. Dominion over social reality and control of the earth have become violent ritual productions of power/truth. They have led to the domination and rape of planet Earth. Culture is construed as the polar opposite of nature; culture needs to control and dominate nature. Eclipsed models of God have led to the dominating nature in the name of the patriarchal God. McFague suggests that God's "universal parenthood cannot be limited to our species and to birth. To limit it to our species displays the anthropocentric focus that fails to appreciate the interdependence and interrelatedness of levels of life. . . . The other direction in which we must universalize parenthood is in extending it beyond birth and an attention to basic nurture, to an attention to the entire well-being of our successors."[29]

Queer Christians must also re-envision themselves as God's lovers and discover a love relation with other species and with the universe itself.[30] They need to become partners in their world with other species and learn to relate to them as friends and lovers. They have to stop acting like abused children repeating cycles of abuse upon nature. McFague suggests re-envisioning nature as God's body, as a lover's body. This begins to correct the patriarchal perspective of dominating and subduing creation.

Just as queers and feminists are freeing themselves from gender politics and its rigid polarizations, so the social constructions of God need to be freed from the gender politics. As new forms of relating between men and women are created, gay men and lesbians can reenvision

God anew without the idolatrous restrictions of gender politics. They restore balance to their constructions of God when they envision God in fluid gender ascriptions and in transgenderal images. Queer theological language about God becomes dimorphic, inclusive, and non-hierarchical. God becomes God/dess. To restore eros into the image of God affirms those who have been marginalized because of their gender or because of their sexual identity.

God is experienced by feminist and lesbian/gay Christians in the movement toward sexual liberation. It is a "shift from understanding salvation as anti-sexual to knowing that there is sexual salvation."[31] God's erotic power transcends the biological determinisms, the cultural constructions, and the power relations that shape the cultural understanding and experience of sexuality. Lesbians and gay men break the tyranny of heterosexism and homophobia with their shared erotic power. God is reconceptualized and experienced as the shared erotic power that liberates lesbians and gay men from sexual alienation, homophobic oppression, gender domination, closetedness, oppression sickness, and abusive violence.

God's erotic power bursts forth on Easter into connectedness or solidarity with the once-dead and now-risen Jesus. God's erotic power is revealed as a shared power with Jesus. In turn, Jesus the Christ becomes the sign of God's erotic power, breaking the linkages of erotic desire and inequality, and Easter becomes the mutual event of heart-connectedness.[32] God and Jesus become mutually connected in solidarity and justice. Jesus becomes the Christa for feminist Christians and the Queer Christ for queer Christians. On Easter, God's erotic power in Jesus is revealed as mutually creative, generative, and liberating. It is the full embodiment of God's love for Jesus and for us. It becomes God's love-making and justice-doing. Easter is the event of mutuality, relational power in the practice of justice and solidarity.

For queer Christians, erotic power is God's empowering way of acting in the world. It is God's way of saying that they are graced as lesbian women and gay men. It affirms their sexual and affectional relatedness as the creative design of God. Sexuality is the practice in which God's erotic power may be embodied, in which queer Christians find connectedness with each other, the oppressed, nature, and God.[33] All ecclesial attempts to change gay/lesbian sexual identities to heterosexual or demand that queers practice celibacy disembody them as human beings.[34] Whatever powerful discursive practices distort the embodied erotic relations of gay men and lesbians, these practices dehumanize and diminish their humanity. By such distortions of gay/lesbian sexuality, the churches neutralize God's erotic power or liberating Spirit in the world; they replace embodied yearning for shared erotic power with necrophilic obsession. They stamp out pleasure; they contain, censor, and repress the erotic. Their demand for celibacy becomes a demand to escape the reality and power of human sexuality. The churches contain and block gay men and lesbians from moving toward mutuality, the interrelatedness of love-making and justice-doing: "Mutuality is the process by which we create and liberate one another."[35] It is the process by which queer Christians liberate one another for the cause of liberation; it is the process by which they experience a glimpse of sexual salvation.

God promises sexual liberation and salvation. Gay men and lesbians name God as the coempowering ground of their erotic practice and spirituality. God is in the midst of their love-making and their justice struggles. God is the heart of gay/lesbian liberation. God is at the heart of their political uprising. God awakens them from the slumbers of apathetic sleep to passionate uprising. God is the eros that connects their sexual love-making to an ecology of love-making and the practice of justice-doing. They are connected in solidarity to other people who are oppressed, and they are connected to a world whose ecology is threatened with domination, exploitation, and destruction.[36] God is the heart of queer erotic insurrection, their transgressive practice of love-making and justice-doing. God is the liberating activity of interrelatedness that will actualize their sexual freedom through the oppression, violence, and the struggle. They live in mutual and sexual relatedness with God and with one another. Erotic power within sexuality becomes the embodied expression of God's love-making and justice-doing. Erotic power becomes an immanent force for political change.

God Coempowers Solidarity and Justice

God's love-making is solidarity with the sexual oppressed. It is embodied or made flesh in justice-doing. Queer theology proclaims that God is in solidarity with queer struggles and their project of sexual liberation. Queer praxis of God's reign is committed to reclaiming Jesus as Liberator of their sexual freedom, retrieving the Bible as an empowering resource for the proclamation of a queer biblical truth, and organizing themselves into base communities to effect political change. These base communities become social groups for focused change and political liberation, critically engaging the social conditions of homophobic/heterosexist oppression and suffering and actualizing freedom. They struggle and battle for sexual justice. They deliberately transgress the social icons of heterosexism.

The practice of God's reign actualizes Jesus' message that God is socially in the midst of the queer struggle for sexual liberation. God has vacated oppressive ecclesial social practices and is there in solidarity with their sexual dissidence. This is the power of erotic struggles for liberation. God is with gay men and lesbians in their love-making and justice-doing. God is there in resistance to and protest against homophobic oppression. God was there in ACT UP's demonstration within St. Patrick's Cathedral. God was with the protesters, stepped upon by the processing clergy and arrested and tried for criminal trespassing and civil disturbance.

Jesus practiced the mutuality of God's reign. He lived God's erotic power in his solidarity with the oppressed, his waging conflict and staging transgressive actions against the oppressive infrastructure of first-century C.E. Palestine. Jesus embodied love-making and justice-doing in his *basileia* practices. Jesus became the Christ, the erotic embodiment of God's power. It was God's sign of shared power, God's sign of keeping the future open for liberation.[37]

What Easter communicates is that God is passionately on the side of gay and lesbian people. The practical implications for the social and cultural change effected by Jesus' praxis of God's coming reign cannot be ignored. Easter is the ultimate social and cultural change, the final sexual liberation. Gods stands against the negative sexual values that oppress people. Easter reveals that God's praxis is grounded in the transformation of human society, the liberation of gay and lesbian oppressed (and all others who are oppressed) from political domination and human suffering. God socially configures liberation and freedom through shared erotic power.

Through his *basileia* activity, Jesus became the Christ, the social symbol of God's solidarity with the sexually oppressed and their liberative praxis. As the queer Christ, Jesus continues to confront, redirect, transgress, and transform the social reality of heterosexism. His praxis and death became God's liberative praxis for us. As the queer Christ, Jesus becomes the symbol of God's promise for social and political change. Jesus stands as God's queer solidarity with lesbians and gay men.

God embodies shared power in love-making and justice-doing. Love between women and love between men embodies the capacity for shared erotic power, which is sacramentalized within queer Christian base communities. As forms of intense interpersonal reaching out, they embody the capacity to live in solidarity with one another and solidarity with the oppressed. Loving in solidarity begins gay/lesbian social action directed toward the doing of justice. For queer Christians, it provides an incentive for insurrection against homophobic oppression. It means that they recognize God's liberating power of love-making and justice-doing within their social practice of liberation and struggle. God will not liberate gay men and lesbians without their participation, their resistance, and their staging direct actions to actualize freedom. Their insurrection against oppression is a sharing of God's erotic power against oppression. They cocreate justice with God.

"No Excluded Ones"[38]

Queer liberation is a thoroughly erotic liberation. It is an erotic liberation from unjust homophobic deployments of power relations. The change that is sought is not just the recognition of queer civil rights or ecclesial recognition of queers as a graced people. What queer Christians seek is a totally egalitarian restructuring of social and cultural deployments of power. It means a radical change in how society experiences, practices, and re-visions gay/lesbian sexuality and sexuality in general. It is sexuality without gender inequalities, violence, and abuse. It is shared erotic power for love-making and justice-doing. Gay/lesbian sexual liberation models a new practice and re-visioning of God. Queer and feminist Christians have a long way to go to correct the sex-negative models of God. As their understanding of human sexuality and God changes, they begin to create an alternative space within society, a new culture within a global network. It provides a means for social and cultural change.

Gay men and lesbians produce an alternative social space between the rigid gender politics of masculine/feminine where they can explore, create, and envision new ways of mutual relating. It is an exile space where they live out sexual dissidence, where they can explore gay-affirming and lesbian-affirming sexuality, where they can make connections for love and for justice, and where they can stage transgressive actions against homophobia/heterosexism. This is the social space where they can make connections for the project of human liberation, what Christians term as God's reign.

Gay/lesbian erotic liberation is not finished with the achievement of their civil rights, ecclesial repentance and recognition, or the end of heterosexist/homophobic social practices. Their liberation is erotically interrelated to the liberation of all the oppressed and the integrity of creation. God is active in gay/lesbian struggles for liberation: "God is clearly with us in our struggles to act, to seek justice, and to effect liberation. Our *a priori* acceptance by God means we have the capacity and responsibility to act justly with and for one another and to demand social justice not only for ourselves but for all persons threatened by heterosexist hierarchies of power."[39]

God is present in the suffering of the poor and the powerless, and gay/lesbian liberated practice is lived in solidarity with the oppressed and the powerless. God is also present in the oppression of nature, and gay/lesbian liberated practice also needs to extend their solidarity to God's body.[40]

What queer liberated practice needs is to link the experience of homophobia with the experiences of other oppressed groups and with oppressed nature. We as queer Christians need to expand our horizons of liberation and provide energy and commitment to the project of human liberation. One effective means of expansion is coalition building with other gay/lesbian justice groups and other non-gay/lesbian groups struggling against oppression. As Foucault aptly points out, power relations coexist within a network of other power relations.[41] The oppression of one group is linked to the oppression and exclusion of other groups. For queer Christian love-making and justice-doing form the base for making creative connections with other social groups. Coalition building, for instance, connects the gay/lesbian movement with the feminist movement. As queers make connections to other groups, they form an ever-expanding global network for change; they take up multiagenda justice issues as their own.

There is a need for a worldly spirituality that makes global connections interdependent. This is appropriate to queer Christians and their project for liberation:

> A worldly spirituality, one born of affirmation and love of the real, tangible cosmos and of our shared humanity within the created world, is possible, but only if it is based on the presupposition that love of neighbor and love of God are coterminous. Any invocation of God to perpetuate injustice, any uncritical respect for the givenness and "authority" of existing social relations of domination, perpetuates

alienated religion. A spirituality motivated by caring and respect for our relation to God, to each other, and to the cosmos depends on our participation in emancipatory history. To love God is to love that concrete power that, through us and the cosmos (always reciprocally) transforms nature, history, society, and human personal life toward community, toward relations of mutual respect. God is personal because God is richly related to all that is, and so must we.[42]

Queer Christian practice means living in solidarity with the social world and with nature. It means affirming plurality and diversity within the social world. It means resisting the dualistic dominations that lead to deforestation, desertification, or high-risk technologies and socioeconomic practices that render a natural region unfit for habitation of plant, animal, or human life. It means resisting the domination of Christianity over other religious traditions. Queer Christian practice is open to making affirming connections with other traditions, their embodied practices of making love and doing justice.

Queer Christians cannot exclude the oppressed from their own practices for liberation. Otherwise, their resistance from the margins is doomed to replicate the social strategies, structures, and value systems of their oppressors. We need to practice solidarity to keep us from repeating the cycles of oppression.Love-making is lived in solidarity, and justice-doing is practiced in anticipation of its fullness. The practice of God's reign is the deprivatization of gay/lesbian erotic power. It makes public our erotic power. Our queer Christian praxis cannot be confined to the closet. Our queer practice and spirituality are radically inclusive, political, social, and ecological. They are oriented toward fundamental social, political, ecological and inclusive change. Queer Christian praxis becomes politically aware, that is, politically and socially conscious of the perspective of the sexual outsider. It expands that awareness of sexual oppression to others who are suffering, exploited, poor, and neglected. The perspective of the sexual outsider includes exploited, dominated, and ravaged nature.[43]

"The Personal Is Political"

A queer theology of liberation is not a private or individual affair. It is not concerned solely with the personal values of private life that promote harmony in interpersonal relations or the personal relations within one's social network. It is not concerned solely with the transformation of the interior life or the development of the spiritual life. In such privatized faith practices, the political, social, and ecological dimensions of human life are left critically unexamined. Privatized faith is the practice of the apathetic God of homophobic/misogynist theology. It is noninvolved practice; it avoids real human pain and suffering. It denies the reality of Jesus' crucifixion and God's passionate uprising against all forms of political, social, and ecological oppression. Human situations of suffering and pain resulting from asymmetrical power relations are not fully felt within private introspective activity. Ecological suffering is ignored as long as it does not affect the development of our own, introspective spiritual lives. This form of religious experience confined to the private and the personal sphere of life is not *basileia* praxis. It is neither love-making nor justice-doing. We as queer Christians must recognize our complicity in compulsory heterosexism and actively change such violent oppression.

Queer Christian sexual liberation is public faith practice. It is the erotic power of love-making and justice-doing set free in the world. Our queer Christian anger and rage are no longer internalized, impeding mutual connectedness. Rather, anger and rage energize queers, queer Christians, and other Christians to mutual connectedness and actions for justice. They are sharpened in their connectedness to their own suffering and in their lived solidarity with other oppressed groups and oppressed nature. Their anger becomes transforming and integrative in justice-doing; it does not withdraw into an apathetic otherworldliness.

Queer faith practices embody erotic power, concrete actions of justice-doing. Queer prayers and liturgies celebrate our embodied erotic power as gift. Our prayers and liturgies are continuously involved in celebrating and making connections. Queer contemplation becomes *basileia* action, discovering our erotic connectedness to the oppressed and the excluded. Our contemplation becomes *basileia* action working for political, social, and ecological change. Our practice of God's reign aims to bring an end to the terror and tragedy of crucifixion—the billions of crucifixions in the world.

Queer Christian political and sexual liberation will not be won when we have become free from homophobic and heterosexist oppression. How can we as gay men and lesbian women be free with millions of homeless in our own country? How can we be free when thirty-three million people in our own country live below the poverty line? How can we be free when fifteen thousand people starve to death each day? How can we be free in a global society where the gulf between rich and poor nations only increases? How can we be free when massive planetary deforestation leads to environmental disaster? How can we be free when God's body is crucified with toxic pollution? We as Christian gay men and lesbian women will not be free until all are free: oppressors, oppressed, and the environment. "No one excluded" is the cry of our queer Christian love-making, and our queer Christian practice is justice for all.

8

Prophetic Queers: ACT UP, FIGHT BACK

Jerry Falwell, Pat Robertson, cardinals O'Connor and Law, and other ecclesial leaders have been in the forefront of the struggle against gay/lesbian civil rights. Jerry Falwell has announced a national battle plan to fight gay/lesbian civil rights. The religious Right is organized to restore traditional family values to American society. The Vatican has instructed American Catholic bishops to oppose lesbian/gay civil rights and promote public discrimination of open gay men and lesbians. Many churches continue to deny and forbid the ordinations of lesbians and gay men who are public about their sexual preference. These churches also continue to refuse to bless same-sex unions. Institutional Christianity blesses, sanctions, and actively promotes systemic violence against gay men and lesbians. Incidences of gay/lesbian bashing find legitimacy in ecclesial hatred. These churches also perpetuate sex-negative statements about lesbians and gay men.

Queer anger is a holy anger. It is time to be angry, to follow Jesus' lead in his Stop the Temple action. Jesus' anger at the Temple's oppression expressed itself in a public demonstration that led to his crucifixion. He violated sacred space because those in charge of the Temple violated God's justice for the undesirables, the outcasts, and the poor. Queer Christians need to follow the lead of ACT UP and Queer Nation in their Stop the Church actions. ACT UP and Queer Nation are more faithful to the gospel of justice than most churches. When queer protesters stage die-ins on the steps of cathedrals, they ritualize the death of the queer Christ. Street theater has become an effective expression of queer anger and the queer thirst for justice. Camp and parody, chants and visibility, street theater and angry protests are techniques that are used to voice the demand for justice.

Queer Christians need to follow in the steps of Jesus, ACT UP, and Queer Nation. They need to act up against the churches and stop the hatred. Queers need to stop the churches before the churches stop queers. It is a life-and-death struggle. Gay men and lesbians are dying and suffering at the hands of fundamentalist Christians in the name of Christ. They are denied their civil rights in the name of national campaigns to restore traditional family values. They are discriminated against in employment, housing, the legal system, foster care, and so forth. Just as the churches are bringing their campaign of hatred into politics, so queer Christians must bring the battle for truth back to the churches.

When a priest or minister gets up in the pulpit and condemns queers, queer Christians need to stand up and demand gospel justice. It is just and right to blow whistles during homophobic homilies. It is appropriate to bring the battle for queer truth into the churches, into the pews, and to the altars. The battle against church hatred requires a commitment to justice. Queer Christians need to intensify their presence within the churches. Invisibility harms the gay/lesbian movement and ignores Jesus' practice of justice-doing. Closeted gay/lesbian Christians and clergy need to come out. It is only by coming out and by affirming the goodness of our sexual diversity that we can change the churches. Many clergy who followed in the footsteps of the queer Christ have suffered exclusion, silencing, and discrimination. Gay/lesbian Christians need to support clergy who come out publicly.

Those gay/lesbian Christians who choose to assimilate within homophobic churches and who remain silent in the face of systemic homophobic violence have betrayed their own as Judas betrayed Jesus the queer Christ. They have not stopped the hatred but continue to crucify gay men and lesbians. Assimilationist gay/lesbian Christians may keep open the dialogue with the churches on gay/lesbian and justice issues. However, they need to speak up in order to maintain a dialogue of justice within the churches. They also need to continue to support the activist queer Christians who bring the battle into the churches themselves.

It is time for queer Christians to act up against the churches and put a stop to their hate campaigns. Queer Christians practice the dissident grace of the Hebrew prophets and Jesus himself. The Hebrew prophets challenged Temple aristocracy and kings for their injustice against the poor (*anawim*). Queer prophets, likewise, challenge Christian leaders for their hate campaigns and promotion of discrimination against gay men and lesbians. Queer activist Christians perform prophetic actions and speak prophetic words. Often their irreverence for sacred space manifests a deeper reverence for God's justice.

Clergy, bishops, and televangelists need to be zapped with questions and challenges. Alternative points of view need to be presented. Kiss-ins, marches, vigils, queer messianic street theater, and visibility actions at liturgical services are appropriate means to act up against the churches. A "Silence = Death" or Queer Nation T-shirt worn to a service raises consciousness and visibility within the congregation. Queer Nation/St. Louis went out "Queermas Caroling" at Christmas, targeting the Catholic cathedral rectory and the archbishop's residence. Traditional Christmas carols were transformed into justice lyrics. It was a small reminder that we are here and that the Catholic church needs to deal with us. Nailing queer demands on church doors follows the good Protestant precedent of Martin Luther. Blessing gay and lesbian unions on the steps of the churches communicates our nonacceptance. It asserts that our loving relationships can also be covenants of grace. Nonviolent civil disobedience is necessary to communicate the seriousness of the homophobic hatred of the churches. Chaining ourselves to the pews, releasing helium-filled condoms inside churches, stickering missals with activist demands, sit-ins and chants during services, and other church events remind Christian leaders and Christian community that they are guilty of crucifying queers.

Many churches are in the grip of religious fundamentalism or literalism. They cannot accept difference; they cannot accept sexual diversity. They cannot accept women as equals. Their theologies and practices are inherently intolerant and hateful. Part of a queer theology is to challenge and discredit heterosexist/homophobic constructions of Christianity and replace such constructions with our own queer constructions. It requires visible presence and articulate voices in universities, colleges, seminaries, and professional associations. The gay/lesbian caucuses in the American Academy of Religion are a beginning. Queer theologians need to reenvision Christianity without misogyny, heterosexism, and homophobia.

Finally, it is our marginality or outsider status as queers that links us to Jesus' practice of God's reign. It is our strength and our grace. Our marginality links us to the marginal and oppressed people of the world. The dissident grace of Jesus can be reclaimed by ourselves in our own sexual dissidence, difference, and political struggles. Jesus' dissident actions in the Temple provide us with a story of resistance and struggle against systemic religious/political oppression of the aristocratic priesthood of the Temple and Roman domination. His struggle was lethal. He was executed for his dissident Stop the Temple action, and the Jewish religious leadership and the Romans seemingly won. But God had the final word and raised up Jesus as the queer Christ, a symbol of dissidence and hope for all queers. Queer dissidence can follow in the footsteps of the queer Christ; they can Stop the Church. Like Jesus, queer Christians can: ACT UP! FIGHT BACK! END HATE!

Michel Foucault: Genealogical Critique

Michel Foucault was a gay French social critic and poststructuralist philosopher. He died of HIV complications in 1984. Most commentators and critics of Foucault remain silent about his gay orientation and his death through HIV complications.[1] Nevertheless, Foucault has been popular in gay and lesbian academic circles for some time. He stood as a socially transgressive critic of culture, its discourse and practices, and its institutional effects. I use Foucault's method of social analysis for two particular reasons. In the first place, his method proceeds from a sociological perspective of conflict and provides a critical grid for analyzing social relations of conflict, power, and domination. New postmodern trends in feminist social analysis of heterosexism and the oppression of women have successfully begun to use Foucault's genealogical critique. The second reason is that Foucault as our gay brother provides us with the critical tools for analyzing heterosexist/homophobic discourse and practice and for constructing a gay and lesbian theological discourse rooted in our own practice. In the process, I hope to reclaim Foucault as part of our gay and lesbian cultural heritage and end the general academic silence about a great gay social critic and thinker.

For Foucault, practice is whatever we do socially. It includes all thinking and communication. Discourse is a human practice. It refers to ideas, specific texts, or theoretical systems. In other words, it is language practiced within a social context. It is formed within the purview of nondiscursive practice. Discourse and practice are closely related to each other. The formation of discourse takes place within the generative matrix of individual and institutional practices, their particular historical situations, and their conflicts and struggles. Discursive practice has particular effects upon the individual and upon society. It determines what we socially experience, perceive, and think.

This means that all forms of discourse are susceptible to social analysis in relation to practice. They are thoroughly context dependent or practice dependent. For Foucault, nondiscursive practices are historical actions that are diffused within individual, social, and institutional actions. Nondiscursive practices include economic strategies, political regulations, institutions, social systems, and cultural mechanisms. Both discursive and nondiscursive practices have a political dimension; they are tactical applications of knowledge.[2] They produce specific effects within mutually generative social fields of competing and conflicting agencies, their discourse, their practices, and their social institutions.

I will explore three other interlocking constellations of Foucault's social analysis: (1) his genealogical method and the "insurrection of subjugated knowledges"; (2) the social grid of knowledge/power in the production of truth; (3) the social construction of sexuality. These three constellations are worked out in his *Power/Knowledge, Discipline and Punish,* and *History of Sexuality,* volume 1. They provide the means for a critique of power relations as they are deployed within discourse/practice.

"The Insurrection of Subjugated Knowledges"

In the early seventies, Foucault made a decisive shift in his method of studying social practices. He began to focus on a genealogical method. Genealogy refers to the "union of erudite and local memories which allows us to establish a historical knowledge of struggles and to make use of this knowledge tactically today."[3] Genealogical method is directed toward activating memories of conflict within contemporary struggle. It brings to the surface what has been excluded from truth claims.

Foucault's genealogical method aims to surface what he calls the "insurrection of subjugated knowledges." By "subjugated knowledges," Foucault has in mind two sets of socially constructed forms of knowledge. In the first instance, subjugated knowledges are the historical contents of discourse that have been buried or disguised within a functionalist coherence or formal systematization. Subjugated knowledges are the historical conflictive contents of discourse that are lost in universalist frameworks or systematizing thought. Such discourse encompasses histories of events and practices. The resistances, struggles, and dominations in events and practices are glossed over or are lost within theoretical frameworks, or they are subsumed into a universal theory. In the second instance, subjugated knowledges are knowledges that are dismissed as lowly, inadequate, irrelevant, or aberrant. They include popular knowledge, which is both regional and marginal and may be disqualified because it is gay, lesbian, or feminist. Various forms of resistance are located within subjugated knowledges.[4]

Foucault's genealogical method tries to explain the present by describing the conflicts and struggles that are papered over in functionalist theories or universal systemizations or confined to the margins of human knowledge. He provides a critique of human attempts at abstraction, reification, and universalization. He correctly understands his genealogical method as thoroughly relativizing discourse and recognizing the perilous production of knowledge. It attempts to deconstruct—that is, reveal the restrictions inherent within—discourse. His method asserts the particularity of discourse, its formation in a context-dependent social matrix, the relativity and fragility of discourse. His method destabilizes discourse by examining what has been excluded, what has been disqualified or has been considered low ranking. For Foucault, subjugated knowledges possess a memory of exclusion, resistance, and struggle in relation to dominant discourse and institutional practices. A genealogical method activates the "dangerous memory" of localized resistance and struggle. It surfaces what has been excluded by discourse.

The theme of subjugated knowledges provides the framework for my articulation of a gay and lesbian theology. In the first instance, my genealogical investigation of subjugated knowledges centers upon the production of homophobic discursive practice in society. Within the horizon of homophobic discursive practice, I include not only all the forms of discourse and practice that are directed at gay and lesbian people but all those forms of universal discursive practice that exclude gay and lesbian people. I include christological discursive practices that have subsumed Jesus into abstract formulations of heterosexist values and ideals. I also include the production of biblical truth as heterosexist truth. My application of genealogical method intends to recover the dangerous memories of Jesus and biblical truth from their captivity within a heterosexist system of discursive practice. Christology is liberated from a pseudouniversal discursive practice and recontextualized to the experience of gay and lesbian people. Likewise, the Bible is rescued from fundamentalism and becomes an empowering resource for gay/lesbian resistance.

The second form of subjugated knowledges is located within the alternative knowledges of gay and lesbian discursive practice. Some alternatives already exist within more than two decades of gay/lesbian writing and activism. Gay and lesbian discursive practice is replete with the vivid memories of resistance to the specific effects of heterosexist power and of struggle against dominant homophobic discourse. Gay and lesbian discourse confronts the oppressive side of heterosexist knowledge and its claims to universality. It exposes a critical alternative that unmasks the claims of universality as specific to the dominant groups within society. It surfaces gay/lesbian social exclusion. Heterosexist discourse is rejected as exclusionary in its universal claims by feminist, lesbian, and gay critics. Gay and lesbian discourse brings the alternative vision of resistance, power, and liberation of an excluded political sexual minority.

Power/Knowledge and the Battle for Truth

As Foucault applied his genealogical method to a variety of social practices, he noticed correlations between power and knowledge in the production of truth. Foucault was not interested in developing a new theory of power. Rather, he focused on a descriptive analysis of particular forms of social resistance and their correlative manifestations of power/knowledge: "Nothing is more material, physical, corporal, than the exercise of power."[5] The goal of power is the management of bodies; it creates docile bodies, controlling human behavior.[6] It is inscribed upon the body and produced in every social interaction. Foucault breaks with the repressive theories of power born from Marxist ideology critique.[7] Within many critiques of ideology, knowledge provides those in power a means of legitimizing their dominant position. A second correlative notion is that a new body of knowledge brings a new group into existence with a different exercise of power.[8] Foucault rethinks the relations between knowledge and power by means of his own genealogical analysis. Power is not organized and structured socially from the top down. It is not merely exercised repressively from a dominant class, competing with other class interests. Rather, power is exercised in a more disguised fashion and in a more complex set of social relationships and operations. Power is positive as well as negative. It produces effects at the level of the body and at the level of knowledge.[9] Thus, language, culture, and society are understood as an open field of interrelations in which power is immanent. Power is everywhere and comes from everywhere.

Power is already socially there, and no one individual remains outside of its reach.[10] Foucault does not conceive it as a property but as a deployment of strategies, maneuvers, techniques, tactics, functions "in a network of relations, constantly in tension, in activity."[11] The multiple relations permeate the depths of society but are "not univocal; they define innumerable points of confrontation, focuses of instability, each of which has its own risks of conflict, of struggles, and of an at least temporary inversion of the power relations."[12] The multiple power relations are the object of unending struggles in which they are strengthened, produced, circulated, transformed, or even reversed.

The operation of power is not centralized but dispersed. It is ubiquitous. It is coextensive with the social body as a network of relations, and the production of power is always relational, strategic, and conflictive: "Where there is power, there is resistance and yet, or rather consequently, this resistance is never in a position of exteriority in relation to power."[13] Where there is a relation of power, there is the possibility of resistance. The exercise of power is conceived by Foucault as a general aspect of discourse and practice—a complex, mobile, and unstable field of interrelations. However, power cannot be limited to the negative forms of prohibition and punishment but takes on multiple productive forms. These productive relations of power are interwoven with other kinds of relations, and their network of interconnections delineates the conditions of domination and oppression and the conditions for social change.

For Foucault, power is immanent in all the social relations, operations, and levels of society.[14] It is diffused in all areas of human knowing and living. Knowledge is not abstract but material and concrete. It is implicated in power. It cannot be separated from the effects of power, nor can power be separated from knowledge. Knowledge is produced through the networklike relations of power, and it, in turn, has effects of power. Power is immanent in every domain of knowledge, organizing all discourses about truth/power. In other words, to know is to use power; it is to use political categories. Knowledge is already embedded in social interpretation; it is a fictive construction guided by the interests of discursive practice. For Foucault, the interpreting subject is embedded in discursive practices.

Foucault's descriptive analysis of the power/knowledge correlation enables him to raise the question of whose knowledge is real or true. He clarifies the "will to truth" as the political production of truth within the social grid of power/knowledge. "Truth is a thing of this world," he claims. It is thoroughly historical and relative to the social conditions that produced it. Foucault defines truth as "the procedure for regulation, production, and distribution of statements" of discourse.[15] Truth claims are made within the generative grid of power/ knowledge, and its claims have effects of power. Truth claims are formed in the struggles and conflicts of power. Thus, Foucault speaks of the "politics of truth" or the "political regime of truth" within society.[16] Each society has a regime of truth with its own particular mechanisms for producing and distributing it. These social mechanisms are the multiple power relations, the interplays of various discursive and nondiscursive fields. The multiplicity of power relations and their effects form an ever-shifting and dynamic field of competing and conflicting mechanisms for the production and the distribution of truth. Thus, Foucault asserts, "There is a battle for truth and around truth."[17] It is a discursive and practical war for truth but also a battle for power.

Each society has its own regime of truth. Repression is real, but it is subordinate to the networklike effects of power. We are subjected to the production of truth through a complex web of power relations within discursive practice:

> There are manifold relations of power which permeate, characterise, and constitute the social body, and these relations of power cannot themselves be established, consolidated, nor implemented without the production, accumulation, and circulation, and functioning of a discourse. There can be no possible exercise of power without a certain economy of discourses of truth which operates through and on the basis of this association. We are subjected to the production of truth through power and we cannot exercise power through the production of truth.[18]

For Foucault, discourse is the material production of truth/power. He defines discourse as a form of power that circulates in the social field. It becomes part of the struggle for power; it is attached to strategies of domination as well as to those of resistance. Discourse has the social effects of power. Discourse may be an instrument of and, at the same time, an effect of power. Foucault writes:

Discourses are not once and for all subservient to power or raised up against it, any more than silences are. We must make allowance for the complex and unstable process whereby discourse can be both an instrument and effect of power, but also a hindrance, a stumbling-block, a point of resistance and a starting point for an opposing strategy. Discourse transmits and produces power; it reinforces it, but also undermines and exposes it, renders it fragile and makes it possible to thwart.[19]

What has been produced in and by discourse can also be a point of resistance. Discourse can be displaced, overthrown, and replaced by other forms of discourse. Foucault states, "We're never trapped by power: it's always possible to modify its hold, in determined conditions and following a precise strategy."[20] The value of discourse is its "production, accumulation, circulation, and functioning" within the network of power relations and social struggle. Power becomes real in the exchange and administration of discourse; it emanates throughout society and its practices.

For gay men and lesbian women, Foucault's genealogical criticism offers an analytical, critical, and strategic framework for understanding the general politics of homophobic truth that has been deployed oppressively against them. It challenges the oppression of homophobic truth by exposing its frailties, instabilities, its failures, and its interlocking exclusions. Genealogical criticism becomes a deconstructive strategy that questions the givenness of homophobic truth. It opens homophobic truth to inherent contradictions within its claims. It can be used to support the specific struggles for gay men and lesbians for liberation.

One of the social effects of homophobic truth is its generation of gay/lesbian resistance. To paraphrase Foucault: Where there is homophobic power there is queer resistance. Queer genealogical criticism is based on the particular social facts of gay/lesbian resistance to the specific effects of homophobic power. Queer critical discourse arises out of gay and lesbian resistance to homophobic oppression and social marginalization. A queer practice of genealogical criticism concentrates on the dominating and exclusionary effects of power in the production and distribution of homophobic truth. Not only does a queer genealogical criticism become a critical practice exposing the dominating and coercive effects of homophobic truth, but it also becomes a critical form of discursive activity whose very practice becomes an exercise of social power. Queer genealogical criticism becomes the practice of its own power, its own production and distribution of truth. It produces its own political regime of truth.

For a queer critical praxis, Foucault's genealogical method offers a strategy for changing society by challenging the homophobic production of and distribution of truth. It understands the operation of homophobic power relations not as centralized but as diffused throughout the network of social relations. This means social change has to be effected within the network of homophobic power relations deployed within our society. Foucault's method offers the path to battle for truth. It points to localized resistance and the production of queer truth claims that challenge the universal claims of homophobic truth. It points to a queer politics of truth that empowers gay men and lesbians to struggle and seek liberation, to realize their human capacity to pour new wine into old wineskins and shatter them. Their "politics of truth" and their "battle for truth" are necessarily innovative, transgressive, and aniconic struggles against the general politics of homophobic truth of our society. They can dismantle homophobic truth only by overthrowing it and replacing it with their discursive truth. It is a battle for and around truth.

The Social Construction of Sexuality

In his *History of Sexuality,* volume 1, Foucault traces the emerging discourse about sexuality as a modern mechanism for organizing knowledge/sexual truth. He observes that modern notions of sexuality have been constructed and deployed within four discursive strategies: (1) a hysterization of women's bodies; (2) a pedagogization of children's sex; (3) a socialization of procreative behavior; and (4) a psychiatrization of perverse pleasure.[21] Foucault noted the power of men over women, parents over their children, the social administrative control over reproductive technology, and psychiatry over the sexually deviant. Sex became a target of social power organized around these four discursive strategies. Sexuality was not repressed; rather, it was produced by power: "Power delineated it, aroused it, and employed it as the proliferating meaning that had always to be taken control of again lest it escape; it was an effect with a meaning-value."[22] As a specific object of knowledge and social control, sexual discourse was produced by relations of power around the above four areas of social concern.

Foucault's thesis is that sexuality was invented as an effect in the spread of power over sex:

> Sexuality must not be thought of as a kind of natural given which power tries to hold in check, or as an obscure domain which knowledge tries to uncover. It is the name that can be given to a historical construct: not a furtive reality that is difficult to grasp, but a great surface network in which the stimulation of bodies, the intensification of pleasures, the incitement to discourse, the formation of special knowledges, the strengthening of controls and resistances, are linked to one another, in accordance with a few major strategies of knowledge and power.[23]

Sexuality is both discourse and practice; it is produced by power. Power is immanent in sexual discourse and practice. Power lays down the laws by which sexuality functions and by which its operations as discursive practice are to be interpreted. Sexuality has its own "regime of truth." As such, it subjects bodies. Bodies are trained, developed, and regulated within sexual discursive practice. To speak of the deployment of sexuality as a "regime of truth" is to acknowledge that sexuality as discursive practice has become a weapons system in service of a particular regime of truth. This I discuss in chapter 1 in investigating the social deployment of homophobia.

Sexual discourse led to the development of scientific and clinical categories for describing, organizing, and regulating sexuality. It made the body an object of knowledge, investing it with power. Sexuality came to be seen as the very essence of human beings, the core of their personality. The medicalization of sexual discourse led to the emergence of the notion of sexual identity.[24] However, to speak of sexuality as constructed and deployed is to challenge the identification of sexuality with nature. Sexuality remains a historical construct that embodies hidden strategies of power/knowledge. For Foucault, heterosexuality and homosexuality were social constructions produced from the power within scientific discourse of sexuality. People are embedded in strategies of sexuality, the discursive practices of sexuality. Thus, Foucault claimed, "sexuality is something we create ourselves."[25] Its construction produced heterosexual bodies and homosexual bodies; it incited heterosexual pleasure and homosexual pleasure.

Foucault's *History of Sexuality,* volume 1 provoked a rethinking of sexual identity not as essential or natural as construed by scientific discourse but as socially constructed. Foucault developed an alternative of examining and re-visioning sexual practices as historical constructs of the scientific discourse of sexuality. Queer critics have expanded his re-visioning of homosexuality as socially constructed practices.[26] Constructionist critics have followed Foucault in comprehending the terms *heterosexual, homosexual,* and *bisexual* as modern labels referring not only to specific sexual practices but also to specific social identities. Constructionists argue against an essentialist position that holds sexual preference is the result of biological forces, hormonal factors, or genetic predisposition.[27] Constructionists do not necessarily deny biological factors but point to the social fact "that sexual desires are learned and that sexual identities come to be fashioned through an individual's interaction with others."[28] Constructionists criticize essentialists for regarding sexual categories as unchanging over time and culture. Constructionists do not deny the existence of same-sex sexual practices in history but claim that "different times and places produce different sexualities."[29] In other words, gay men and lesbian women may share same-sex sexual practices with particular Greek men in Athens and women on Lesbos during the fourth century B.C.E., but those similar sexual practices have different social constructions of meaning. Contemporary lesbians and Greek women from the fourth century B.C.E. do not share the same cultural definitions of sex, nor do they have the same social experience of sex. Same-sex sexual practices have been variously constructed over time by different societies; they exist in different historical formations and cultural configurations. Jeffrey Weeks claims that a universalistic history of homosexuality is no longer possible with the recognition of the culturally specific social constructions of same sex-sexual practices.[30] What we find is the different historical configurations of same-sex sexual desires and practices.

Gay and lesbian sexual identities are the product of a long process of social definition and self-definition.[31] It required the development of the definitions, categories, and social regulations of the nineteenth- and twentieth-century discursive practice. It required what Foucault calls the "reverse discourse" of homosexuals.[32] Homosexuality and heterosexuality are cultural constructions organized around the nineteenth century clinical need to describe normal and abnormal sexuality. These are nineteenth- and twentieth-century constructs produced not at the level of the body but on the level of discourse and social practices.

Notes

Introduction

1. Michel Foucault, "Politics and Ethics: An Interview," in *The Foucault Reader,* ed. Paul Rabinow (New York: Pantheon, 1984), 374.
2. I want to explain the usage of certain terms of exclusion, privilege, and power and to rescue them from a heterosexist/homophobic usage without traveling the route of Mary Daly in creating a new vocabulary. *God* when used in a gay/lesbian social context refers to God/dess. Likewise, *the Christ* is a relational term inclusive of Christa; it will also refer to the gay/lesbian Christ/a as distinguished from the usages of other authors. Both *God* and *Christ* are understood as gender inclusive and gay/lesbian inclusive in my theological discourse. I do use *reign of God or basileia* for kingdom; they are more gender-neutral terms.
3. Mary Hunt, *Fierce Tenderness: A Feminist Theology of Friendship* (New York: Crossroad, 1990), 48.
4. James Wolf, ed., *Gay Priests* (San Francisco: Harper & Row, 1989). See my book review of *Gay Priests* in *Harvard Divinity Bulletin* 20, no. 3 (1990–91): 23. See also: Zalmos Sherwood, *Kairos: Confessions of a Gay Priest* (Boston: Alyson Publications, 1987); Rosemary Curb and Nancy Manahan, *Lesbian Nuns* (Tallahassee: Naiad Press, 1985); Jeannine Gramick, ed., *Homosexuality in the Priesthood and Religious Life* (New York: Crossroad, 1990).
5. Mary Daly asserts, "Patriarchy is itself the prevailing religion of the planet, and its essential message is necrophilia"; Mary Daly, *Gyn/Ecology: The Metaethics of Radical Feminism* (Boston: Beacon Press, 1978), 39; Rosemary Ruether, *New Woman/New Earth: Sexist Ideologies and Human Liberation* (New York: Seabury Press, 1975); Sharon Welch, *A Feminist Ethic of Risk* (Minneapolis: Fortress Press, 1990); Carter Heyward, *Our Passion for Justice* (New York: Pilgrim Press, 1984); Heyward, *Touching Our Strength* (San Francisco: Harper & Row, 1989).
6. James H. Cone, *A Black Theology of Liberation* (Philadelphia: J. B. Lippincott, 1970); Cone, *God of the Oppressed* (New York: Seabury Press, 1985).

7. Gustavo Gutiérrez, *A Theology of Liberation* (Maryknoll, NY: Orbis Books, 1973); Gutiérrez, *The Power of the Poor in History* (Maryknoll, NY: Orbis Books, 1983); Leonardo Boff, *Jesus Christ Liberator* (Maryknoll, NY: Orbis Books, 1986); Jon Sobrino, *Christology at the Crossroads* (Maryknoll, NY: Orbis Books, 1985); Juan Luis Segundo, *Liberation of Theology* (Maryknoll, NY: Orbis Books, 1976); Segundo, *Faith and Ideologies* (Maryknoll, NY: Orbis Books, 1984).

8. Sharon D. Welch, *Communities of Resistance and Solidarity: A Feminist Perspective* (Maryknoll, NY: Orbis Books, 1985), 80.

9. Theo Witvliet, *The Way of the Black Messiah* (Oak Park, IL: Meyer-Stone Books, 1987), 97. For a good summary of different contextual theologies, see Witvliet, *A Place in the Sun* (Maryknoll, NY: Orbis Books, 1985).

10. S. D. Collins, "Theology in the Politics of Appalachian Women," in *Womanspirit Rising: A Feminist Reader,* ed. C. Christ and J. Plaskow (San Francisco: Harper & Row, 1979), 152.

11. Hans Küng adopts this notion of "dangerous and liberating memory" from J. B. Metz; Küng, *On Being a Christian* (New York: Doubleday, 1976), 121.

12. Welch, *Feminist Ethic of Risk,* 157.

13. Hunt, *Fierce Tenderness,* 45.

14. Julia Penelope, *Call Me Lesbian: Lesbian Lives, Lesbian Theory* (Freedom, CA: Crossing Press, 1992), xiii.

15. Penelope uses *heteropatriarchy* in her lesbian cultural analysis, *Call Me Lesbian.*

16. John Boswell gives a good social history of the word homosexuality. Boswell, *Christianity, Social Tolerance, and Homosexuality* (Chicago: Univ. of Chicago Press, 1980).

17. Penelope notes the wide diversity within the lesbian community, *Call Me Lesbian,* 78–97. All usages of *lesbian* reflect this wide diversity. The correlative usage of *gay* similarly reflects such a diversity.

18. Michel Foucault, *Language, Counter-Memory, Practice* (Ithaca: Cornell Univ. Press, 1977), 146.

19. Welch, *Communities of Resistance,* 20. In this work, Welch works out the application of using Foucault's genealogical critique within feminist theology. In *A Feminist Ethic,* she practices genealogical criticism in her theological constructions.

Chapter 1. The Social Organization of Homophobia

1. Eduardo Galeano, *The Book of Embraces* (New York: W. W. Norton, 1991), 159.

2. Audre Lorde, *Sister Outsider* (New York: Crossing Press, 1984), 120.

3. George Weinberg introduced the term *homophobia,* in *Society and the Healthy Homosexual* (New York: St. Martin's Press, 1972). The underlying presupposition of homophobia is that heterosexuality is normative and superior to all other sexual practices. See Jeannine Gramick, "Prejudice,

Religion, and Homosexual People," in *A Challenge to Love*, ed. Robert Nugent (New York: Crossroad, 1983), 3–39; William Paul, "Minority Status for Gay People: Majority Reaction and Social Context," in *Homosexuality*, ed. William Paul and James Weinrich (Beverly Hills: Sage Publications, 1982), 351–70; Marshall Kirk and Hunter Madsen, *After the Ball* (New York: Penguin Books, 1990), 3–133; Warren Blumenfeld ed., *Homophobia: How We All Pay the Price* (Boston: Beacon Press, 1992); and Robert Baird and Stuart Rosembaum eds., *Bigotry, Prejudice and Hatred* (Buffalo, NY: Prometheus Books, 1992).

4. Adrienne Rich, "Compulsory Heterosexuality and Lesbian Experience," in *Powers of Desire: The Politics of Sexuality*, ed. Ann Snitow, Christine Stanell, and Sharon Thompson (New York: Monthly Review Press, 1983), 177–205. Compulsory heterosexuality pervades the networks of power relations within our society. See Gary Kinsman's analysis of the emergence of heterosexuality: Kinsman, *The Regulation of Desire: Sexuality in Canada* (Montreal: Black Rose Books, 1987), 37–61.

5. Carter Heyward, *Touching Our Strength* (San Francisco: Harper & Row, 1989), 50. See also Jonathan Dollimore, *Sexual Dissidence* (Oxford: Clarendon Press, 1991), 236, and Suzanne Pharr, *Homophobia: A Weapon of Sexism* (Little Rock: Chardon Press, 1988).

6. Gay males threaten heterosexist males because they embody the symbolism of woman. See: James B. Nelson, *Between Two Gardens* (New York: Pilgrim Press, 1983), 51–53; Nelson, *The Intimate Connection* (Philadelphia: Westminster Press, 1988), 59–64. Beverly Harrison makes a strong connection between misogyny and homophobia. She connects the hatred of women, subjugation of sexual passion, and homophobia. She observes, "Homo-erotic men are perceived as failed men, no better than females." See Harrison, "Misogyny and Homophobia: The Unexplored Connections," in *Making the Connections*, ed. Carol Robb (Boston: Beacon Press, 1985), 140. Lesbian women become a threat to heterosexist males because of their independence; they break the political dependency of women trapped in heterosexist relationships; see Pharr, *Homophobia*, 19–20.

7. Rodney Karr, "Homosexual Labeling and the Male Role," in *GaySpeak: Gay Male and Lesbian Communication*, ed. James Chesbro (New York: Pilgrim Press, 1981), 3–11, also Stephen Morin and Ellen Garfinkle, "Male Homophobia," in the same volume, 117–29. See Julia Penelope's discussion of "heteropatriarchical semantics," *Call Me Lesbian: Lesbian Lives, Lesbian Theory* (Freedom, CA: Crossing Press, 1992), 78–97.

8. Howard S. Becker, *Outsiders* (Glencoe, IL: Free Press, 1963), 19.

9. Karr, "Homosexual Labeling," 3–11.

10. Michel Foucault, *The History of Sexuality* (New York: Vintage Books, 1990), 1:53–73.

11. Ibid., 62–73.

12. Ibid., 43.

13. Ibid. Arnold Davidson notes that the term *perversion* is derived from moral theology and that perversion was applied to ethical choice and not

to identity; see Davidson, "Sex and the Emergence of Sexuality," *Critical Inquiry* no. 14 (1987): 45–48.

14. Foucault, *History of Sexuality,* 1:101. For a lesbian view of medical discourse, see Shane Phelan, *Identity Politics* (Philadelphia: Temple Univ. Press, 1989), 19–35.

15. Jonathan Katz, ed., *Gay American History* (New York: Harper & Row, 1975), 134–207.

16. Irving Bieber, *Homosexuality: A Psychoanalytic Study of Male Homosexuals* (New York: Basic Books, 1962); Bieber, "Homosexuality," in *Comprehensive Textbook of Psychiatry,* ed. Alfred Freedman and Harold Kaplan (Baltimore: William & Wilkins, 1967); Bieber, "Clinical Aspects of Male Homosexuality," in *Sexual Inversion: The Multiple Roots of Homosexuality* (New York: Basic Books, 1965), 248–67. See Dollimore's discussion of the discrimination perpetuated by psychiatry and psychoanalysis, *Sexual Dissidence,* 169–90.

17. Charles Socarides, *The Overt Homosexual* (New York: Grune and Stratton, 1968); Socarides, "Homosexuality," in *American Handbook of Psychiatry,* 2d edition, ed. Silvano Areti (New York: Basic Books, 1974); Socarides, *Homosexuality* (New York: Jason Aronson, 1978).

18. Richard C. Pillard, "Psychotherapeutic Treatment for the Invisible Minority," in *Homosexuality,* ed. Paul and Weinrich, 99–113; John Money, *Gay, Straight, and In-Between* (New York: Oxford Univ. Press, 1988).

19. John DeCeco, "Homosexuality's Brief Recovery: From Sickness to Health and Back Again," *Journal of Sex Research,* 23 (1987): 106–29; W. Ricketts, "Biological Research on Homosexuality: Ansell's Cow or Occam's Razor?" *Journal of Homosexuality* 9, no. 4 (1984): 65–93.

20. Allan Berube points out that psychiatric discourse on homosexuality influenced the creation of a Selective Service screening process to weed out homosexuals and affects the military's current policies of discriminating against gay/lesbian candidates. See Berube, *Coming Out Under Fire* (New York: Penguin, 1991), 149–74. Psychiatric discourse on homosexuality, for the most part, has reinforced ecclesial homophobia. The emerging plurality of psychiatric discourse in the mid-seventies has led to the emergence of alternative voices within Christian discourse.

21. Foucault, *History of Sexuality,* 1:101.

22. Eva Sedgwick, *The Epistemology of the Closet* (Berkeley and Los Angeles: Univ. of California Press, 1990), 43. Dr. Simon Levay, a gay neuroanatomist, reported a difference in the brain structure of the hypothalamus in gay men from heterosexual men. This suggests a possible genetic etiology for sexual orientation.

23. David Greenberg suggests that latent homoerotic impulses within the clergy were fended off by a social mechanism of intolerance and hatred. Fear and loathing of homoerotic feelings and practices developed as a "psychological defense mechanism against the inner conflict created by the imposition of clerical celibacy and the rigid repression of all sexual expression." See Greenberg, *The Construction of Homosexuality* (Chicago: Univ. of Chicago Press, 1988), 289. Greenberg situates the need

to repress homosexual impulses in the institutional arrangements of the late medieval church. Institutional efforts to control homoerotic impulses among the clergy would have been extended by an anxious clergy. "A priest trying to repress his own homosexual desires would have felt as much anxiety over a lay-person's homosexuality as over another priest's or nun's." It explains the intense social responses toward same-sex feelings and practices (290–91). His full argument can be found on 279–92. See also Greenberg's "Christian Intolerance of Homosexuality," *American Journal of Sociology* 88 (1982): 515–46.

24. See Paul Siegel, "Homophobia: Types, Origins, Remedies," *Christianity and Crisis* 39 (Nov. 12, 1979): 280–84.

25. Morin and Garfinkle, "Male Homophobia," in *GaySpeak*, ed. Chesbro, 119, 332. See also Kenneth Plummer, "Homosexual Categories: Some Research Problems in the Labelling Perspective of Homosexuality," in *The Making of the Modern Homosexual*, ed. K. Plumer (London: Hutchison, 1981), 62; Michael L. Stemmler and J. Michael Clark, eds., *Homophobia and the Judeo-Christian Tradition* (Dallas: Monument Press, 1990).

26. The Quakers, Moravians, and Unitarian Universalists have taken active steps to welcome gay/lesbian people within their churches and to fight homophobia. See Edward Batchelor, *Homosexuality and Ethics* (New York: Pilgrim Press, 1980), 235–42.

27. See, for instance, John J. Spong, *Living in Sin* (San Francisco: Harper & Row, 1988), 135–55; Batchelor, *Homosexuality and Ethics*, 235–42; Robert Nugent and Jeannine Gramick, "Homosexuality: Protestant, Catholic, and Jewish Issues; A Fishbone Tale," in *Homosexuality and Religion*, ed. Richard Hasbany (New York: Harrington Park Press, 1989), 7–46; Richard Woods, *Another Kind of Love* (Ft. Wayne, IN: Knoll Publishing, 1988).

28. MCC met all five qualifications for National Council of Churches membership: (1) a basis of association as a Christian body; (2) autonomous and stable corporate identity; (3) demonstrated respect and cooperation with other communions; (4) definite and centralized church polity to train its ordained members; (5) a minimum of fifty churches with a membership of twenty thousand. See Troy D. Perry and Thomas Swicegood, *Don't Be Afraid Anymore* (New York: St. Martin's Press, 1990), 236–37. Members of the National Council of Churches drew out the application process and finally denied admission. Some of the churches threatened to leave the NCC if MCC was admitted. Others felt that MCC membership would compromise its pastoral ministry to homosexuals; See Perry and Swicegood, 230–68.

29. Cardinal Ratzinger in his "Letter to the Bishops" writes,

It is deplorable that homosexual persons have been and are the object of violent malice in speech or in action. Such treatment deserves condemnation from the Church's pastors whenever it occurs. . . . But the proper reaction to crimes committed against homosexual persons should not be to claim that the homosexual condition is not disordered. When such a claim is made and when homosexual activity is consequently condoned, or when civil legislation is introduced to protect behavior to which no one has any conceivable right, neither the Church nor society at large should be surprised when other distorted notions and practices gain ground, and irrational and violent reactions increase.

Joseph Cardinal Ratzinger, "Letter to the Bishops of the Catholic Church on the Pastoral Care of Homosexual Persons," in *The Vatican and Homosexuality*, ed. Jeannine Gramick and Pat Furey (New York: Crossroad, 1988), 5–6. Ratzinger's statement has not produced any outcry against gay/lesbian bashing and hate crimes from the pulpits. The second part of his statement negates the first about "violent malice in speech and in action." It has sanctioned Catholic opposition to hate crimes and civil rights bills that protected against discrimination in housing and employment. I have used a Catholic example here but could well have used many other examples from other churches.

30. Quoted in Greenberg, *Construction of Homosexuality*, 467.

31. Anita Bryant, *The Anita Bryant Story: The Survival of Our Nation's Families and the Threat of Militant Homosexuality* (Old Tappan, NJ: Fleming H. Reve II, 1977), 62. For a gay response see Martin Duberman, *About Time: Exploring the Gay Past* (New York: Penguin Books, 1991), 342–54, and John D'Emilio and Estelle B. Freedman, *Intimate Matters* (New York: Harper & Row, 1988), 346–47.

32. Roger E. Biery, *Understanding Homosexuality: The Pride and the Prejudice* (Austin: Edward William Publishing, 1990), 143.

33. National Gay and Lesbian Task Force Policy Institute (NGLTFPI), *Anti-Gay/Lesbian Violence, Victimization, and Defamation in 1990* (Washington, DC, NGLTFPI, 1991), 19. Hereafter, NGLTFPI.

34. Quoted in Greenberg, *Construction of Homosexuality*, 467.

35. Dollimore, *Sexual Dissidence*, 237. See also: Dollimore, *Sexual Dissidence*, 54–58, 89–91, 235–40; Greenberg, *Construction of Homosexuality*, 298, 323.

36. Dollimore, *Sexual Dissidence*, 237–38.

37. P. J. Leithart, "Sodomy and the Future of America," *The Biblical World* (Feb. 1988), 7–8.

38. Exodus International is the umbrella organization for seventy-five worldwide "ex-gay ministries." Two Exodus cofounders, Gary Cooper and Michael Bussee, fell in love and left Exodus ministries for one another. They describe the ministry, "Exodus is homophobia with a happy face." From all the hundreds of gay men and lesbian women that went through the program, only thirty have maintained a heterosexual practice, and many hundreds suffered emotional anguish trying to be saved. See Frederic Millen, "Exodus Cofounders Tell Ex-Gay Movement to Get Real," *The Advocate* no. 565 (Dec. 4, 1990): 39.

39. *Exodus Policy Statement* (unsigned, undated brochure), 2. A newsletter from Metanoia Ministries states, "It is somewhat comforting to know that biological aspects of man play little to no role in the development of homosexuality." See Douglas A. Houck, *Biological Determinism* (Seattle: Metanoia Ministries, n.d.).

40. *Exodus Policy Statement*, 2; *Regeneration Teachings and Testimonies* (unsigned, undated brochure). Gary Cooper, cofounder of Exodus, says, "As a Christian, I experienced liberation, but it was conditional. I had the feeling I was gay. But I was a new person in Christ, so I was no longer gay." Quoted by Millen, "Exodus Cofounders," 39.

41. Elizabeth Moberly argues that homosexuality is caused by psychological factors: Moberly, *Homosexuality, A New Christian Ethic* (Greenwood, SC: Attic Press, 1983); Moberly, *Psychogenesis: The Early Development of Gender Identity* (London: Routledge and Kegan Paul, 1983).

42. One of the founders of Homosexuals Anonymous, Colin Cook, identifies homosexuality with sinful, fallen nature. He uses a fourteen-step program to treat homosexuality as an addiction or spiritual disease that one needs to combat. The fourteen-step program is a form of social control to gain freedom from homosexuality. See Colin Cook, *We're Finding Freedom* (Homosexuals Anonymous, 1988). David Caligiuri, another founder of Homosexuals Anonymous, has rejected his exgay ministry and embraced his own gay orientation; see Robert Pella, "The Founder of an Ex-gay Support Group Chooses Homo over Hetero," *The Advocate* no. 606 (June 30, 1992).

43. Ratzinger, "Letter to the Bishops," 2. Further on, Ratzinger consistently equates homosexuality with genital activity. The Missouri Synod Lutheran Church has adopted Catholic language in labeling homosexuals as "intrinsically sinful." "Homophile Behavior Is Intrinsically Sinful," *Christian News* 30, no. 31 (Aug. 3, 1992): 1. See Robert Nugent's criticism, "Sexual Orientation in Vatican Thinking," in *The Vatican and Homosexuality*, ed. Gramick and Furey, 48–58. To gay men and lesbians, the institutional discourse of the Catholic church has consistently dehumanized and demonized them.

44. Ratzinger, "Letter to the Bishops," 8.

45. Courage was set up as a Catholic organization to assist gay/lesbian Catholics to disavow homosexual activity and to live celibate lives. Courage has not drawn the numbers of Catholics that Dignity has, nor has it been very successful in assisting gay/lesbian Catholics to practice chastity. Courage has been replaced by the latest parody of Dignity, Diocesan Gay/Lesbian Outreach ministries, which celebrate liturgy for gay/lesbian Catholics but require that they follow church teaching on sexuality. This tactic has successfully divided many Dignity chapters who have been expelled from churches. Some Dignity chapters have moved to lay-led liturgical celebrations rather than be co-opted into giving up their belief in gay/lesbian sex as "loving, life-giving, and life-affirming." Membership in Dignity has declined. Pat Windsor, "Dignity, Church Find Ways to Peacefully Coexist," *National Catholic Reporter* 27 (Aug. 16, 1991): 7–8.

46. Robert Nugent and Jeannine Gramick, *Building Bridges: Gay and Lesbian Reality and the Catholic Church* (Mystic, CT: Twenty-third Publications, 1992), 73. See their worldwide survey of Catholic bishops, 137–145,

157–171. They conclude that there appears to be little hope with the Catholic bishops.

47. Barry Adkins, "Battle for Gay Rights Bill Begins in City," *New York Native* (Jan. 27–Feb. 2, 1986), 11.

48. Charles Curran, "Homosexuality and Moral Theology: Methodological and Substantive Considerations," *The Thomist* 30 (1971): 447–81; Curran, "Moral Theology and Homosexuality," in *Homosexuality and the Catholic Church,* ed. Jeannine Gramick (Chicago: Thomas More Press, 1983), 138–68.

49. McNeill's earlier work viewed gay/lesbian experience positively; it attempted to rework Catholic moral teaching with critical biblical exegesis and psychological studies on homosexuality. He was silenced for his creative pastoral outreach to the gay/lesbian community. See John J. McNeill, *The Church and the Homosexual* (Kansas City: Sheed Andrews and McMeel, 1976). When McNeill broke his silence and followed the dictates of his conscience by speaking out against Cardinal Ratzinger's letter, he was expelled from the Society of Jesus. There was no judicial recourse for an appeal. His more recent works expand on his earlier theology; they affirm gay/lesbian sexuality and spirituality as life giving, welcoming, hospitable. See McNeill, "Homosexuality, Lesbianism, and the Future: The Creative Role of the Gay Community in Building a More Humane Society," in *A Challenge to Love,* ed. Robert Nugent (New York: Crossroad, 1983), 52–64; McNeill, *Taking a Chance on God* (Boston: Beacon Press, 1988).

50. Some recent discourse from the Catholic Right on homosexuality has been institutionally sanctioned: James P. Hannigan, *Homosexuality: A Test Case for Christian Social Ethics* (Mahwah, NJ: Paulist Press, 1988); John F. Harvey, *The Homosexual Person* (San Francisco: Ignatius Press, 1987). Rueda's book is one of the most homophobic books of the Catholic Right. He postulates a gay/lesbian conspiracy to subvert the church: Rueda, *The Homosexual Network* (Old Greenwich, CT: Devin Adair, 1982). See a gay critique of the Catholic theological perspective: Kevin Gordon, "The Sexual Bankruptcy of the Christian Traditions: A Perspective of Radical Suspicion and of Fundamental Trust," in *AIDS Issues: Confronting the Church,* ed. David Hallman (New York: Pilgrim Press, 1989), 169–212; Craig Wesley Plant, "The Evolution of Pastoral Thought Concerning Homosexuality in Selected Vatican and American Documents from 1975–1986," in *Homophobia and the Judeo-Christian Tradition,* ed. Stemmeler and Clark, 117–46.

51. The 1990 attempt to repeal a Denver ordinance banning discrimination against gay men and lesbians was defeated in a general election by a 55 percent to 45 percent margin. The hate campaign was supported by Denver's Catholic archbishop and fundamentalist churches. Cardinal Law and the Massachusetts bishops sent a letter to Boston Mayor Flynn, Governor Weld, and to state and city legislators. In their statement, they defined a family as "a man and a woman in lawful union together with

their children." The bishops asserted, "The extension of the title family to gay and lesbian couples and the granting of economic privileges to domestic partners on an equal plane with true families must be opposed and rejected as undermining the family in our society today. If family life is ignored or despised or undermined, there is no natural foundation for social and civil life." Chris Bull, "Catholic Officials' Opposition Raps Boston Partners Bill," *The Advocate* no. 579 (June 18, 1991): 19. See also Richard Mohr, *Gay Ideas* (Boston: Beacon Press, 1992), 90.

52. "Some Considerations Concerning the Catholic Response to Legislate Proposals on the Nondiscrimination of Homosexual Persons," unsigned document, *National Catholic Reporter* 28, no. 35 (July 31, 1992): 10. Hereafter: "Some Considerations." See some responses: New Ways Ministry Press Release, "Human Dignity and the Common Good: A Response of New Ways Ministry to the Vatican Gay Rights Document," July 15, 1992; John Gallagher, "Vatican Statement Condones Anti-gay Discrimination," *The Advocate* no. 610 (Aug. 25, 1992): 21; Peter Gomes, "Homophobic? Re-Read Your Bible," *New York Times,* Aug. 17, 1992.

53. "Some Considerations," 10.

54. Ibid.

55. Rob Schwitz, an ROTC student who came out as gay at Washington University and who was expelled from the ROTC program, had his registration with the Boy Scouts permanently revoked. See Bruce Mirken, "Boy Scout Confidential," *The Advocate* no. 593 (Dec. 31, 1991): 52–55. Blake Lewis, national spokesperson for the BSA, states the policy of the Boy Scouts of America:

> For over eighty-one years, the Boy Scouts of America has placed a strong emphasis on the traditional family unit and family values. The Scouting program is designed to be a shared, family experience. The BSA believes that homosexuality is not consistent with this family focus.

In the case of Tim Curran, an openly gay man who was denied leadership of a troop by the Boy Scouts of America, the Los Angeles Superior Court upheld the BSA position as not violating the state's antibias laws. This response presupposes that gay men and lesbian women cannot be good role models. It also fails to recognize that out of the four million Boy Scouts in the U.S.A., four hundred thousand are gay. The Girl Scouts of America feels no need for such restrictive policies.

56. Tim Jeal speaks of Baden-Powell's homosexual relationship with Kenneth McLean in *The Boy-Man: The Life of Lord Baden-Powell* (New York: William Morrow, 1990), 74–109.

57. Thomas S. Weinberg, *Gay Men, Gay Selves: The Social Construction of Homosexual Identities* (New York: Irvington Publishers, 1983), 60–78.

58. NGLTFPI, 15–16.

59. Ibid., 16.

60. James Holobaugh in 1990 and Rob Schwitz in 1991 were expelled from the ROTC program at Washington University for wrestling with their sexual orientation and coming out as gay. Both students chose to be

honest and wanted to serve their country. Despite opinion polls showing that 64 percent of the American public agrees that gay/lesbian people be allowed to serve in the military, the Department of Defense has opposed it. It seems that change will ultimately be effected by the colleges and universities. Many threatened to close their ROTC programs if the Department of Defense does not change its discriminatory policies against gay/lesbian candidates. A survey commissioned by the Human Rights Campaign Fund found that 80 percent of the respondents opposed the military policy. See Rick Harding, "Top Pentagon Official During Reagan Tenure Blasts Military Policy," *The Advocate* no. 578 (June 4, 1991): 25.

61. Editors of the *Harvard Law Review, Sexual Orientation and the Law* (Cambridge: Harvard Univ. Press, 1990), 44. Military police from Lackland Air Force Base in Texas sometimes assisted by San Antonio and Bexar County law enforcement officials periodically block exits from gay bar parking lots and search inside for armed forces personnel. Lackland Air Force Base has declared gay bars and establishments off-limits to military personnel: *The Advocate* no. 583 (Aug. 13, 1991): 10.

62. *Review* editors, *Sexual Orientation*, 46–47.

63. Ibid., 51–52.

64. Allan Berube, *Coming Out Under Fire* (New York: Penguin Books, 1991), 278–79.

65. Berube, *Coming Out*, 3. See also Harper Barnes, "Gays in the Army: What Is the Trouble?" *St. Louis Post-Dispatch*, Dec. 29, 1991, 2D.

66. *Review* editors, *Sexual Orientation*, 50. D'Emilio & Freedman, *Intimate Matters*, 293–95.

67. *Review* editors, *Sexual Orientation*, 66.

68. Ibid., 73. Two-thirds of the two thousand respondents to a market survey reported having witnessed at least some hostility in the workplace. See "Gay in Corporate America," *Fortune* (Dec. 16, 1991), 44.

69. The stereotypes are: (1) homosexuals molest children; (2) they recruit children into a homosexual lifestyle; (3) homosexuals are immoral role models. These stereotypes are built upon prejudice, misinformation, and no factual evidence. See Rhonda Rivera, "Homosexuality and the Law," in *Homosexuality*, ed. Paul and Weinrich, 327.

70. Rhonda Rivera, "Queer Law: Sexual Orientation Law in the Mid-Eighties," *University of Dayton Law Review* 2, no. 2 (1986): 329; *Review* editors, *Sexual Orientation*, 150–53. Section 212(a)(4), subsection 11882(a)(4) of the Immigration and Nationality Act denies entry into the U.S. to people who are "afflicted with psychopathic personality, or sexual deviation." In *Boutilier v. Immigration and Naturalization Service*, the Supreme Court ruled that Congress intended to exclude homosexuals from entry under the category of "psychopathic personality"; *Review* editors, *Sexual Orientation*, 151.

71. Greenberg, *Construction of Homosexuality*, 466.

72. *Review* editors, *Sexual Orientation*, 119–32.

73. One psychiatrist hired by the defense testified that Dan White suffered from depression, aggravated by eating Twinkies. The defense did not deny the shootings but argued diminished capacity. A number of psychiatrists portrayed White as an upright, moral citizen who broke under pressure. See David J. Thomas, "San Francisco's 1979 White Night Riot: Injustice, Vengeance, and Beyond," in *Homosexuality*, ed. Paul and Weinrich, 337–50. For a gay/lesbian reaction; see Warren Hinckle, "Dan White's San Francisco, the Untold Story," *Inquiry* (Oct. 29, 1979).

74. John D'Emilio, "Gay Politics and Community in San Francisco Since World War II," in *Hidden from History: Reclaiming the Gay and Lesbian Past*, ed. Martin Duberman, Martha Vicinus, and George Chauncey (New York: Penguin Books, 1990), 471.

75. *Review* editors, *Sexual Orientation*, 33–38.

76. Congressional Representative Dannemeyer states in defense of the restoration of state sodomy laws: "In passing such laws, we would also affirm a normative way of life for all Americans: that they are born and nurtured in traditional families where children have both mothers and fathers and hence learn to understand the marvelous union of man and woman that continually leads to the rebirth of life and love and hope on earth." William Dannemeyer, *Shadow in the Land* (San Francisco: Ignatius Press, 1989), 219. See a gay/lesbian interpretation of the effects of *Bowers v. Hardwick:* Richard C. Mohr, *Gay/Justice* (New York: Columbia Univ. Press, 1988).

77. See *Review* editors, *Sexual Orientation*, 93–119. The editors conclude, "Gay and lesbian relationships are qualitatively similar to heterosexual relationships in many essential aspects and are not inherently harmful either to partners or to society. . . . Society's disapproval of the gay and lesbian lifestyle should not, therefore, entail legal exclusion of gay men and lesbians from private law entitlements," 118.

78. The Coalition for Lesbian and Gay Civil Rights in Cambridge, Massachusetts, issued the following statement:

> Although many gay men and lesbians observe the institution of marriage today, they are not afforded the legal protection that the full state recognition would confer: certain legal and property rights; custody rights for jointly raised children; inheritances; tax and insurance benefits; and visitation rights. There is a societal cost to not recognizing gay marriages. The lack of legal and societal recognition makes it far more difficult and stressful to remain in relationships.

Lesbian and Gay Marriage (Cambridge, MA: The Coalition of Lesbian and Gay Civil Rights, n.d.).

79. *Review* editors, *Sexual Orientation*, 170.

80. Quoted in NGLTFPI, 19.

81. Ibid., 18.

82. Paula Treichler, "AIDS, Homophobia, and Biomedical Discourse: An Epidemic of Signification," in *AIDS: Cultural Analysis, Cultural Activism*, ed. Douglas Crimps (Cambridge: MIT Press, 1988), 60; see especially

31–70; Sander L. Gilman, "AIDS and Syphilis: The Iconography of Disease," in the same volume, 87–108.

83. Randy Shilts, *And the Band Played On* (New York: Penguin Books, 1988).
84. Ibid.
85. William Buckley, "Crucial Steps in Combating the AIDS Epidemic: Identify All the Carriers," *New York Times*, Mar. 16, 1986, 27.
86. Douglas Crimps, "Introduction," in *AIDS: Cultural Analysis*, 8.
87. Ratzinger obliquely refers to threat of HIV infection: "Even when the practice of homosexuality may seriously threaten the lives and the well-being of a large number of its people, its advocates remain undeterred and refuse to consider the magnitude of the risks involved." Ratzinger goes on, "The Church can never be so callous." *The Vatican and Homosexuality,* ed. Gramick and Furey, 5. In fact, the institutional church has been callous and is responsible for the spread of HIV infection to countless numbers of people. ACT UP activists assert that the church hierarchy remains guilty of the genocidal spread of HIV infection.
88. Quoted in Crimps, "Introduction," 8.
89. NGLTFPI, 16.
90. Ibid., 16.
91. Jerry Falwell, "AIDS: The Judgment of God," *Liberty Report* no. 2 (April 1987): 5, 2. See Bruce Mills's discussion of religious homophobia and AIDS-phobia: Mills, "Fear and Passion: A Psychological Reflection on the Construction of Homophobia in the Context of AIDS," in *Homophobia and the Judeo-Christian Tradition,* ed. Stemmler and Clark, 165–87.
92. Earl Shelp and Ronald Sunderland, *AIDS and the Church* (Philadelphia: Westminister Press, 1987), 19.
93. Task Force on Gay/Lesbian Issues/San Francisco, *Homosexuality and Justice* (San Francisco: Consultation on Homosexuality, Social Justice, and Roman Catholic Theology, 1986), 210.
94. Mills, "Fear and Passion," in *Homophobia,* ed. Stemmler and Clark, 165–87.
95. Shelp and Sunderland, *AIDS and the Church,* 23.
96. Gary Comstock, *Violence Against Lesbians and Gay Men* (New York: Columbia Univ. Press, 1992), 110. Comstock's study is an excellent social analysis of homophobic violence.
97. NGLTFPI, 9.
98. Ibid., 12–17.
99. Ibid., 25.
100. *Review* editors, *Sexual Orientation,* 31.

Chapter 2. Gay and Lesbian Silence Is Broken

1. Jeffrey Weeks, "Capitalism and the Organization of Sex," in *Homosexuality: Power and Politics* (London: Allison and Busby, 1989), 20.

2. Michel Foucault, *The History of Sexuality* (New York: Vintage Books, 1990), 1:101. See also John Coleman, "The Homosexual Revolution and Hermeneutics," *Concilium* 173 (1984): 55–64.

3. Thomas S. Weinberg, *Gay Men, Gay Selves: The Social Construction of Homosexual Identities* (New York: Irvington Publishers, 1983), 45–78; Eli Coleman, "Developmental Stages of the Coming-Out Process," in *Homosexuality* ed. William Paul and James Weinrich (Beverly Hills: Sage Publications, 1982), 150–51; Roger Biery, *Understanding Homosexuality: The Pride and the Prejudice* (Austin: Edward William Publishing, 1990), 268–77.

4. Joel Hencken, "Homosexuality and Psychoanalysis," in *Homosexuality* ed. Paul and Weinrich, 124.

5. Rodney Karr, "Homosexual Labeling and the Male Role," in *GaySpeak: Gay Male and Lesbian Communication* ed. James Chesbro (New York: Pilgrim Press, 1981), 3–11; Stephen Morin and Ellen Garfinkle, "Male Homophobia," in the same volume, 117–29.

6. Morin and Garfinkle, "Male Homophobia."

7. Martin S. Weinberg, and Colin J. Williams, *Male Homosexuals: Their Problems and Adaptations* (New York: Oxford Univ. Press, 1974); Alan Bell and Martin Weinberg, *Homosexualities: A Study of Diversity Among Men and Women* (New York: Simon & Schuster, 1978), 162, 166.

8. Bell and Weinberg, *Homosexualities*, 160–61.

9. Public awareness of the many cases of child molestation by priests points to the need for a complete revamping of Catholic sexual theology and its disciplinary practices regarding priesthood. The studies on noncelibate priests reinforce the need for allowing married clergy (both female and male), gay/lesbian priests in blessed unions, and a recognition of those few who are called to a celibate life. James Wolf, ed., *Gay Priests* (San Francisco: Harper & Row, 1989).

10. Eva Koskofsky Sedgwick has undertaken excellent cultural studies of the variations of homophobia and closetedness in literature: Eva Sedgwick, *Between Men: English Literature and Male Homosexual Desire* (Ithaca: Cornell Univ. Press, 1985); Sedgwick, *Epistemology of the Closet* (Berkeley and Los Angeles: Univ. of California Press, 1990).

11. Foucault maintains that a person's body is a blank slate on which society writes its scripts. The body is the field upon which social and cultural forces exercise power to create; it is patterned with sexuality and identity. The making of gay and lesbian bodies refers to the creation of visible bodies and identities in society. Gay/lesbian identities and bodies are correlative. For the effects of World War II in the making of modern gay/lesbian bodies, see Allan Berube, *Coming Out Under Fire* (New York: Penguin Books, 1991); Berube, "Marching to a Different Drummer: Lesbian and Gay GIs in World War II," in *Hidden from History: Reclaiming the Gay and Lesbian Past* ed. Martin Duberman, Martha Vicinus, and George Chauncey (New York: Penguin Books, 1990), 383–94.

12. Berube, *Coming Out*, 220–54.

13. John D'Emilio and Estelle B. Freedman, *Intimate Matters* (New York: Harper & Row, 1988), 289. See also Berube, *Coming Out,* 271–73.

14. Alfred Kinsey, Wardell Pomeroy, and Clyde Martin, *Sexual Behavior in the Human Male* (Philadelphia: W. B. Saunders, 1948).

15. Michael Bronski discusses *The Ladder, One,* and *The Mattachine Review.* These magazines would come in unmarked envelopes because gay/ lesbian people feared being discovered. The magazines mark the beginnings of gay/lesbian discourse in the postwar period. See Michael Bronski, *Culture Clash: The Making of Gay Sensibility* (Boston: South End Press, 1984), 80–84.

16. Ronald Bayer, *Homosexuality and American Psychiatry: The Politics of Diagnosis* (Princeton: Princeton Univ. Press, 1987), 71.

17. Edmund Bergler, *Homosexuality: Disease or Way of Life?* (New York: Hill and Wang, 1956).

18. Bayer, *Homosexuality and American Psychiatry,* 75–88.

19. Salvatore Liccata, "The Homosexual Rights Movement in the United States," in *The Gay Past,* ed. Salvatore Liccata and Robert Petersen (New York: Harrington Park Press, 1985), 170–78.

20. Bayer, *Homosexuality and American Psychiatry,* 88.

21. Ibid., 90–91.

22. It is a little-known fact outside of the gay/lesbian community that many gay and lesbian bars in the pre-Stonewall period were Mafia owned. The Mafia paid off police to avoid harassment and raids. Those bars that were owned by gays or lesbians found themselves in the same cycle of extortion and harassment. The Stonewall Inn owned by gays, had refused to pay increased extortion monies to the police. Thus the raid of June 27, 1969, was initiated to force compliance. Raids affected the customers who frequented the bars; such harassment of customers was a means to force compliance with payoffs.

23. Eric Marcus, *Making History: An Oral History* (New York: HarperCollins, 1992), 192.

24. Conversation with Jack W. at the Sharing Center for HIV people in St. Louis, June 1991. I am protecting Jack's identity because of HIV discrimination.

25. Toby Marotta, *The Politics of Homosexuality* (Boston: Houghton Mifflin, 1983), 128–33; Dennis Altman, *Homosexual Oppression and Liberation* (New York: Outerbridge & Dienstfrey, 1971), 179–84. Another excellent account of gay/lesbian activism: Barry Adam, *The Rise of the Gay and Lesbian Movement* (Boston: Twayne Publishing, 1987).

26. Marotta, *Politics of Homosexuality,* 134–95.

27. Marcus, *Making History,* 265. See also Marotta, *Politics of Homosexuality,* 229–303.

28. Coleman, "Developmental Stages," 151–53.

29. Weinberg, *Gay Men, Gay Selves,* 162–217.

30. Gay men and lesbian women must seek out the mental health resources within their community to work to heal all internalized homophobia.

They need to heal themselves from oppression sickness in the cylces of abuse, low self-esteem, and internalized hatred in a therapeutic milieu that is either lesbian affirming or gay affirming; see Don Clark, *The New Loving Someone Gay* (Berkeley: Celestial Arts, 1987), 219–61.

31. Kirk and Madsen argue for using persuasive not transgressive strategies for changing homophobia in America. They argue for coming out, portraying gay men and lesbian women as victims, not aggressive challengers. Kirk and Madsen disregard the accomplishments achieved by transgressive activists. They want to wage a public relations campaign to make gay/lesbian people look good to America. Marshall Kirk and Hunter Madsen, *After the Ball* (New York: Penguin Books, 1990), 161–270.

32. Bronski, *Culture Clash*, 198; Bronski, "Reform or Revolution? The Challenge of Creating a Gay Sensibility," in *Gay Spirit*, ed. Mark Thompson (New York: St. Martin's Press, 1987), 10–19; Don Kilhefner, "Gay People at a Critical Crossroad: Assimilation or Affirmation?" in *Gay Spirit*, 121–30; Mark Thompson, "The Evolution of a Faerie: Notes Toward a New Definition of Gay," in *Gay Spirit*, 292–302.

33. See Penelope's discussion of lesbian attempts to reclaim derogatory labels: Julia Penelope, *Call Me Lesbian: Lesbian Lives, Lesbian Theory* (Freedom, CA: Crossing Press, 1992), 90. Judy Grahn attempts to reclaim gay/lesbian epithets in a comparative cultural study: Judy Grahn, *Another Mother Tongue: Gay Words, Gay Worlds* (Boston: Beacon Press, 1984).

34. The full statement of the press release from William A. Bridges, corporate vice president of human resources of Cracker Barrel Old Country Store:

> Cracker Barrel is founded upon a concept of traditional American values, quality in all we do, and a philosophy of 100 percent guest satisfaction. It is inconsistent with our concepts and values, and is perceived to be inconsistent with those of our customer base, to continue to employ individuals in our operating units whose sexual preferences fail to demonstrate normal heterosexual values which have been the foundation of families in our society. Therefore, it is felt this business decision is in the best interests of the company.

35. In another press release from Mr. Bridges dated Feb. 22, 1991, Cracker Barrel supposedly rescinded the policy:

> In the past, we have always responded to the values and wishes of our customers. Our recent position on the employment of homosexuals in a limited number of stores may have been well-intentioned over-reaction to the perceived values of our customers and their comfort level with these individuals. We have re-visited our thinking on the subject and feel it only makes good business sense to continue to employ those folks who will provide the quality service our customers have come to expect from us.

The company to date has refused to rehire or make reparations to the terminated employees. It has continued to fire employees on the assumption that they were homosexual, regardless of job performance.

36. Trixi Burke, "Mohr on Outing and Maupin," in *The News*, vol. 11, issue 14, Dec. 7, 1992. For Mohr's full position, see Mohr, *Gay Ideas* (Boston: Beacon Press, 1992), 11–48.

37. Jonathan Dollimore, *Sexual Dissidence* (Oxford: Clarendon Press, 1991), 324. See his particular discussion of camp, 315–22, and his discussion of transgressive reinscription, 279–325; Mark Thompson, "Children of Paradise: A Brief History of Queens," in *Gay Spirit*, ed. Thompson, 49–68.

38. Geoff Mains, "Urban Aboriginals and the Celebration of Leather Magic," in *Gay Spirit*, ed. Thompson, 99–117; Mains, *Urban Aboriginals: A Celebration of Leathersexuality* (San Francisco: Gay Sunshine, 1984).

39. Thompson, "Children of Paradise," in *Gay Spirit*, ed. Thompson, 60–61.

40. Evelyn Hooker, "A Preliminary Analysis of Group Behavior of Homosexuals," *Journal of Psychology* 42 (1956): 217–25; Hooker, "Male Homosexuals and Their Worlds," in *Sexual Inversion: The Multiple Roots of Homosexuality* ed. Judd Marmor (New York: Basic Books, 1965); 83–107; Hooker, "The Homosexual Community," in *Sexual Deviance*, ed. John Gagnon and William Simon (New York: Harper & Row, 1967), 167–84; Thomas Szasz, *The Myth of Mental Illness* (New York: Dell, 1961); Szasz, *The Manufacture of Madness* (New York: Harper & Row, 1970); Judd Marmor, ed., *Sexual Inversion;* Marmor, *Homosexuality: A Modern Reappraisal* (New York: Basic Books, 1980).

41. Bayer, *Homosexuality and American Psychiatry*, 92.

42. Ibid., 103.

43. Ibid.

44. Ibid., 99.

45. Ibid.

46. Ibid., 105.

47. Dr. Robert Cabaj, president of the Association of Gay and Lesbian Psychiatrists, wrote against the continued stigmatization of gay and lesbian people with the remaining diagnostic category of ego-dystonic homosexuality: "Needless to say with the AIDS crisis and the growing attempts by the military and insurance companies to screen out gay people, the diagnosis has very frightening potential for abuse"; Bayer, *Homosexuality and American Psychiatry*, 213.

48. The American Psychological Association stated, "Homosexuality per se implies no impairment in judgment, or general social or vocation responsibilities. Further, the American Psychological Association urges all mental health professionals to take the lead in removing the stigma of mental illness that has long been associated with homosexual orientations." See Edward Batchelor, ed., *Homosexuality and Ethics* (New York: Pilgrim Press, 1980), 243.

49. Audre Lorde, "Uses of the Erotic: The Erotic as Power," in *Take Back the Night*, ed. Laura Lederer (New York: William Morrow, 1980), 298.

50. Bronski, *Culture Clash*, 213–14.

51. Grahn, *Another Mother Tongue*, 23.

52. Nugent and Nugent, "Homosexuality: Protestant, Catholic and Jewish Issues," in *Homosexuality and Religion*, 7–46.

53. For a list of famous men and women in history who practiced their same-sex attractions, see Warren J. Blumenfield and Diane Raymond, *Looking at Gay and Lesbian Life* (New York: Philosophical Library, 1988), 378–81.

54. Judith Plaskow, "Jewish Memory from a Feminist Perspective," in *Weaving the Visions: New Patterns of Feminist Spirituality*, ed. J. Plaskow and C. Christ (San Francisco: Harper & Row, 1989), 45.

55. Martin Duberman, *About Time: Exploring the Gay Past* (New York: Penguin Books, 1991), 452.

56. Those not cited in the notes: Judith Brown, *Immodest Acts: The Life of a Lesbian Nun in Renaissance Italy* (New York: Oxford Univ. Press, 1986.); Bret Hinsch, *Passions of the Cut Sleeve: The Male Homosexual Tradition in China* (Berkeley and Los Angeles: Univ. of California Press, 1990). See *Hidden from History* ed. Martin Duberman, Martha Vicinus, and George Chauncy (New York: Penguin Books, 1989). See also Christine Downing, *Myths and Mysteries of Same-Sex Love* (New York: Continuum, 1989); John Winkler, *The Constraints of Desire: The Anthropology of Sex and Gender in Ancient Greece* (New York: Routledge, 1990).

57. Bronski, *Culture Clash*, 197–98.

58. Shilts, *And the Band Played On*, xxii.

59. Larry Kramer, *Reports from the Holocaust* (New York: St. Martin's Press, 1989).

60. Shilts, *And the Band Played On*, xxii.

61. Ibid., 618–20; Cindy Ruskin, *The Quilt: Stories from the Names Project* (New York: Pocket Books, 1988). Mohr maintains that the quilt is best understood as expressing sacred values and ritual in attempting to deal with mass death and individual loss. Mohr, *Gay Ideas*, 115–117.

62. The pink triangle is appropriated and inverted from the pink triangle that gay internees were forced to wear in the Nazi death camps. Lesbian internees were stigmatized with black triangles. The triangles were an insignia of subhumanity like the yellow Star of David worn by Jewish internees. "Silence = Death" refers to the inaction and lack of resistance to the internment of gay/lesbian people and their deaths. "Silence = Death" declares that oppression and annihilation of gay people, then and now, must be broken as a matter of survival," Douglas Crimp with Adam Rolston, *AIDS Demo Graphics* (Seattle: Bay Press, 1990), 14.

63. Peter Staley, "Has the Direct Action Group ACT UP Gone Astray?" *The Advocate* no. 582 (July 30, 1991), 98.

64. Burroughs Wellcome has claimed that the high price was intended to recover research costs for AZT. However, AZT was first synthesized by the Institute of Cancer Research, supported by federal funds. Burroughs Wellcome secured the patent for AZT with minimal preclinical trials costs. It raped the HIV community by initially charging each individual $10,000 per year for AZT, while production cost per capsule ranged between seven and fifteen cents. Burroughs Wellcome profited while

many HIV-positive people died from their inability to pay. For instance, indigent HIV-positive people in Missouri had to sue the state of Missouri to provide Medicaid reimbursement for AZT. How many HIV-positive people died prematurely because of the corporate greed of Burroughs Wellcome? Crimp, *AIDS Demo Graphics*, 114–21.

65. Chris Bull, "New York's Peter Staley: Activism as the Best Therapy," *The Advocate* no. 544 (Feb. 13, 1990): 32; Crimp, *AIDS Demo Graphics*, 46–50.

66. Cardinal O'Connor spearheaded opposition to an earlier position of the National Conference of Catholic Bishops that viewed condom usage as a medical issue to prevent HIV transmission rather than a sexual issue. O'Connor and other conservative bishops forced the rescinding of the earlier position.

67. Chris Bull, "Mass Action," *The Advocate* no. 542 (Jan. 16, 1990): 7. Crimp, *AIDS Demo Graphics*, 30–41.

68. Didiere Eribon, *Michel Foucault* (Cambridge: Harvard Univ. Press, 1991), 314–16.

69. Ed Cohen, "Foucauldian Necrologies: 'Gay' 'Politics'? Politically Gay?" *Textual Practice* 2, no. 1 (1988): 87–101. See Foucault's discussion of the gay/lesbian movement: G. Barbadette, "The Social Triumph of the Sexual Will: A Conversation with Michel Foucault," *Christopher Street* no. 64 (1982): 36–41; Bob Gallagher and Alexander Wilson, "Sex and the Politics of Identity: An Interview with Michel Foucault," in *Gay Spirit*, ed. Thompson, 25–35; Foucault, *Michel Foucault: Politics, Philosophy, Culture* (New York: Routledge, 1990), 286–303.

70. Cohen, "Foucauldian Necrologies," 91.

71. Gallagher and Wilson, "Sex and the Politics of Identity;" in *Gay Spirit*, ed. Thompson, 28.

72. Cohen, "Foucauldian Necrologies," 92.

73. Barbadette, "Social Triumph," 39.

74. Foucault defines asceticism:

> Asceticism as a renunciation of pleasure has got a bad name. But being ascetic is different: it's the way you work at yourself in order to change you or to make yourself appear, which fortunately it never does. Isn't that what our problem is today? We've said goodbye to a certain form of asceticism. It's now up to us to step forward into a gay asceticism, which would involve us working on ourselves and inventing—I don't mean discovering—an as yet uncertain way of being. What we ought to be working towards, I feel, is not so much the liberation of our desires, but making ourselves infinitely more open to enjoyment. (Cohen, "Foucauldian Necrologies," 92)

Foucault in his *The Use of Pleasure* and *The Care of the Self* turns his attention to asceticism, the production of the self, and the issue of pleasure. Michel Foucault, *The History of Sexuality*, vol. 2, *The Use of Pleasure* (New York: Vintage Books, 1990); *The History of Sexuality*, vol. 3, *The Care of the Self* (New York: Vintage Books, 1990).

75. Cohen, "Foucauldian Necrologies," 97.

Chapter 3. From Christ the Oppressor to Jesus the Liberator

1. Michel Foucault, *Power/Knowledge* (New York: Pantheon Books, 1980), 133.
2. Michel Foucault, *Language, Counter-Memory, Practice* (Ithaca: Cornell Univ. Press, 1977), 151.
3. Raymond E. Brown, *The Birth of Messiah* (New York: Doubleday, 1977); Eta Ranke-Heinemann, *Eunuchs for the Kingdom of Heaven* (New York: Doubleday, 1990).
4. Hubert Dreyfus and Paul Rabinow, *Michel Foucault, Beyond Structuralism and Hermeneutics* (Chicago: Univ. of Chicago Press, 1983), 255. Christian discourse between the second and fourth centuries C.E. gave a lot of attention to sexual desire/pleasure. 1 Corinthinians 7:1, and 8 recommends refraining from sex because the end is near. The Acts of Paul and Thecla, an enormously popular text in the early Christian movement, maintains that only virgins will be resurrected. See Elaine Pagels's discussion of Thecla in *Adam, Eve, and the Serpent* (New York Random House, 1988), 18–20. See also: Ranke-Heinemann, *Eunuchs*, 18–20, Foucault, *History of Sexuality*, vol. 3 (New York: Vintage Books, 1990); E. R. Dodds, *Pagan and Christian in an Age of Anxiety* (Cambridge: Cambridge Univ. Press, 1965), 32–33; James A. Brundage, *Law, Sex, and Christian Society in Medieval Europe* (Chicago: Univ. of Chicago Press, 1987), 60–76. Peter Brown, *The Body and Society* (New York: Columbia Univ. Press, 1988), 65–209.
5. Samuel Laeuchli, *Power and Sexuality: The Emergence of Canon Law at the Synod of Elvira* (Philadelphia: Temple Univ. Press, 1977), 56–113; Beverly Harrison and Carter Heyward, "Pain and Pleasure: Avoiding the Confusions of Christian Tradition in Feminist Theory," in *Christianity, Patriarchy, and Abuse*, ed. Joanne Carlson Brown and Carole Bolin (New York: Pilgrim Press, 1989), 150–166.
6. Foucault observes, "These two options, that sex is at the heart of all pleasure and that its nature requires that it should be restricted and devoted to procreation, are not of Christian but of Stoic origin; and Christianity was obliged to incorporate them when it sought to integrate itself in the State structure of the Roman Empire in which Stoicism was virtually the universal philosophy. Sex then became the code of pleasure"; Michel Foucault, "On Genealogy," in Hubert Dreyfus and Paul Rabinow, *Michel Foucault* (Chicago: Univ. of Chicago Press, 1985), 242. See also Elizabeth A. Clark, "Foucault, the Fathers, and Sex," *Journal of the American Academy of Religion* 56 no. 4 (1989): 619–41. See John McNeill's summary of the incorporation of Stoicism into Christian discourse on human nature; McNeill, *The Church and the Homosexual* (Kansas City: Sheed Andrews and McMeel, 1976), 89–107, also Brown, *Body and Society*, 122–37.
7. Foucault, *Power/Knowledge*, 191. See also Foucault, "Sexuality and Solitude," in *On Signs*, ed. Marshall Blonsky (Baltimore: Johns Hopkins Univ. Press, 1985), 369.

8. W. E. Phipps, *Was Jesus Married? The Distortion of Sexuality in the Christian Tradition* (New York: Harper & Row, 1970), 120–63; Dodds, *Pagan and Christian.*

9. Beverly Harrison notes that misogyny and homophobia are sustained by the depth of anti-body, antisensual discourse in dominant Christianity. The phobic fear of eroticism as foreign and evil permeated Christianity from early in the second century C.E. Misogyny is reflected in the phobic projection of female stigma onto any males who need to be distanced from dominant norms of manhood, such as men attracted to same-sex practices. See Beverly Harrison, "Misogyny and Homophobia: The Unexplored Connections," in *Making the Connections,* ed. Carol Robb (Boston: Beacon Press, 1985), 135–51. Rosemary Ruether similarly connects homophobia and heterosexism in Christian history; see Ruether, "Homophobia, Heterosexism, and Pastoral Practice," in *Homosexuality in the Priesthood and Religious Life,* ed. Jeannine Gramick (New York: Crossroad, 1990), 21–35. See also James B. Nelson, *Embodiment: An Approach to Sexuality and Christian Theology* (Minneapolis, Augsburg Press, 1979), 37–69, and McNeill *Church and the Homosexual,* 189.

10. In his detailed study, *Law, Sex, and Christian Society,* James Brundage documents Christian hostility to sexual pleasure in its discursive and nondiscursive practices from its origin to the Reformation. Peter Brown, in *Body and Society,* examines Christianity's anti-body and antisexual perspective from its enculturation into the Hellenistic world to the early Middle Ages. Thomas Aquinas appeared to acknowledge pleasure as positive value. He said, "Pleasure is the perfection of activity," quoted by Matthew Fox, *Sheer Joy* (San Francisco: HarperSanFrancisco, 1991), 34. Thomas stood against the Augustinian tradition in this regard. However, his view of female sexuality remained narrow. See Fox's discussion, 37–45. I would include his statements on same-sex practices as well. It is bizarre for Catholic hierarchs and theologians to canonize an outdated view of sexuality.

11. Dorothee Soelle speaks about *apatheia,* "literally non-suffering. . . . Apathy is a form of the inability to suffer. It is understanding as a social condition in which people are dominated by a goal of avoiding suffering that it becomes a goal to avoid human relationships and contacts altogether"; Soelle, *Suffering* (Philadelphia: Fortress Press, 1975), 36. Jürgen Moltmann asserts, "In the physical sense, *apatheia* means unchangeableness; in the psychological sense, insensitivity; and in the ethical sense, freedom"; Moltmann, *The Crucified God* (New York: Harper & Row, 1974), 267. Literature on the theme of God's passibility/impassibility: J. K. Mozley, *The Impassability of God* (London: Cambridge Univ. Press, 1926); Terrence Fretheim, *The Suffering of God: An Old Testament Perspective* (Philadelphia: Fortress Press, 1977); S. Paul Schilling, *God and Human Language* (Nashville: Abingdon Press, 1977); Warren McWilliams, *The Passion of God* (Macon, GA: Mercer Univ. Press, 1985).

12. Augustine, *City of God* 8, 17. Passion is identified with demons and the pagan gods and rationality with the Christian God.

13. What we have in the Christian apologists was a synthesis of the biblical God with Stoic philosophy. The Hebrew God was transformed into the Stoic, apathetic God. Thus, the Hebrew God lost both compassion and passion for justice-doing.

14. Carter Heyward, *The Redemption of God: A Theology of Mutual Relation* (Washington, D.C.: University of America Press, 1989), 12; Moltmann, *Crucified God*, 222, 248.

15. Tertullian, *On the Flesh of Christ*, 20. See Brown's discussion, *Body and Society*, 76–79.

16. Jerome, *Letter 48, To Pammachoius*, 2, quoted in Elaine Pagels, *Adam, Eve, and the Serpent*, 95. Ambrose and Augustine also condemned Jovinian for his heresy. See Pagels's description of the dispute between Jerome and Jovinian, 91–96. See Brown's treatment of Jerome, *Body and Society*, 366–86.

17. Reay Tannahill, *Sex in History* (New York: Stein and Day, 1980), 136–53; Brown, *Body and Society*, 285–322, 341–65.

18. Augustine's legacy has been fifteen hundred years of hostility to sexual pleasure. He maintains that in Eden the connection between man and woman is asexual (*De gen. contra Manichaeos* 1.19). Sexual pleasure was considered an evil (*City of God* 22.24; *Against Julian* 5.9, 5.46; *De homo conjugali* 3.3, 8.9, 17.9). In *Epistles* 262.4, Augustine advises a woman, "Your husband does not cease to be your spouse because of joint abstinence from carnal relations. You will remain all the more devout as spouses the more you keep this resolution." Virginity thus was a higher state of holiness than marriage with sexual relations. Abstinence from pleasure and lust-inspired sexual actions became a preoccupation for Christianity into the modern era. See Pagels, Miles, and Brown on Augustine and sexuality: Pagels, *Adam, Eve, and the Serpent*, 98–150; Margaret Miles, *Augustine on the Body* (Missoula, MT: Scholars Press, 1979), 41–72; Brown, *Body and Society*, 387–427.

19. *On Marriage and Concupiscence* 1.13. "That semen itself," Augustine argues, "already 'shackled by the bonds of death,' transmits the damage incurred by sin." Hence, Augustine concludes, "Every human being ever conceived through semen is born contaminated with sin." Pagels summarizes the concept of flesh and sin in *City of God* 13.14: Pagels; *Adam, Eve, and the Serpent*, 109.

20. Foucault, "On Genealogy," in Dreyfus and Rabinow, *Michel Foucault*, 370; Pagels, *Adam, Eve, and the Serpent*, 110–12.

21. Foucault defines self-technology: "In every culture, I think, this self-technology implies a set of truth obligations: learning what is truth, discovering the truth, being enlightened by the truth, telling the truth. All these are considered important either for the constitution or for the transformation of the self"; Foucault, "On Genealogy," in Dreyfus and Rabinow, *Michel Foucault*, 367. See Michel Foucault, "Technologies of the Self," in *Technologies of the Self*, ed. Luther Martin, Huck Gutman, and Patrick Hutton (Amherst: Univ. of Massachusetts Press, 1988), 16–49; Foucault, "The Political Technology of Individuals," in *Technologies of the Self*, 145–62.

22. Foucault, "On Genealogy," in Dreyfus and Rabinow, *Michel Foucault,* 371.
23. Dorothee Soelle, *Death by Bread Alone* (Philadelphia: Fortress Press, 1978), 9–10. Anti-body dualism emerged in Christian discourse and practice from basic assimilation of cultural/philosophical misogyny. The basic hatred and fear of women were incorporated into the Christian social production and distribution of a complex web of antisexual, misogynistic, and homophobic power relations. Maleness was asserted as superior to femaleness; it became a rejection of the body with all its pleasures; see Harrison "Misogyny and Homophobia," in *Making the Connections,* ed. Robb, 136–51. Cf. Nelson, *Embodiment,* 37–69.
24. Leo Steinberg presents compelling evidence of the Renaissance shift toward the sexuality of Jesus: Leo Steinberg, *The Sexuality of Christ in Renaissance Art and in Modern Oblivion* (New York: Pantheon Books, 1983), 1.
25. Steinberg, *Sexuality of Christ,* 13. See also Arnold Davidson, "Sex and the Emergence of Sexuality," in *Forms of Desire,* ed. Edward Stein (New York: Routledge, 1992), 102–10.
26. James B. Nelson, *The Intimate Connection* (Philadelphia: Westminster Press, 1988), 106.
27. Luther refers to sexual desire and union as instances of shame and disgust: Luther, "Lectures on Genesis," *Luther's Works,* ed. Jaroslav Pelikan (St. Louis: Concordia, 1968) 1:62–63, 71, 105. On the other hand, Luther affirms the goodness of marriage and sexuality: Luther, "Estate of Marriage," *Luther's Works,* ed. Jaroslav Pelikan 45:17, 36–37.
28. John Calvin, *A Harmony of the Gospels* (Edinburgh: Saint Andre Press, 1972), 2:249.
29. John Paul II in *Familiaris consortia* praises periodic continence in marriage through the use of the rhythm method of birth control. He maintains married (oppposite-sex) sexual actions may serve procreation or abstinence. In John Paul's gospel of continence, birth control would allow unbridled pleasure/lust.
30. Tom F. Driver, "Sexuality and Jesus," *Union Seminary Quarterly Review* 20 (1965): 243, 240.
31. D. H. Lawrence, *The Later D. H. Lawrence* (New York: Knopf, 1952), 391.
32. Phipps, *Was Jesus Married?;* Phipps, *The Sexuality of Jesus* (New York: Harper & Row, 1975).
33. John Meier disputes Phipps's use of the scriptural evidence to argue for a married Jesus and instead assumes the traditional position of Jesus' celibacy: Meier, *A Marginal Jew: Rethinking the Historical Jesus* (New York: Doubleday, 1991), 1:332–45.
34. Tom Driver argues against the current Christian practice of keeping Jesus the Christ as centrist model. Such a centrist model leads to normative practices that are exclusive; see Driver, *Christ in a Changing World: Toward an Ethical Christology* (New York: Crossroad, 1981), 32–56.
35. George Edwards, "A Critique of Creationist Homophobia," in *Homosexuality and Religion,* ed. Richard Hasbany (New York: Harrington Park Press, 1989), 95–118.

36. Phyllis Trible, *God and the Rhetoric of Sexuality* (Philadelphia: Fortress Press, 1978), 12.
37. Norman Gottwald shares Trible's conclusions; Gottwald, *The Hebrew Bible: A Socio-literary Introduction* (Philadelphia: Fortress Press, 1985), 239.
38. Patricia Wilson-Kastner, *Faith, Feminism, and the Christ* (Philadelphia: Fortress Press, 1983); Rosemary Ruether, *To Change the World: Christology and Cultural Criticism* (New York: Crossroad, 1981); Elisabeth Schüssler Fiorenza, *In Memory of Her* (New York: Crossroad, 1989).
39. Schüssler Fiorenza, *In Memory of Her*, 118–54.
40. The sculpture by Edwina Sandys was on display during Lent in 1984. See Carter Heyward, *Touching Our Strength* (San Francisco: Harper & Row, 1989), 114.
41. Rita Nakashima Brock, *Journeys by Heart* (New York: Crossroad, 1991), 113.
42. Ibid., 52.
43. Heyward, *Touching Our Strength*, 114.
44. Norman Perrin, *Jesus and the Language of the Kingdom* (London: SCM, 1976); J. D. Crossan, *In Parables* (San Francisco: Harper & Row, 1973); Bruce Chilton and J. I. H. McDonald, *Jesus and the Ethics of the Kingdom* (Grand Rapids: Eerdmans, 1987).
45. Some good treatments of the historical Jesus: E. P. Sanders, *Jesus and Judaism* (Philadelphia: Fortress Press, 1987); Richard Horsley, *Jesus and the Spiral of Violence: Popular Jewish Resistance in Roman Palestine* (San Francisco: Harper & Row, 1987); Marcus Borg, *Jesus: A New Vision* (San Francisco: Harper & Row, 1987); J. D. Crossan, *The Historical Jesus: The Life of a Mediterranean Jewish Peasant* (San Francisco: HarperSanFrancisco, 1991); Paul Hollenbach, "Liberating Jesus for Social Involvement," *Biblical Theology Bulletin* 15 (1985): 151–57.
46. Chilton and McDonald, *Jesus*, 110–34.
47. Norman Perrin, *Rediscovering the Teachings of Jesus* (New York: Harper & Row, 1967), 102–8; Crossan, *Historical Jesus*, 261–64, 341–44.
48. Crossan, *Historical Jesus*, 341, 346.
49. Schüssler Fiorenza, *In Memory of Her*, 140–50.
50. Douglas Oakman, *Jesus and the Economic Questions of His Day* (Lewiston, NY: Edwin Mellen Press, 1986), 213–15; Halvor Moxnes, *The Economy of the Kingdom* (Philadelphia: Fortress Press, 1988), 157–59.
51. For a good picture of first-century Judaism, see: Richard Horsley and John Hanson, *Bandits, Prophets, and Messiahs* (San Francisco: Harper & Row, 1985); Horsely, *Jesus and the Spiral;* Oakman, *Jesus and the Economic Questions;* Gerd Theissen, *The Sociology of Early Palestinian Christianity* (Philadelphia: Fortress Press, 1988); Anthony Saldarini, *Pharisees, Scribes, and Sadducees* (Wilmington, DE: Michael Glazier, 1988); Crossan, *Historical Jesus;* Martin Goodman, *The Ruling Class of Judea: The Origins of the Jewish Revolt Against Rome* A.D. 66–70 (Cambridge: Cambridge Univ. Press, 1987); Sheldon Isenberg, "Power Through the Temple and

Torah in Greco-Roman Palestine," in *Christianity, Judaism, and Other Greco-Roman Cults*, ed. Jacob Neusner (Leiden: E. J. Brill, 1975), 24–52.

52. Oakman, *Jesus and the Economic Questions*, 155, 153–55. See also: Horsley, *Jesus and the Spiral*, 246–84; John Kloppenborg, "Alms, Debt, and Divorce: Jesus' Ethics in their Mediterranean Context," *Toronto Journal of Theology* 6 (1990): 182–200; Crossan, *Historical Jesus*, 294.

53. E. P. Sanders recognizes the lethal consequences of Jesus' action in the Temple, yet he does not realize the full political implications of the action. Horsley does recognize the political implications; Sanders, *Jesus and Judaism*, 75, 296–306; Horsley, *Jesus and the Spiral*, 297–317.

54. Francis Schüssler Fiorenza, *Foundational Theology* (New York: Crossroad, 1986), 45.

55. Moltmann, *Crucified God*, 252.

56. Dorothee Soelle, *The Strength of the Weak* (Philadelphia: Westminster Press, 1984), 71–76.

57. *Newsweek*, Aug. 7, 1967, 83; Hugh Montefiore, *For God's Sake* (Philadelphia: Fortress Press, 1969), 182. Phipps argues that if Montefiore's speculations are perceived as plausible, it may be due to the effeminate way that artists represented Jesus. He notes that artists frequently used women as models to capture Jesus' tender qualities: *Was Jesus Married?* 7. Phipps wants a total heterosexual construction of Jesus' sexual practices. He demonstrates heterosexist stereotypic understanding of people inclined to same-sex practices as effeminate.

58. Malcolm Boyd, "Was Jesus Gay?" *The Advocate* no. 565 (Dec. 4, 1990): 90. Boyd also quotes the Rev. Sharon Robinson, dean of Samaritan College:

> I never knew how to separate my spirituality from my sexuality. . . . Sleeping with a woman was both natural and fulfilling. It's unthinkable to me that Jesus could be uncomfortable with my lesbianism. He understands fully that being lesbian or gay isn't simply a matter of genital behavior but is a whole way of being. Jesus was just as queer in his time as we are in ours. What a gift.

59. Robert Williams, *Just as I Am: A Practical Guide to Being Out, Proud, and Christian* (New York: Crown Publishers, 1992), 122. See Williams's full reconstruction of Jesus as gay and sexual, 116–22. I had the privilege of reading Williams's manuscript *The Beloved Disciple*. In that work, Williams reconstructs a fictional story of Jesus and Lazarus as lovers. One of the many valuable aspects of the work is the vivid description of the lovemaking between Jesus and Lazarus. *The Beloved Disciple* directly confronts the sexphobic and homophobic attitudes of Christians regarding Jesus, and at the same time, it expresses the widespread intuition shared by many gay Christians about Jesus.

60. Rosemary Ruether, "The Sexuality of Jesus: What the Synoptics Have to Say," *Christianity and Crisis* 38, no. 8 (1978):136–37.

61. The African American reclamation of Jesus as black has been an empowering resource for their liberation practice. See James Cone, *A Black Theology of Liberation* (Philadelphia: J. B. Lippincott, 1970), 212–19;

Cone, *God of the Oppressed* (New York: Seabury Press, 1975), 133–37. Some feminist theologians have started to speak about the Christ/a as the woman-affirming experience of Jesus the Christ: Heyward, *Touching Our Strength,* 114–18; Brock, *Journey by Heart,* 52–53, 67-70.

62. Ruether, "Sexuality of Jesus," 136, 137.

63. See Clark's reconstruction of a gay-sensitive Jesus. J. Michael Clark, *A Place to Start: Towards an Unapologetic Gay Liberation Theology* (Dallas: Monument Press, 1987), 108–117. E. M. Barrett argues for an embodied, sexual Jesus: Barrett, "Gay People and Moral Theology," in *The Gay Academic,* ed. Louie Crew (Palm Springs: ETC Publications, 1978), 329–34.

64. The Jesus traditions in the Bible do not provide us with any information on the sexual practices of Jesus, whether those practices were opposite sex or same sex or nonexistent. The silence of the biblical sources and the idealization of celibate practice by the later church does not prove that Jesus was celibate. The question of Jesus' sex practice remains unanswerable. However, Jesus broke gender lines and roles of his first-century society in his relationships with women disciples. His washing the feet of his disciples was a function frequently performed by a wife for her husband or a servant for his master. Jesus had a great deal of social freedom that appeals to gay/lesbian Christians.

65. An early Christian apologetic to shift blame from Pilate and the Romans to the Jewish leadership takes place in the formation of the passion accounts in the four Gospels. The fact of Jesus' crucifixion presented problems to citizens in the Greco-Roman world. Paul encountered obstacles in preaching a crucified messiah (1 Cor. 1:23). There was no more heinous crime than political revolution. If Jesus was regarded as a political revolutionary (*lestes*), than his whole movement came under suspicion. The depoliticizing of Jesus and his death and the subsequent spiritualizing of the Christ led to an inculturation of Christian discourse within Greco-Roman philosophy. Depoliticizing, spiritualizing, and the idealization of celibacy are integrally woven in Christian discourse on God, Christ, and sexuality.

66. National Gay and Lesbian Task Force Policy Institute, *Anti-Gay/Lesbian Violence, Victimization, and Defamation in 1990* (Washington, D.C.: NGLTFPI, 1991), 13.

Chapter 4. A Queer Biblical Hermeneutics

1. Michel Foucault, *Michel Foucault: Politics, Philosophy, Culture* (New York: Routledge, 1988), 155.

2. Elisabeth Schüssler Fiorenza, *Bread Not Stone* (Boston: Beacon Press, 1984); Schüssler Fiorenza, *In Memory of Her* (New York: Crossroad, 1989), *But She Said* (Boston: Beacon Press, 1990). Kevin Gordon asserts that a gay/lesbian theological methodology shares many contours with a feminist liberation theology. Kevin Gordon, "The Sexual Bankruptcy of

Christian Traditions: A Perspective of Radical Suspicion and Fundamental Trust," in *AIDS Issues: Confronting the Challenge*, ed. David Hullman (New York: Pilgrim Press, 1989), 185–86.

3. Schüssler Fiorenza, *Bread Not Stone*, xviii.

4. Ibid., xiii.

5. Phyllis Trible, *Texts of Terror* (Philadelphia: Fortress Press, 1984), 1. See Gen. 16:1–16, 21:9–21; 2 Samuel 13:1–22; Judges 19:1–30; Judges 11:29–40.

6. Trible, *Texts of Terror*, 3.

7. Schüssler Fiorenza, *Bread Not Stone*, 30–31.

8. Ibid., 45.

9. Michel Foucault, *Discipline and Punish: The Birth of the Prison* (New York: Pantheon Books, 1979), 27.

10. Schüssler Fiorenza, *Bread Not Stone*, 50.

11. Norbert Lohfink does a very concise study in the Hebrew Scriptures on God's preferential option for the poor and the oppressed: Norbert Lohfink, *Option for the Poor* (Berkeley: Bibal Press, 1987).

12. Elisabeth Schüssler Fiorenza observes, "Fundamentalist apologetics has linked the theological concept of inerrancy to the historic understanding of truth. Roman Catholicism shares in this fundamentalist Biblicism insofar as it is reluctant to accept biblical criticism and to free itself from precritical doctrinal positions," *Bread Not Stone*, 29; James Barr, *Fundamentalism* (Philadelphia: Westminster Press, 1978).

13. "Report of the Special Committee on Human Sexuality," in *Presbyterians and Human Sexuality 1991* (Louisville, KY: Offices of Presbyterian General Assembly, 1991). This is one of the best theologically crafted statements on human sexuality and justice that I have read. The minority report in the same volume is a classic example of blending biblical fundamentalism, heterosexism, and homophobia.

14. Stephen Morin and Ellen Garfinkle, "Male Homophobia," in *GaySpeak: Gay male and Lesbian Communication*, ed. James Chesbro (New York: Pilgrim Press, 1981), 119, 332; George R. Edwards, "A Critique of Creationist Homophobia," in *Homosexuality and Religion*, ed. Richard Hasbany (New York: Harrington Park Press, 1989), 95–118.

15. The Bible is frequently read as a singular text. However, it consists of many books with many diverse, developing, and conflicting traditions. Cardinal Ratzinger's usage is an example of Catholic biblical interpretation grounded in a fundamentalism of the church's teachings. He states, "The Scriptures are not properly understood when they are interpreted in a way which contradicts the Church's living Tradition. To be correct, the interpretation of Scripture must be in substantial accord with Tradition"; Ratzinger, "Letter to the Bishops of the Catholic Church on the Pastoral Care of Homosexual Persons," in *The Vatican and Homosexuality*, ed. Jeannine Gramick and Pat Furey (New York: Crossroad, 1988), 3. Ratzinger's usage of the alleged biblical texts on same-sex practices does not substantially differ from Jerry Falwell's usage.

16. Both Von Rad and Westermann interpret the sin of Sodom as unnatural sin and the lack of hospitality: G. Von Rad, *Genesis* (Philadelphia:

Westminster Press, 1961), 210–17; C. Westermann, *Genesis 12–36* (Minneapolis: Augsburg Publishing, 1985), 301. Vawter interprets the text as a traditional Roman Catholic exegete; the sin of Sodom is homosexuality. He reads back homosexuality as a preference/identity back into the text; B. Vawter, *On Genesis: A New Reading* (Garden City, NY: Doubleday, 1977), 233–36. All three above authors are affected by traditional Sodom discourse.

17. Hospitality and protection of the sojourner (*ger*) are important to God in the Hebrew Scriptures. God reminds the Hebrews that they too were once sojourners: "You shall not oppress a sojourner (*ger*); you know the heart of a sojourner; you were sojourners (*gerim*) in the land of Egypt" (Exod. 23:9). D. S. Bailey was the first in recent times to suggest that the sin of Sodom was wickedness in general and lack of hospitality in particular; Dereck Sherwin Bailey, *Homosexuality and the Western Christian Tradition* (Hamden, CT: Archon Books, 1975), 8. See also John Boswell, *Christianity, Social Tolerance, and Homosexuality* (Chicago: Univ. of Chicago Press, 1980), 92–98. James Loader argues that there are antiurban sentiments and issues of hospitality in the Sodom story: Loader, *A Tale of Two Cities: Sodom and Gomorrah* (Kampen, the Netherlands: J. K. Kok, 1990), 15–47.

18. Kenneth Dover, *Greek Homosexuality* (Cambridge: Harvard Univ. Press, 1978), 105; Loader, *Tale of Two Cities*, 37.

19. Walter Brueggemann places the sin of Sodom in the turbulence of the narrative. He argues that not only is it a violation of hospitality but the violence of gang rape. He notes that *outcry* in 19:13 argues for an abuse of justice; Brueggemann, *Genesis* (Atlanta: John Knox Press, 1982), 164.

20. Norman Gottwald challenges the cultic interpretation:

> Biblical scholars have been inclined to think that homosexuality was stigmatized in ancient Israel because of its practice in Canaanite fertility religion; recently, however, doubts have been raised about whether cult prostitution was practiced as widely in Israel's environment as once thought. There is also the real possibility that male homosexuality (lesbianism is not mentioned in the Hebrew Bible) was abhorred in ancient Israel because it seemed to involve a prodigal waste of "male seed" which according to ancient misunderstanding was thought to be limited in quantity or potency. In that event, to be a homosexual was to be derelict in fathering the large families that were the cultural norm for agricultural Israelites.

Gottwald, *The Hebrew Bible* (Philadelphia, Fortress Press, 1985), 477.

21. George R. Edwards notes the indiscriminate modernizing of biblical references to cult prostitutes as referring to noncultic same-sex practices: Edwards, *Gay/Lesbian Liberation: A Biblical Perspective* (New York: Pilgrim Press, 1984), 68. Robin Scroggs notes that biblical statements can only be applied to situations similar to those addressed: Scroggs, *The New Testament and Homosexuality* (Philadelphia: Fortress Press, 1983), 125. See Comstock's treatment of biblical texts on anti-gay/lesbian violence: Gary Comstock, *Violence Against Lesbians and Gay Men* (New York: Columbia Univ. Press, 1992), 128–40.

22. Victor Furnish, *The Moral Teaching of Paul* (Nashville: Abingdon Press, 1979), 73–78.
23. Furnish, *Moral Teaching*, 58–68, 73–74; Boswell, *Christianity*, 108–12; Scroggs, *New Testament*, 89, 114–15; Edwards, *Gay/Lesbian Liberation*, 85–100; L. William Countryman, *Dirt, Greed, and Sex* (Philadelphia: Fortress Press, 1988), 109–16.
24. Edwards, *Gay/Lesbian Liberation*, 77. Victor Furnish also concludes, "Since Paul offered no direct teaching to his own churches on the subject of homosexual conduct, his letters certainly cannot yield any specific answers to the questions being faced in the modern church"; Furnish, *Moral Teaching*, 79.
25. Furnish, *Moral Teaching*, 54. Boswell's appendix on lexicography and Paul is excellent: Boswell, *Christianity*, 335–53.
26. Boswell, *Christianity*, 107.
27. Ibid., 352.
28. Ibid., 107.
29. Ibid., 106–7; Countryman, *Dirt, Greed, and Sex*, 128.
30. Furnish, *Moral Teaching*, 73; Boswell, *Christianity*, 107, 353. Scroggs differs from Boswell. He advances the hypothesis that *malakoi* and *arsenokoitai* refer respectively to passive and active partners in male same-sex intercourse: Scroggs, *New Testament*, 62–65, 101–9. Scroggs believes that Paul is condemning pederasty, not adult same-sex practices.
31. Countryman, *Dirt, Greed, and Sex*, 133–35; Edwards, *Gay/Lesbian Liberation*, 100–2.
32. Edwards, *Gay/Lesbian Liberation*, 28. John J. McNeill and Loader have good summaries of the development of the homosexual interpretation of the story of Sodom: McNeill, *The Church and the Homosexual* (Kansas City: Sheed Andrews and McMeel, 1976), 68–87; Loader, *A Tale of Two Cities*, 75–138.
33. Boswell, *Christianity*, 333.
34. *Summa Theologica* 153.2; 154.11–12.
35. *Confessions* 3.8.
36. Boswell, *Christianity*, 203.
37. Ibid., 203–4.
38. Ibid., 316.
39. *Summa Theologica* 154.11.
40. James A. Brundage, *Law, Sex, and Christian Society in Medieval Europe* (Chicago: Univ. of Chicago Press, 1987), 7.
41. Bailey, *Homosexuality*, 73–75. See also Bailey's and Boswell's discussions of Justinian: Bailey, *Homosexuality*, 73–81; Boswell, *Christianity*, 170–79. See also Brundage, *Law*.
42. Quoted in Boswell, *Christianity*, 289.
43. Ibid., 293.
44. Ibid., 93 n. 2.
45. Ibid., 272–75. Jonathan Dollimore, *Sexual Dissidence* (Oxford: Clarendon Press, 1991), 238; Brundage, *Law*, 472–73, 493–94. Brundage notes

Jacques de Vitry's claim during the twelfth century that Muhammad introduced sodomy to the Arab world, 399.

46. Dollimore, *Sexual Dissidence*, 237. See David Greenberg's discussion of the Buggery Act of 1533 in England: Greenberg, *The Construction of Homosexuality* (Chicago: Univ. of Chicago Press, 1988), 323–24.

47. Boswell, *Christianity*, 272–75; Brundage, *Law*, 313; Dollimore, *Sexual Dissidence*, 237. Dollimore also cites an interesting article by Arthur Gilbert about the correlation of social and political crises provoking the policing of sexual deviance: Gilbert, "Sexual Deviance and Disaster During the Napoleonic Wars," *Albion* no. 9 (1977): 98–113.

48. Dollimore, *Sexual Dissidence*, 238. See similar arguments on sexual dissidence: Jeffrey Richards, *Sex, Dissidence, Damnation: Minority Groups in the Middle Ages* (New York: Routledge, 1991).

49. Boswell, *Christianity*, 338.

50. Boswell, *Christianity*, 348.

51. *Summa contra gentiles* 3.122.

52. Ibid., 204–5, 353.

53. Boswell, *Christianity*, 338 and 338 n. 7; Furnish, *Moral Teaching*, 53–58.

54. Fred W. Burnett asserts, "The phrase 'the Bible is the Church's book' establishes boundaries which can be shown to be ideological and arbitrary, but also have material, discursive effects." See Burnett, "Postmodern Biblical Exegesis: The Eve of Historical Criticism," *Semeia* 51 (1991): 67. Burnett is correct to point out the ideological possession of the Bible by the churches. The churches view biblical scholars as inscribed within their own discursive field but in a subordinate position. See Cardinal Ratzinger's *Instruction on the Ecclesial Vocation of the Theologian* (U.S. Conference of Catholic Bishops, Washington, D.C.: Congregation for the Doctrine of the Faith, 1990).

55. Dollimore, *Sexual Dissidence*, 90.

56. Foucault, *Michel Foucault*, 126–27, 138.

57. Burnett, "Postmodern Biblical Exegesis," 68–71; J. Michael Clark, *A Lavender Cosmic Pilgrim* (Garland, TX: Tangelwuld Press, 1990), 18–25.

58. I do not object, in principle, to the extension of ecclesial discursive practice into the political arena. I applaud statements for justice. My objection centers on statements that lack compassion and justice. This is apparent in their political campaigns against homosexuality and women.

59. J. Michael Clark, *A Place to Start: Towards an Unapologetic Gay Liberation Theology* (Dallas: Monument Press, 1987), 11.

60. Foucault, 208.

61. To name only a few: E. Schüssler Fiorenza, *Bread Not Stone* and *In Memory of Her*; Sharon Welch, *Communities of Resistance and Solidarity: A Feminist Perspective* (Maryknoll, NY: Orbis Books, 1985); Welch, *A Feminist Ethic of Risk* (Minneapolis: Fortress Press, 1990); Carter Heyward, *Touching Our Strength* (San Francisco: Harper & Row, 1989); Leonardo Boff, *Jesus Christ Liberator* (Maryknoll, NY: Orbis Books, 1986); Jon Sobrino, *Christology at the Crossroads* (Maryknoll, NY: Orbis Books, 1985); Gustavo Gutiérrez, *A Theology of Liberation* (Maryknoll, NY: Orbis

Books, 1973); Gutiérrez, Clodovis Boff, *Theology and Praxis* (Maryknoll, NY: Orbis Books, 1987).

62. Alternative gay/lesbian publishing houses were needed for the production and circulation of gay/lesbian discourse. Edisol W. Dotson, *Putting Out 1991* (San Francisco: Putting Out Books, 1991).

63. J. M. Clark, *Place to Start*, 45. See also Mary Hunt, *Fierce Tenderness: A Feminist Theology of Friendship* (New York: Crossroad, 1990), 60–62.

64. Foucault, *Michel Foucault*, 154–55.

65. Ibid., 155.

66. Gary A. Phillips, "Exegesis as Critical Praxis: Reclaiming History and Text from a Postmodern Perspective," *Semeia* 51 (1991): 7–49. See Richard Palmer, "Postmodern Hermeneutics and the Act of Reading," *Notre Dame English Journal: A Journal of Religion in Literature* 15 (1983): 55–84. Also Schüssler Fiorenza's defense of feminist postmodern reconstructions; Schüssler Fiorenza, *But She Said*, 88–101.

67. Foucault, *Michel Foucault*, 156.

68. Richard Plant, *The Pink Triangle* (New York: Henry Holt, 1986); Larry Kramer, *Reports from the Holocaust* (New York: St. Martin's Press), 1989.

69. Foucault, *Michel Foucault*, 154.

70. Elisabeth Schüssler Fiorenza has pioneered imaginative feminist reconstructions of biblical texts. Her reconstruction points to a parallel direction of development for queer reconstructions: Schüssler Fiorenza, *But She Said*. For gay/lesbian attempts to use their experience to interpret the Bible, see: Carter Heyward, *Our Passion for Justice* (New York: Pilgrim Press, 1984); Chris Glaser, *Come Home* (San Francisco: Harper & Row, 1990); Maury Johnston, *Gays Under Grace* (Nashville: Winston-Derek Publishers, 1991); J. M. Clark, *Place to Start*.

71. Elisabeth Schüssler Fiorenza, "The Politics of Otherness: Biblical Interpretation as a Critical Praxis for Liberation," in *The Future of Liberation Theology: Essays in Honor of Gustavo Gutiérrez*, ed. Marc Ellis and Otto Maduro (Maryknoll, NY: Orbis Books, 1989), 310–25; Lee Cormie, "The Hermeneutical Privilege of the Oppressed: Liberation Theologies, Biblical Faith, and Marxist Sociology of Knowledge," *Proceedings of the Catholic Theological Society of America*, 32 (1978), 155–81.

72. Sharon Welch understands the important of resistance for liberation discourse:

> Resistance narratives criticize the "master narratives" of Western literature, with their conventions of causality and closure. Resistance literature is postmodern in its rejection of a self-referential closure. Like the deconstructionists, resistance writers see their work as endlessly "textual," or better, referential, understandable only as embedded in a play of historical references and having as its function the evocation of political action. Such action reconstitutes the context and the meaning of the text.

Welch, *Feminist Ethic of Risk*, 142. I strongly agree with Welch's description of resistance narratives as postmodern. A gay/lesbian biblical hermeneutics is a postmodern project. See Welch's discussion of postmodern literature, 123–51. For postmodern biblical hermeneutics see: Phillips, "Exegesis as Critical Praxis," 7–49; David Jobling, "Writing the Wrongs of the World: The Deconstruction of the Biblical Text in the Context of Liberation Theologies," *Semeia* 51 (1991): 81–117; Burnett, "Postmodern Bibilical Exegesis," 61–80; Stephen Moore, *Literary Criticism and the Gospels* (New Haven: Yale Univ. Press, 1989), 108–70. I would balance deconstructive strategies with reconstructive hermeneutics. See Francis Schzüssler Fiorenza, *Foundational Theology* (New York: Crossroad, 1986), 285–311.

73. As gay/lesbian Christians feel their pain and the pain of other oppressed peoples, they commit themselves to transform the social conditions that lead to the pain. Their hermeneutics of solidarity opens them to conflict when they commit themselves to change the social conditions of oppression. There is resistance from already existing deployments of social power as they practice justice-doing. There is no escape from social and political conflict in the practice of solidarity and justice.

74. See Ched Myers for a good sociological exegesis of the exorcisms: Myers, *Binding the Strong Man* (Maryknoll, NY: Orbis Books, 1988), 192–94.

75. Paul Hollenbach, "Jesus, Demoniacs, and Public Authorities: A Socio-Historical Study," *Journal of the American Academy of Religion* 49 (1981): 573. Hollenbach's article is an excellent application of sociohistorical interpretation to Jesus' practice of exorcisms.

76. Hollenbach, "Jesus," 575. Gerd Theissen comes to the same conclusion: Theissen, *The Miracle Stories of the Early Christian Tradition* (Philadelphia: Fortress Press, 1983), 256.

77. Welch asserts, "Dangerous memories are a people's history of resistance and struggle, of dignity and transcendence in the face of oppression," *Feminist Ethic,* 155. See her discussion of dangerous memories: *Communities,* 32–54 and *Feminist Ethic,* 153–56. Jana Sawicki arrives at similar conclusions: Sawicki, *Disciplining Foucault: Feminism, Power, and the Body* (New York: Routledge, 1991), 57. A gay/lesbian biblical hermeneutics becomes a double-edged retrieval of the dangerous memories of Jesus' *basileia* practice and resistance to oppression and of gay/lesbian resistance and struggle against interlocking deployments of homophobic power. These two retrievals intensify dangerous memories of gay/lesbian Christians.

Chapter 5. Embracing the Exile

1. Michel Foucault, *Michel Foucault: Politics, Philosophy, Culture* (New York: Routledge, 1990), 156.

2. James Wolf, ed., *Gay Priests* (San Francisco: Harper & Row, 1989); Rosemary Curb and Nancy Manahan, *Lesbian Nuns* (Tallahassee: Naiad Press, 1985); Zalmos Sherwood, *Kairos: Confessions of a Gay Priest* (Boston: Alyson Publications, 1987); Jeannine Gramick, ed., *Homosexuality in the Priesthood and Religious Life* (New York: Crossroad,

1990); Malcolm Boyd, "Telling a Lie for Christ?" in *Gay Spirit,* ed. Mark Thompson (New York: St. Martin's Press, 1987), 78–87. See a gay/lesbian reading of gay Catholic priests: G. Destefano, "Gay Under the Collar: The Hypocrisy of the Catholic Church," *The Advocate* no. 439 (1986): 43–48. See also Robert Nugent and Jeannine Gramick, *Building Bridges: Gay and Lesbian Reality and the Catholic Church* (Mystic, CT: Twenty-third Publications, 1992), 89–134.

3. Peter Brown, *The Body and Society: Men, Women and Sexual Renunciation in Early Christianity* (New York: Columbia Univ. Press, 1988).

4. James Drane, "Condoms, AIDS, and Catholic Ethic: Open to the Transmission of Death?" *Commonweal* 118 (Mar. 22, 1991): 188–92. For a summary of the evolution of natural law arguments, see John J. McNeill, *The Church and the Homosexual* (Kansas City: Sheed Andrews and McMeel, 1976), 67–107; Nugent and Gramick, *Building Bridges,* 32–47.

5. For example, no ethicist addresses the social construction of sexuality. See Jeffrey Weeks, *Against Nature: Essays on History, Sexuality and Identity* (London: Rivers Ram Press, 1991); *Sexuality and Its Discontents* (New York, Routledge & Kegan Paul, 1985); Edward Stein, ed., *Forms of Desire: Sexual Orientation and the Social Constructionist Controversy* (New York: Routledge, 1990).

6. James A. Brundage; *Law, Sex, and Christian Society in Medieval Europe* (Chicago: Univ. of Chicago Press, 1987), 7. See also Mohr's criticism of the natural/unnatural usage: Richard Mohr, "Gay Basics: Some Questions, Facts, and Values," in *Bigotry, Prejudice and Hatred,* ed. Robert M. Baird and Stuart Rosenbau, (Buffalo, NY: Prometheus Books, 1992), 174–77.

7. Four of the most gay- and lesbian-sensitive authors: Rosemary Ruether, "Homophobia, Heterosexism, and Pastoral Practice," in *Homosexuality in the Priesthood and the Religious Life,* ed. Jeannine Gramick (New York: Crossroad, 1990) 21–35; Daniel Maguire, "The Shadow Side of the Homosexuality Debate," in the same volume, 36–55; Andre Guindon, *The Sexual Creators: An Ethical Proposal for Concerned Christians* (New York: University Press of America, 1986), 63–83, 167–79; James B. Nelson, *Embodiment: An Approach to Sexuality and Christian Theology* (Minneapolis: Augsburg Press, 1978), 180–210.

8. Marvin Ellison, "Common Decency: A New Christian Sexual Ethics," *Christianity and Crisis* (Nov. 12, 1990), 354.

9. Xavier John Seubert, "The Sacramentality of Metaphors: Reflection on Homosexuality," *Cross Currents* 41, no. 1 (Spring 1991): 62–63.

10. *Presbyterians and Human Sexuality 1991* (Louisville, KY: Offices of Presbyterian General Assembly, 1991), 9.

11. The long centuries of Christian intolerance and hatred to people with homoerotic attraction and Jewish people contributed to the Nazi discourse of hatred. It was Christian intolerance of the sexually and religiously/socially different that ratified Nazi brutality. A quarter of a million gay/lesbian Germans and hundreds of thousands of gay/lesbian non-Germans died in the Holocaust. See Louis Crompton, "Gay

Genocide from Leviticus to Hitler," in *The Gay Academic,* ed. Louie Crew, (Palm Springs: ETC Publications, 1978), 67–91.

12. The churches' lack of leadership on healthy sexuality has infantilized people. Those of the Christian Right who have opposed education on safer sex practices and HIV transmission have contributed to the active spread of HIV infection. Larry Kramer's metaphor of the "holocaust" has led gay/lesbian and AIDS activists to perceive the campaign against safer sex practices as genocidal.

13. Wolf, ed., *Gay Priests,* 29.

14. The Presbyterian General Assembly issued a pastoral letter to be read in every congregation that forbade the ordination of gay/lesbian candidates. It reaffirmed its earlier statements that called for gay/lesbian people to transform their sexual desires or remain celibate. The Presbyterian Church is not alone in its failure to educate and revise its fundamentalistic stance on gay/lesbian people. Two San Francisco congregations were put on ecclesial trial and suspended by the Evangelical Lutheran Church of America for the ordination of two lesbian women and a gay man. The United Methodist Church set up a committee studying sexual issues, which recommended deleting from the law the phrase "homosexuality is incompatible in Christian teaching." The committee recommendations have been received with widespread opposition, and the general consensus is that it will be voted down at the next General Convention. The Metropolitan Community Church applied for membership in the National Council of Churches over ten years ago; the application was overwhelmingly rejected. The Episcopalian bishops chose to table the proposals that included the ordination of openly gay/lesbian priests and the blessing of same-sex unions.

15. John Gallagher, "Rights Issues Split Protestant Churches; More Battles Expected," *The Advocate* no. 581 (July 16, 1991): 16.

16. Nancy Hardesty, "Holy Wars: Gays and Lesbians Fight Organized Religion," *The Advocate* no. 565 (Dec. 4, 1990): 34–38. The United Methodist minister Rose Mary Denman lost her ministerial status in an ecclesial trial. She was defrocked because she was lesbian. See Wickie Stamps, "No Church Lady," *The Advocate* no. 565 (Dec. 4, 1990): 40.

17. Craig O'Neill and Kathleen Ritter, *Coming Out Within* (San Francisco: HarperSanFrancisco, 1992). In a statement released to the Fresno priests, Bishop Steinbock claims that the Reverend Craig O'Neill "condones and promotes homosexual and lesbian sexual activity. . . . Automatically one who teaches a morality that is against the official teaching of the church is not able to teach in the name of the church."

18. The notion of the exile was articulated as a healing journey for gay/lesbian Christians by John Fortunato in *Embracing the Exile* (San Francisco: Harper & Row, 1982). Similarly, Rosemary Ruether speaks of an "exodus from patriarchy," *Women-Church: Theology and Practice of Feminist Liturgical Communities* (San Francisco: Harper & Row, 1985). See some attempts at nonapologetic theologies: J. Michael Clark, *A Place to Start: Towards an Unapologetic Gay Liberation Theology* (Dallas:

Monument Press, 1987); Clark, *A Defiant Celebration: Theological Ethics and Gay Sexuality* (Garland, TX: Tangelwuld Press, 1990); Robert Williams, "Re-Visioning Christianity for Radical Gay Men and Lesbians," *Christopher Street* no. 145 (March 1991): 23–27.

19. Gay/lesbian Christian groups such as Integrity, Dignity, etc., have suffered ecclesial sanctions, synodal condemnations, and overwhelming votes in favor of exclusionary practices. One has just to look at the failures of the Presbyterian General Assembly, the Episcopalians, United Methodists, and the National Conference of Catholic Bishops to adopt justice-doing practices in favor of gay/lesbian Christians.

20. Base or basic communities evolved with Latin American Christianity as a new way of doing church for and with the poor. They might be described as politically involved faith communities. See Arthur McGovern, *Liberation Theology and Its Critics* (Maryknoll, NY: Orbis Books, 1989), 201–4. Some gay/lesbian Christians are attempting a similar definition of a Christian base community: Kevin Calegari, "Dignity: A Basic Ecclesial Community," *Creation* (Sept./Oct. 1990), 18–21; Robert Williams, "Re-Visioning Christianity for Radical Gay Men and Lesbians," *Christopher Street* no. 145 ( ): 23–27; John J. McNeill, *Taking a Chance on God* (Boston : Beacon Press, 1988), 179–85.

21. Joseph Cardinal Ratzinger, "Letter to the Bishops of the Catholic Church on the Pastoral Care of Homosexual Persons," in *The Vatican and Homosexuality*, ed. Jeannine Gramick and Pat Furey (New York: Crossroad, 1988), 7–8.

22. Dorothee Soelle, *The Strength of the Weak* (Philadelphia: Westminister Press, 1984), 71–76.

23. Mary Hunt points out the need for reconstructing the meaning of church within the justice experience of women. Hunt calls it the "ekklesia of justice." Women-Church is a base community attempting to contextualize ritual practices to the experience of women; Hunt, *Fierce Tenderness: A Feminist Theology of Friendship* (New York: Crossroad, 1990), 159–61; Ruether, *Women-Church*.

24. Chris Glazer, *Come Home* (San Francisco: Harper & Row, 1990), 131–51; M. Clark, *Place to Start*; J.M. Clark, *Defiant Celebration*; Carter Heyward, *Our Passion for Justice* (New York: Pilgrim Press, 1984); Heyward, *Touching Our Strength* (San Francisco: Harper & Row, 1989).

25. Hunt, *Fierce Tenderness*, 117. Hunt suggests sacramentalizing friendship, 116–18. Gordon notes the sacramentality of gay/lesbian sexuality: Gordon, "The Sexual Bankruptcy of Christian Traditions," 191–92. See also Clark's discussion on developing new rituals and symbols. Clark, *Place to Start*, 175–79. Hunt and Clark are correct in their observations on the need for sacramentalizing and ritualizing gay/lesbian experience. I would push their observations to define a sacrament as composed of a symbolic gesture linked to an interpretative word about God's reign. It is not merely the *proclamation* of God's reign in "our" midst but the *practice* of God's reign in "our" midst. It is an intense, practical enounter

with God in our social world, which calls to work with God in transforming that world. Sacraments are moments of love-making and justice-doing. The whole base community tries to become a visible sacrament of God's reign.

26. Heyward, *Our Passion for Justice*, 86. See her discussion on how passion as lovers fuels rage at injustice, 83–93. Heyward develops the connection of love-making and justice-doing in her more recent work, *Touching Our Strength*. See also a ground-breaking attempt to sacramentalize gay/ lesbian experience by Xavier John Seubert, "Sacramentality of Metaphors," 52–68.

27. Robert Williams, *Just as I Am*, 226–39. Walter Williams, *The Spirit and the Flesh* (Boston: Beacon Press, 1992), Mitch Walker, "Visionary Love: The Magical Gay Spirit-Power," in *Gay Spirit*, ed. Thompson, 210–36; Judy Grahn, *Another Mother Tongue: Gay Words, Gay Worlds* (Boston: Beacon Press, 1984), 37–38.

28. Some recent portrayals of Jesus that deal with the shamanistic aspects of his ministry: James D. G. Dunn, *Jesus and the Spirit* (Philadelphia: Westminster Press, 1975), 11–92; Morton Smith, *Jesus the Magician* (Cambridge: Cambridge Univ. Press 1978); J. D. Crossan, *The Historical Jesus: The Life of a Mediterranean Jewish Peasant* (San Francisco: HarperSanFrancisco, 1991); Marcus Borg, *Jesus: A New Vision* (San Francisco: Harper & Row, 1987), 39–76.

29. See Malina's and Neyrey's presentation of Jesus the Witch: Bruce Malina and Jerry Neyrey, *Calling Jesus Names* (Sonoma: Polebridge Press, 1988), 1–32.

30. The notion of liminality was developed by Victor Turner's ritual studies of Ndembu initiation rituals. See his list of the characteristics of liminality, *The Ritual Process* (Chicago: Aldine Publishing, 1969), 92–93. See also Tom F. Driver, *The Magic of Ritual* (San Francisco: HarperSanFrancisco, 1991), 152–65.

31. Driver, *Magic of Ritual*, 73.

32. Ibid., 74.

33. Robert Williams, *Just as I Am*, 229. Grahn also recognizes that liminal spaces where queers inhabit have transcendent potentialities: Grahn, *Another Mother Tongue*, 270.

34. Matthew Fox, "The Spiritual Journey of the Homosexual and Just About Everyone Else," in *A Challenge to Love: Gay and Lesbian Catholics in the Church*, ed. Robert Nugent (New York: Crossroad, 1983), 198.

35. Driver, *Magic of Ritual*, 116.

36. Heyward, *Touching Our Strength*, 36.

37. Ibid., 82.

38. Gay/lesbian spirituality must be embodied. It is a joyful celebration of being gay/lesbian; it is erotic, empowering, and political. It is a spirituality that comprehends love-making and justice-doing as one activity. See: Richard Woods, *Another Kind of Love* (Ft. Wayne, IN: Knoll Publishing, 1988), 120–41; McNeill, *Taking a Chance*, 1–26, 121–36, 200–6; Heyward, *Touching Our Strength*, 87–118; O'Neill and Ritter; *Coming Out*

Within; Clark, *Place to Start,* 121–29. R. Williams, *Just as I Am,* 228–41. See also J. M. Clark's most recent work: *A Lavender Cosmic Pilgrim: Further Ruminations on Gay Spirituality, Theology, and Sexuality* (Las Colinas, CA: Liberal Press, 1990).

39. Dermot Lane makes a strong argument for the connection of the Eucharist to the practice of justice: Dermot A. Lane, *Foundations for a Social Theology* (Ramsey, NJ: Paulist Press, 1984), 141–69.

40. Breaking bread and sharing the cup are empowering actions for a Christian gay/lesbian base community. In an AIDS base community that I have participated in as priest for five years, the breaking of bread and sharing of the cup are practices of theodicy, solidarity, and hope. They energize members in their service to the HIV-positive community and share their grief. After breaking bread and sharing the cup, members participate in a litany of remembrance (*anamnesis*) of those who have died of HIV illness.

41. O'Neill and Ritter, *Coming Out Within;* Fortunato, *Embracing the Exile.*

42. McNeill, *Taking a Chance,* 95–107; J. Michael Clark, *Diary of a Southern Queen: An HIV-positive Vision Quest* (Dallas: Monument Press, 1990).

43. John E. Fortunato, *AIDS: The Spiritual Dilemma* (San Francisco: Harper and Row, 1987), 100–9; J. M. Clark, *Lavender Cosmic Pilgrim,* 33–40.

44. The Episcopal Church proclaimed, "Our Church has AIDS," with a banner hung in Grace Cathedral in San Francisco. See also Letty M. Russell, ed., *The Church with AIDS* (Louisville, KY: Westminster/John Knox, 1990).

45. I refrain from using the term *marriage* for gay/lesbian unions; the term is too encoded with a heterosexist and heterosexual social history. I believe in the sacramentality of gay/lesbian unions on a par with healthy heterosexual marriages and the need to legally recognize those unions. I want to discourage the use of marriage for our unions; it remains too narrow and restrictive a model for same-sex unions.

46. John Boswell has discovered Christian liturgical blessings of same-sex relationship dating back to the fourth century. These are still performed in some rural areas as Eastern Catholic rites. See his preliminary findings in a videotaped address entitled *1500 Years of the Church's Blessing Lesbian and Gay Relationship: It's Nothing New* (Place: Integrity, 1988). Bishop Spong calls for the blessing of gay/lesbian commitments: John Spong, *Living in Sin* (San Francisco: Harper & Row, 1988), 196–207. See also Robert Williams, "Toward a Theology for Lesbian and Gay Marriage," *Anglican Theological Review* 72 (1990); 134–57; R. Williams, *Just as I Am,* (New York: Crown Publishing, 1992), 208–18. The Episcopal bishop of California, The Right Reverend William Swing, covened a theology group to study a proposed rite for the blessing and celebration of same-sex unions: *A Study Document Based on the Proposed Rite: The Celebration and Blessing of a Covenant in Love* (unpublished paper, 1987). Sam Potaro, "Homosexuality as Vocation," *The Witness* (June 1991), 18–25.

47. Xavier Seubert takes such a defense of gay/lesbian sexual activity; Seubert, "Sacramentality of Metaphors," 61. Andre Guindon applies the notion of sexual fecundity as integrated, relational, and loving to

gay/lesbian relationships. André Guindon, *The Sexual Creators: An Ethical Proposal for Concerned Christians* (New York: Univ. of America Press, 1986), 63–83, 167–79.

48. Guidon, *The Sexual Creator,* 176.

49. Ibid., 179.

50. Communication problems within same-sex couples often result from attempts to pattern their unions after heterosexist models of marriage. Our unions need not take on the heterosexist politics of many dysfunctional heterosexist marriages/relationships. See Don Clark, *The New Loving Someone Gay* (Berkeley: Celestial Arts, 1987), 171; J. Michael Clark, *A Defiant Celebration,* 35–81. Mary Hunt observes that differences in power between partners lead to breakdowns in intimate communication; See Hunt, *Fierce Tenderness,* 126.

51. David McWhirter and Andrew Mattison, *The Male Couple* (Englewood Cliffs, NJ: Prentice-Hall, 1984); Tina Tessina, *Gay Relationships for Men and Women* (Los Angeles: Joseph Tarcher, 1989); Betty Berzon, *Permanent Partners: Building Gay and Lesbian Relationships That Last* (New York: E. P. Dutton, 1988); Eric Marcus, *The Male Couple's Guide to Living Together* (HarperCollins: New York, 1988).

52. During my years with various base communities, I have discovered that priestly ministry is actively alive in different grass-roots groups. It has been common practice in different base communities to designate nonordained women and men, alternating facilitators to preside in eucharistic celebrations.

Chapter 6. The Struggle for Sexual Justice

1. Quoted in Allan Boesak, *Farewell to Innocence* (Maryknoll, NY: Orbis Books, 1977), 72.

2. For example, the president of Dignity National, Patrick Roche, wrote to Cincinnati archbishop Daniel Pilarczyk, president of the National Conference of Catholic Bishops, seeking dialogue on civil rights issues, AIDS, and anti-gay/lesbian violence. Roche met with NCCB's general secretary, Monsignor Robert Lynch. Lynch found little hope in future dialogue and did not feel that "there was anything productive to be gained from further meetings." Pat Windsor, "Dignity, Church Find Ways to Peacefully Coexist," *National Catholic Reporter* 27, (Aug. 16, 1991): 8.

3. Robert McClory, "Bishops Buck Criticism, Attend Gay Symposium in Chicago," *National Catholic Reporter* 28, no. 23 (Apr. 10, 1992): 6.

4. Openly gay/lesbian writers who have begun a theological discourse: John McNeill, Carter Heyward, Mary Hunt, J. Michael Clark, Malcolm Boyd, Chris Glazer, Robert Williams, Maury Johnston, Michael Stemmeler, Gary Comstock.

5. Beverly Harrison, "The Power of Anger in the Work of Love," in *Weaving the Visions,* ed. Judith Plaskow and Carol Christ (San Francisco: Harper & Row, 1989), 220.

6. Ched Myers, *Binding the Strongman* (Maryknoll, NY: Orbis Books, 1988), 291. Myers applies this term to Jesus' last meal. His analysis of the Marcan portrayal of Jesus' showdown with the powers in Jerusalem is excellent; see 290–382. He brings out the political nature of Jesus' provocative ministry in Jerusalem.

7. Martin Hengel, *The Charismatic Leader and His Followers* (New York: Crossroad, 1982), 16–17.

8. E. P. Sanders, *Jesus and Judaism* (Minneapolis: Augsburg Fortress, 1985), 70.

9. William Wilson, *The Execution of Jesus* New York: Charles Scribner's Sons, 1970), 98.

10. Gerd Theissen, *The Sociology of Palestinian Judaism* (Philadelphia: Fortress Press, 1988), 52.

11. James H. Charlesworth, *Jesus Within Judaism* (New York: Doubleday, 1988), 118.

12. Richard Horsley, *Jesus and the Spiral of Violence* (San Francisco: Harper & Row, 1987), 297–317.

13. The initial document allowed the discussion of prophylatic devices. This was the controversial issue that led to O'Connor forcing the withdrawal of the pastoral letter. See *The Many Faces of AIDS* (Washington, D.C.: United States Catholic Conference, 1987), 18.

14. See Myers' political interpretation, *Binding the Strongman,* 369–82. In his chapter, "Holy Anger: Protest as Vocation," Robert Williams treats Jesus and the Temple demonstration as a "Stop the Church" action; see *Just as I Am* (New York: Crown Publishing, 1992), 219–27. See also Douglas Crimp and Adam Rolston, *AIDS Demo Graphics* (Seattle: Bay Press, 1990), 130–41.

15. Robert Williams, *Just As I Am,* 217–25.

16. Horsley, *Jesus and the Spiral;* Paul Hollenbach, "Jesus, Demoniacs, and Public Authorities: A Socio-Historical Study," *Journal of the American Academy of Religion* 49 (1981): 561–88; Douglas Oakman, *Jesus and the Economic Questions of His Day* (Lewiston, NY: Edwin Mellen Press, 1986).

17. Public Broadcasting Corporation canceled a Point of View documentary film, *Stop the Church.* The film, produced by Altar Ego Productions, was a documentary on the Dec. 10, 1989, ACT UP demonstrations at St. Patrick's Cathedral. The film was too controversial because of the action taken against sacred space. The British movie *Over Our Dead Bodies* shows Cardinal O'Connor and the other celebrants stepping on and over demonstrators to get to the altar. The visual stepping on bodies embodied the homophobic and AIDS-phobic oppression of the cardinal.

18. Stop the Church Coalition, St. Louis, Media Packet, April 19, 1992.

19. Thomas Yingling, "AIDS in America: Postmodern Governance, Identity, and Experience," in *Inside/Out: Lesbian Theories, Gay Theories,* ed. Diana Fuss (New York: Routledge, 1991), 299.

20. Don Aucoin, "Gay Activists Stage Wedding at Holy Cross Cathedral," *Boston Globe,* Aug. 19, 1991, 13–14.

21. Robert Williams, *Just as I Am,* 161.

22. Ibid., 161.

23. Documents of the Thirty-first and Thirty-second General Congregations of the Society of Jesus (St. Louis: The Institute of Jesus Sources, 1977), no. 47, p. 427. See the next statement on solidarity (no. 48). In particular, Decree 4 of the Thirty-second General Congregations contains many statements committing the mission of the Society of Jesus to justice and solidarity with the oppressed. The statements for justice were minimal from the Thirty-third General Congregation of the Society of Jesus; it was closely supervised by John Paul II.

24. Organized mass nonviolent civil disobedience (*ahimsa*) originated with Mahatma Gandhi in 1906 in South Africa and later was used against colonial British control in India. Gandhi was influenced by Emmeline Pankhurst, who championed women's rights in England through non-violent action. Rosa Parks and Dr. Martin Luther King, Jr., popularized modern nonviolent sit-ins, freedom rides, and boycotts. Vietnam War protesters employed the burning of draft cards, mass demonstrations, sit-ins, and the blocking of induction centers. That civil disobedience is nonviolent does not mean that it does not disrupt or transgress. The ethic of love and justice is at the center of all nonviolent civil disobedience.

25. Strong homophobic reactions in people are usually what is called "reaction conversion" by social scientists. It is quite fair to engage in public debate to point this fact out. Not only do people suffer from reaction conversion but also do such ostensibly homophobic institutions as the military and the Catholic hierarchy. See David Greenberg, *The Construction of Homosexuality* (Chicago: Univ. of Chicago Press, 1988), 279–92.

26. Sharon D. Welch, *A Feminist Ethic of Risk* (Minneapolis: Fortress Press, 1990), 75.

27. See Robin Stevens, "Eating Our Own," *The Advocate* no. 609 (Aug. 13, 1992): 33–42.

28. Ibid., 37.

29. *Horizontal hostility* is the term used by Julia Penelope to describe the internecine criticism and trashing within the gay/lesbian community. See *Call Me Lesbian: Lesbian Lives, Lesbian Theory* (Freedom, CA: Crossing Press, 1992), 60–77.

30. Ibid., 69–70.

31. For criticism of sadomasochism, see Penelope, *Call Me Lesbian*, 113–31. In counterattack and defense, see Pat Califia, *Sapphistry: The Book of Lesbian Sexuality* (Tallahassee: Naiad Press, 1980).

Chapter 7. God as Love-Making and Justice-Doing

1. Carter Heyward, *Touching Our Strength* (San Francisco: Harper & Row, 1989), 189–90.

2. Mary Daly, *Beyond God the Father* (Boston: Beacon Press, 1985), 19.

3. Sallie McFague, "Imaging a Theology of Nature: The World as God's Body," in *Liberating Life: Contemporary Approaches to Ecological*

Theology, ed. Charles Birch, William Eakin, and Jay McDaniel (Maryknoll, NY: Orbis Books, 1989), 201–27, 140.

4. Mary Daly, *Gyn/Ecology: The Metaethics of Radical Feminism* (Boston: Beacon Press, 1978), 38.

5. Daly, *Beyond God the Father,* 34–35.

6. Beverly W. Harrison points out the danger of Daly's metaphorical leap into "otherworldly Womanspace"—the danger of turning anger inward. Harrison maintains that feminist spirituality must reject world-denying elements and be committed to profound social change. It becomes a feminist ethic that is "deeply and profoundly worldly, a spirituality of sensuality." See Harrison, "The Power of Anger in the Work of Love: Christian Ethics for Women and Other Strangers," in *Making the Connections,* ed. Carol Robb (Boston: Beacon Press, 1985), 6–8.

    Elizabeth Schüssler Fiorenza points out that Daly's understanding of sisterhood does not sustain feminist solidarity because it fails to perceive the feminist movement as the bonding of the oppressed, viewing it instead as a pure network of sisterhood. See Schüssler Fiorenza, *Bread Not Stone* (Boston: Beacon Press, 1984), 166. Welch defines a theology of immanence with four social contours: (1) an imperative for ethical action; (2) the human community's celebration of the wonder and beauty of life; (3) transcending the conditions of oppression through loving life, self, and others despite social forces that deny these values; (4) a movement toward social transformation; see Welch, *A Feminist Ethic of Risk* (Minneapolis: Fortress Press, 1990), 179–80. Mary Hunt gives a different reading of Daly as proposing a powerful political model for change; see Hunt, *Fierce Tenderness: A Feminist Theology of Friendship* (New York: Crossroad, 1990), 64–67.

7. McFague looks at three interrelated models for God: Mother, Lover, and Friend. Sallie McFague, *Models of God: Theology for an Ecological, Nuclear Age* (Philadelphia: Fortress Press, 1987), 97–180. Heyward attempts to move in the same direction; Carter Heyward, *The Redemption of God* (Washington, DC: University Press of America, 1982).

8. McFague, *Models of God,* 130.

9. See Warren McWilliams for the discussion of the tradition of the apathetic God; McWilliams, *The Passion of God* (Macon, GA: Mercer Univ. Press, 1985), 6–24. Welch rejects the classical theistic models that valorize absolute power. She states, "I find the god of classical theism irrational and unworthy of worship." Welch, *Feminist Ethic of Risk,* 175, 111–16.

10. Phyllis Trible explored the sexual diversity of images for God in Genesis, the Song of Songs, and the book of Ruth. The Hebrew biblical tradition is more erotically diverse and full of conflicting traditions. The tendency of heterosexist biblical scholars has been to gloss over the differences into a patriarchal systematization. See Phyllis Trible, *God and the Rhetoric of Sexuality* (Philadelphia: Fortress Press, 1978).

11. McFague, *Models of God,* 130–32. Hunt's notion of friendship includes embodiment or the erotic; Hunt, *Fierce Tenderness,* 167–69. See also

James B. Nelson, *The Intimate Connection* (Philadelphia: Westminster Press, 1988), 55.

12. Adrienne Rich, Audre Lorde, Haunani-Kay Trask, Carter Heyward, Mary Hunt, Michel Foucault, Jeffrey Weeks, J. Michael Clark, Kevin Gordon.

13. James Nelson's *Embodiment* begins a reenvisioning of both sexuality and the model of God that recent feminist theologies pioneered; Nelson, *Embodiment: An Approach to Sexuality and Christian Theology* (Minneapolis: Augsburg Publishing House, 1979), 14, 16–37.

14. Foucault, *History of Sexuality*, 1: 83–102.

15. Beverly Harrison and Carter Heyward, "Pain and Pleasure: Avoiding the Confusions of Christian Tradition in Feminist Theory," in *Christianity, Patriarchy, and Abuse*, ed. Joanne Carlson Brown and Carole Bolin (New York: Pilgrim Press, 1989), 166.

16. Haunani-Kay Trask, *Eros and Power: The Promise of Feminist Theory* (Philadelphia: Univ. of Pennsylvania Press, 1986), 92–93; Audre Lorde, "Uses of the Erotic," in *Weaving the Visions*, ed. Judith Plaskow and Carol Christ (San Francisco: Harper & Row, 1989), 208–13; Heyward, *Touching Our Strength;* Hunt, *Fierce Tenderness;* Rita Nakashima Brock, *Journeys by Heart* (New York: Crossroad, 1991); J. Michael Clark, *A Lavender Cosmic Pilgrim* (Garland, TX: Tangelwuld Press, 1990), 49–53.

17. Trask, *Eros and Power,* 93.

18. Brock, *Journeys by Heart,* 26.

19. Guindon, *The Sexual Creators,* 63–83, 167–79.

20. Brock, *Journeys by Heart,* 26.

21. McFague, *Models of Gods,* 131.

22. Harrison, "Power of Anger," in *Making Connections,* 217.

23. Heyward, *Touching Our Strength,* 99. One of the strengths of Carter Heyward's *Touching Our Strength* is her connecting love-making to justice. Her theological enterprise opens itself to a hermeneutics of solidarity. This is the basis of all liberation theology.

24. Ibid., 3.

25. McFague speaks of justice-doing with her conceptual model of God as mother; McFague, *Models of God,* 117–23.

26. Ibid., 135. Hunt argues for a wider notion of the divine, God as friend. God as friend includes the model of God as lover; Hunt, *Fierce Tenderness,* 167–69.

27. James Nelson wrote this in a statement to the Presbyterian Task Force on Human Sexuality; "Report of the Special Committee on Human Sexuality," in *Presbyterians and Human Sexuality 1991* (Offices of Presbyterian General Assembly, 1991), 9.

28. Nelson, *Embodiment,* 37–69; Hunt, *Fierce Tenderness,* 116.

29. McFague, *Models of God,* 120–21.

30. Ibid.

31. Nelson develops the notion of sexual salvation. It forms a corrective to dualisms within which Christian practices have been constructed; Nelson, *Embodiment,* 70–103; Nelson, *The Intimate Connection*

(Philadelphia: Westminster Press, 1988), 120.

32. Brock does this with the relational notion of Christ/a; Brock, *Journeys by Heart*, 52–53, 67–72. Heyward begins an initial exploration of the notion of Christ/a; Heyward, *Touching Our Strength*, 114–18. *Christ* is a relational term of erotic power. There is a need to develop a Christology that incorporates the Queer Christ and the Christ/a.

33. There is a direct correlation with models for God and sexuality. Some of the past models have been impoverished; thus, there have been impoverished social constructions of sexual desire. Just as we are in our infancy in revising models of God, so we are in our infancy in comprehending the full potentiality, diversity, and creativity of our human sexuality.

34. Ecclesial attempts to change our sexual identity and practices are attempts to dehumanize us, or they disembody us by encouraging us to involuntary celibacy. Such attempts manifest a basic erotophobia.

35. Heyward, *Touching Our Strength*, 105.

36. Birch, Eakin, and McDaniel, eds., *Liberating Life;* Thomas Berry, *The Dream of the Earth* (San Francisco: Sierra Club Books, 1988); Matthew Fox:1979:140–75.

37. Welch, *Feminist Ethic of Risk*, 153–80.

38. The phrase is from Jules Girardi. It is quoted by Beverly Harrison, "Power of Anger," in *Making the Connections*, ed. Robb, 224.

39. Clark, *Place to Start*, 95.

40. McFague, *Models of God*, and "Imaging a Theology of Nature," in *Liberating Life*, ed. Birch et al. See also Rosemary Radford Ruether, *Gaia & God: An Ecofeminist Theology of Earth Healing* (San Francisco: HarperSanFrancisco, 1992).

41. Foucault, *The History of Sexuality* (New York: Vintage Books, 1990), 1:92–102.

42. Beverly Harrison, "Theological Reflection in the Struggle for Liberation: A Feminist Perspective," in *Making the Connections*, ed. Robb, 260.

43. Lois K. Daly, "Ecofeminism, Reverence for Life, and Feminist Theological Ethics," in *Liberating Life*, ed. Birch et al., 88–108. See also Hunt, *Fierce Tenderness*, 173–76.

Appendix

1. Ed Cohen, "Foucauldian Necrologies: 'Gay' 'Politics'? Politically Gay?" *Textual Practice* 2, no. 1 (1988): 87–101. See Didier Eribon's excellent biography of Foucault and his discussion of Foucault's struggles with sexuality: Eribon, *Michel Foucault* (Cambridge: Harvard Univ. Press, 1991).

2. Foucault claims that "power produces knowledge (and not by encouraging it because it serves power or by applying because it is useful); that power and knowledge directly imply another; that there is no power relation without the relative constitution of a field of knowledge, nor any knowledge that does not presuppose and constitute at the

same time power relations"; Foucault, *Discipline and Punish* (New York: Vintage Books, 1979), 27. See Jana Sawicki, *Disciplining Foucault: Feminism, Power, and the Body* (New York: Routledge, 1991), 20–26.

3. Michel Foucault, *Power/Knowledge* (New York: Pantheon Books, 1980), 83.
4. Ibid., 82.
5. Ibid., 58.
6. Foucault, *Discipline and Punish*.
7. Ibid., 141–42.
8. Sharon D. Welch, "The Battle for Truth: Foucault, Liberation Theology, and the Insurrection of Subjugated Knowledges" (Ph.D. dissertation, Vanderbilt University, 1982), 147–51.
9. Foucault, *Power/Knowledge*, 59.
10. Ibid., 141–42.
11. Foucault, *Discipline and Punish*, 26.
12. Ibid., 27.
13. Michel Foucault, *The History of Sexuality* (New York: Vintage Books, 1990), 1:95.
14. Ibid., 93–94.
15. Foucault, *Power/Knowledge*, 133.
16. Ibid., 131.
17. Ibid., 132. See Jonathan Dollimore's excellent study of sexual transgression and discursive battle for truth; Dollimore, *Sexual Dissidence* (Oxford: Clarendon Press, 1991).
18. Foucault, *Power/Knowledge*, 93.
19. Foucault, *History of Sexuality*, 1:100–1.
20. Ibid., 13.
21. Ibid., 103–14.
22. Ibid., 148.
23. Ibid., 105–6.
24. Ibid., 53–73.
25. Bob Gallagher and Alexander Wilson, "Sex and the Politics of Identity: An Interview with Michel Foucault," in *Gay Spirit*, ed. Mark Thompson (New York: St. Martin's Press, 1987), 28.
26. Padgug argues that our sexuality is a rich and ever-varying set of potentialities. He maintains the history of sexual practices as ever-changing social constructions. Same- and opposite-sex practices and other variations of sexual practices may be universal in history. However, sexual identity is a recent social construction; Robert Padgug, "Sexual Matters: Rethinking Sexuality in History," in *Hidden from History: Reclaiming the Gay and Lesbian Past*, ed. Martin Duberman, Martha Vicinus, and George Chauncey (New York: Penguin Books, 1990), 54–64. Similar arguments are found among other gay and lesbian authors: Dollimore, *Sexual Dissidence*; David Halperin, *One Hundred Years of Homosexuality* (New York: Routledge, 1990), 1–53; Halperin, "Sex Before Sexuality: Pederasty, Politics, and Power in Classical Athens," in *Hidden from History*, ed. Duberman et al., 37–53. John D'Emilio and Estelle B. Freedman, *Intimate Matters: A History of Sexuality in America* (New York: Harper & Row,

1988); Gary Kinsman, *The Regulation of Desire: Sexuality in Canada* (Montreal: Black Rose Books, 1987), 23–61; Martin Duberman, *About Time: Exploring the Gay Past* (New York: Penguin Books, 1991), 436–67; Jeffrey Weeks, "Capitalism and the Organization of Sex," in *Homosexuality: Power and Politics, Gay Left Collective* (London: Allison and Busby, 1980), 11–20; Weeks, *Sex, Politics, and Society* (New York: Longman, 1981), 96–97; John D'Emilio, "Capitalism and Gay Identity," in *Powers of Desire: The Politics of Sexuality,* ed. Ann Snitow, Christine Stanell, and Sharon Thompson (New York: Monthly Review Press, 1983), 100–16. For feminist and lesbian arguments, see: Shane Phelan, *Identity Politics* (Philadelphia: Temple Univ. Press, 1989); Irene Diamond and Lee Quigley, "American Feminism and the Language of Control," in *Feminism and Foucault: Reflections on Resistance,* ed. Irene Diamond and Lee Quigley (Boston: Northeastern Univ. Press, 1988), 193–206; Jana Sawicki, *Disciplining Foucault: Feminism, Power, and the Body* (New York: Routledge, 1991); Celia Kitzinger, *The Social Construction of Lesbianism* (London: Sage Publications, 1987), 90–124. Debate on the social constructionist position: Julia Penelope, *Call Me Lesbian: Lesbian Lives, Lesbian Theory* (Freedom, CA: Crossing Press, 1992), 17–38. Judy Grahn, *Another Mother Tongue: Gay Words, Gay Worlds* (Boston: Beacon Press, 1984). Richard Mohr, *Gay Ideas* (Boston: Beacon Press, 1992), 221–42.

27. Boswell defends himself against the essentialist accusation for his study of same sex-practices in *Christianity, Homosexuality, and Social Tolerance* (Chicago: Univ. of Chicago Press, 1980). He removes his usage of *gay* and *lesbian* from sexual identity politics; Boswell, "Revolution, Universals, and Sexual Categories," in *Hidden from History,* ed. Duberman et al., 17–36.

28. Halperin, *One Hundred Years,* 42.

29. Ibid.

30. Weeks, *Sex, Politics, and Society,* 96–97.

31. Weeks, "Capitalism," in *Homosexuality: Power and Politics,* 19.

32. Foucault, *History of Sexuality,* 1:101.

Index